STUDIES IN

AFRICAN AMERICAN HISTORY AND CULTURE

edited by

GRAHAM RUSSELL HODGES
COLGATE UNIVERSITY

RACE, CLASS, AND THE STRUGGLE FOR NEIGHBORHOOD IN WASHINGTON, D.C.

NELSON F. KOFIE

Routledge
Taylor & Francis Group

NEW YORK AND LONDON

First published 1999 by Garland Publishing, Inc.

This edition published 2014 by Routledge
711 Third Avenue, New York, NY 10017
2 Park Square, Milton Park, Abingdon, Oxon, OX14 4RN

Routledge is an imprint of the Taylor & Francis Group, an informa business

First issued in paperback 2016

Library of Congress Cataloging-in-Publication Data

Kofie, Nelson F.
Race, class, and the struggle for neighborhood in Washington, D.C. / Nelson F. Kofie.
     p.   cm. — (Studies in African American history and
culture)
    Includes bibliographical references and index.
    ISBN 0-8153-3114-2 (alk. paper)
    1. Afro-Americans—Washington (D.C.)—Social conditions—
Case studies. 2. Washington (D.C.)—Social conditions—Case
studies. 3. Washington (D.C.)—Race relations—Case studies.
4. Community development—Washington (D.C.)—Case studies.
5. Poor—Washington (D.C.)—Political activity—Case studies.
6. Social change—Washington (D.C.)—History—20th century—
Case studies. 7. Apartment houses, Cooperative—Washington
(D.C.)—Case studies. I. Title. II. Series.
F205.N4K64 1999
305.896'0730753—dc21
                                             98-55171

ISBN13: 978-0-8153-3114-8 (hbk)
ISBN13: 978-1-138-98438-7 (pbk)

For my wife, Nancy, and my son, Omar

Contents

List of Charts

List of Tables

Acknowledgments

While writing I benefited from the goodwill and financial support of several individuals and institutions. Without the generousity of these people, my effort to tell the story of Sun-Hope neighborhood-community's residents would have been difficult. This book started with a suggestion by Dr. William Chamblis to consider conducting an ethnographic study of Sun-Hope community for my doctoral dissertation. I accepted the challenge and received further assistance from other people associated with the community. Having acquired Hope Mansions, the president of Shelter Incorporated was most delighted to provide as much assistance as I asked. The People's Advocacy, which was tasked with assisting the tenants to establish a co-operative organization, granted me internship position. This enabled me truly to participate in and observe events taking place in the community. The residents were most generous in reflecting and sharing their varied stories with me. Some of them wanted the best for me in the pursuit of my Ph.D., so that they were willing to call and keep me informed about the "going-ons" during times when I was absent from the community. Their phone calls were invaluable sources of critical information that made the story of Sun-Hope complete. After each day spent in the community—whether participating in a meeting or Bible study, listening to complaints about the living conditions, watching transactions between drug dealers and buyers or the police conduct drug raids—I always retreated to the comfort of my home in the suburbs evermore conscious of the privileges I enjoy and the many blessings bestowed on my life.

One organization which provided financial support deserves mention. The Center for Nonprofit Governance and Philanthropy,

Indiana University-Purdue University, funded my research for 2 years, and provided me the opportunity to present pieces of my work at conferences. More funding came from Goucher College's summer grant which enabled me to conduct follow-up interviews and research, and to cover the cost of editorial service.

Some special individuals nurtured my thinking about the Sun-Hope and its residents. My thanks to my grad school buddy Cheryl-Ann B. Repetti who always listened, questioned and responded wisely to my theoretical renderings pertaining to the case of Sun-Hope. Ronald Weitzer spent considerable time combing through the original manuscript for flaws and provided invaluable suggestions to improve it. Jennifer Bess came to the rescue; her editing was priceless. I am deeply greatful.

Dr. Nelson Kofie
Towson, September 1998.

Race, Class, and the Struggle for Neighborhood in Washington, D.C.

CHAPTER 1

African Americans and Urban Neighborhood Communities

The urban experience and the emergence of predominantly African American neighborhoods continues to be focus of academic research.[1] Unlike other ethnic enclaves, predominantly African American neighborhoods were planned, structured and maintained by the white dominant group, either by plan or by default. Enforced *de jure* segregation laws, local ordinances, discriminatory banking and real estate practices, as well as a general atmosphere of racist attitudes, ensured that African Americans, regardless of income, were clustered into congested, dilapidated, and underserved neighborhoods in urban areas. From their inception, predominantly impoverished black neighborhoods were, and continue to be, sustained by a white culture of segregation.[2]

Besides defining the form and content of race relations, the culture of segregation shaped social class relations as well. Historically, Richard Meister noted, "[t]he urban experience has not been the same for the black American as it has been for the white. For whites, the city has offered opportunity and mobility. The city has not offered blacks these same avenues of progress."[3] The culture of segregation, by plan or default, determined where they lived, the kinds of employment open to them in the segment economy, and the inflated interest rate loans which financial agencies were willing to offer them to buy a home or start a business. The culture of segregation was, in effect, another structural blockage thwarting the upward mobility of urban African Americans.[4]

This apt observation, while not completely obsolete, requires reexamination. There have been marked changes in the social factors which encouraged the differing opportunities and mobility of blacks and whites in the city. Since the Civil Rights Act of 1964, overt racial discrimination in employment, housing and educational attainment have all abated considerably due to favorable legal and attitudinal changes. The result has been a notable increase in opportunity and mobility for black Americans who have education and marketable skills. Thus, what remains constant within the black urban experience, compared to experiences of other white ethnics, is the continuing destabilization process within previously mixed-race and -income neighborhoods, and the emergence of a seemingly entrenched black underclass.[5]

Following the "white flight" in the 1960s, a disproportionate number of the black middle- and working-class families exited many black urban neighborhoods too.[6] For those who were unskilled, inadequately educated and who lacked the economic means to move out, these neighborhoods took a turn for the worse. Replacing the outgoing tenants were predominantly poor people. In tandem, landlords felt no pressure from the poor tenants to improve services, and city governments experiencing a dwindling tax-base shifted resources and services to predominantly middle-class or white neighborhoods. The outcome has been the concentration of predominantly impoverished residents in declining and decaying public and assisted housing in the inner-city areas. In these areas, the disproportionate number of residents are families with female heads of households, living below the poverty line or on the threshold of poverty, and welfare dependent. Young males are frequently unemployed and teenage girls have babies out of wedlock. All of these strains, combined with a general malaise people feel, account for the structure of the *de facto* black ghettos.[7]

The consequences of the situations in the black ghettos are the same across the country. These neighborhoods characteristically lack, or at best, have weak community-based mediating institutions and leadership. Active, traditional leaders in the ghettos have lost status to gang leaders and druglords.[8] Both informal and formal social control mechanisms are ineffective, and lawlessness is pervasive. Law-abiding residents live in fear, crime is rampant, drug-related deaths are frequent, ordinary disputes get settled with gun battle, human life is devalued, and the youth and young adult males are arrested and incarcerated disproportionately. It is not uncommon to hear children talk about death frequently, and expect to die in their teens.[9] There is a prevailing sense of hopelessness and powerlessness.

The unique African American internal migration from the deep south to urban areas in the north in search of better opportunities—escaping racism and economic dislocation—has been the subject of various studies.[10] Although the racial problems encountered in the north were not that different from those of the south, the economic growth in the north provided blacks with better avenues than indentured servitude. The experiences of the urban African Americans, and especially those trapped in the ghettos, have been the subjects of copious studies, so much as to earn them labels such as the working poor, the dispossessed, the underclass, and the truely disadvantaged[11].

During the 1960s, the dominant phrase coined to capture the conditions in which the urban poor African American lived was the "tangle of pathology."[12] Studies pointed to the African American's internalized culture of poverty which prevents them from assimilating into the mainstream society, and thus from seeing a need to engage in actions to change their living conditions.[13] A representative author argued that the poor are poor because they lack cultural capital—cognitive ability, education, marketable skills, linguistic skills—without which their participation in the socioeconomic mainstream is impossible.[14] Since then, others have pointed to the prevailing antithetical middle-class values by which the urban poor live their lives.[15] The source of the problems plaguing the urban poor, then, is the poor themselves.

Each of these authors acknowledge, in varying degrees, that the source of poverty is rooted in the social structure. They share, however, a view that the antidote to poverty is the assimilation of core American values: rugged individualism and self-motivation, thriftiness, self-sufficiency, competitiveness in the labor market, a faith in equal opportunity which is accessible to everyone, and the drive to succeed which inevitably engenders a rewarding work-ethic. Guided by these values, the theoritsts explain, the poor can bring themselves up by their own bootstraps.

These kinds of myopic analyses draw attention to attitudinal and behavioral patterns which thwart the individual's social advancement. There is an underlying assumption, however, that the individual's failure to compete and succeed in the land of opportunity proves that he/she has a character flaw. The idea that the individual is solely responsible for the circumstances circumscribing his/her life is good ideology but bad sociology. Using the individual as a unit of analysis is problematic. It is reductionist and psychologically driven. It overlooks the various contexts giving rise to urban ghettos in the first place, and the social forces impinging on the lives of the poor.

Another weakness of the individualistic interpretation of life in the urban ghetto is the tendency to treat all the residents in these areas a monolith. Various people are residents there for various reasons. For some, the ghetto is a trap from which they find no escape. They live there independent of choice. The ghetto neighborhoods are the few places they can afford rental units. Others can afford to move out but continue to live there because they have established and maintained a life-time of social networks. Others are attracted to the ghetto for its weak internal social control, which is conducive to various deviant and victimless crimes.

There are other people, however, who continue to live in these neighborhoods because of their sense of civil responsibility. They use their know-how to draw needed resources into the community and to empower others to initiate change. Thus, from a more panoramic and inclusive perspective, this sociological case study of a neighborhood community seeks to explore the historical, economic, sociocultural, political, and ideological contexts and structures shaping the choices people make and to examine how they strategically conduct themselves when faced with certain kinds of opportunities and constraints.[16]

Sociology is the study of people doing things. It seeks to examine the patterns of collective behavior under various circumstances. As active participants in social life, people struggle to maintain, alter, submit to or create institutions shaping their life chances. In the main, people interpret a social condition affecting them as a private trouble without realizing, more often than not, that it is rooted in a public issue. These two spheres are linked but separable for analytical purposes. Private troubles "occur within the character of the individual and within [the] range of . . . immediate relations with others; they have to do with the self and with those limited areas of social life of which [one] is directly and personally aware."[17] Ideas about and solutions to private troubles often occur within the immediate milieux, such as a person's family, tenant council, or school. This is not the case, however, with public issues. They are social problems which are beyond the individual's immediate environment, affecting a large number of people with obvious ramifications. They involve systemic crises confronting society, or differentially affecting a subgroup, and they demand addressing by the state apparatus. The sociological imagination of the urban neighborhood community, then, must explore the relationship between private troubles and public issues. Employing the sociological imagination as a paradigm provides a fruitful means by which to understand the social processes of the ghetto, the interactions among people, institutions and organizations. The sociological imagination addresses some essential complexities by placing the individual problems within a context that includes more than the forces at work within the ghetto limits: a) it implicates both institutions and individuals (active or alienated) as agents in the formation and transformation of the urban ghetto. b) It recognizes the inherent contradictions in social institutions, the adverse effects of which are felt disproportionately by ghetto residents. c) It recognizes the varied and intense coercive agencies at work in the everyday life of the ordinary ghetto resident.

BACKGROUND AND OVERVIEW

This is a study of neighborhood community change in the northeastern section of Washington, D.C. Special attention is given the factors contributing to the destabilization of this previously stable, working- and middle-class black community. Associated with the destabilization process is the emergence of the neighborhood as a haven for drug dealers and criminals. The study also examines the efforts of some community members to form mediating institutions, mobilizing their neighbors in a grassroots plan to regenerate the community through the vehicle of cooperative homeownership. In addition, the junctures at which the residents and other agencies struggle over power, leadership and strategies for addressing the problems of joblessness, drug dealing, and gun violence in the community will be examined. Further attention is given to the process of group formation, the consciousness-raising endeavors of residents to transform previously private troubles into community/public issues, and the subsequent collective action to address these issues.

The study focuses on three apartment complexes—Riverside Apartments, a public housing project, Sunrise Apartments and Hope Mansions. Sunrise Apartments and Hope Mansions (or Sun-Hope) were built in 1954 and 1960, respectively, by a black preacher, Father Jonas, founder of the Faith Church of Christ (FCC). During the 1950s and 1960s, the community was inhabited by black lawyers, doctors, professors and other middle-class professionals living in close proximity to working-class residents of the public housing project, Riverside Apartments. The dismantling of restrictive housing covenants, however, enabled many middle-class professionals to move out of the community. Following this exodus, not only Riverside Apartments, but Sunrise and Hope Mansions as well, became home to predominantly low-income residents.

Attendant to this demographic change was an increased prevalence of crime and disorderly behavior in the neighborhood. In 1974, Riverside Apartments was demolished due to decay, and Sunrise and Hope Mansions apartments became centers of illicit drug activity, theft and violence. By the late 1980s, the police had given up any effort to control the intense and frequent illegal activities and began referring to the area as "Little Beirut" and "Hell's Horseshoe."

In 1985, there were some significant developments that aimed to improve the living conditions in the community. Among these was the acquisition of Hope Mansions by Shelter Incorporated. In the same manner, another group of investors led by Jason Saunders acquired Sunrise. At the core of the community rejuvenation was an unsuccessful attempt by tenants, especially those in Hope Mansions, to gain ownership/management of their apartment units through a nonprofit, grassroots, cooperative structure. A similar effort by the tenant group leadership at Sunrise failed.

Cooperative tenant ownership and management, unlike traditional public housing, requires tenant participation in community activities such as organizing neighborhood patrols, evaluating and screening residents, and securing public and private services. Collaborative tenant initiative, recruitment, and participation in identifying and solving the problems plaguing their neighborhood encourages the formation of informal social controls. This is the case especially when tenants feel the formal control agencies, such as the police, have failed them.

The aim of this book is to examine the efforts of low-income residents to mobilize internal and external resources to address problems facing their neighborhood community. This is especially significant because there is widespread assumption that all ghetto is an internally disorganized neighborhood where residents either are apathetic or passively accept the problems of gangs, drug dealing and deviance prevalant in their community. This is not always the case. Sometimes a few determined residents, disregarding the threats by gun-touting drug dealers, are able to empower others and solicit services from formal agencies to act to restore some order in their community.

EMPOWERMENT OF LOW-INCOME RESIDENTS

There is a renewed interest in the U.S. to attempt to reduce poverty, housing crises and the neighborhood blight among the urban low-income population. Coincidentally, there has been an ideological shift embraced by both liberals and conservatives. The current approach is "community empowerment," wherein tenant initiative and responsibility are necessary steps to reducing the myriad of problems facing the urban poor. According to Bratt:

> Empowerment may be defined as the control a people have over the course of their lives, or the amount of power and influence a group has in affecting its community.[18]

The interdependent components of empowerment begin with: a) the collective consciousness of residents regarding the impoverished conditions in which they live. In this sense, information is a source of power. Well-informed residents are aware of the origins of and the strategies needed to deal with neighborhood problems. b) Tenants' political knowledge about their common cause—this is possible by translating individual (household) private troubles into public (community) issues. Typical of many impoverished neighborhoods, residents tend to underestimate their collective power to effect change through influencing their elected officials or management. For instance, a leaky faucet might be a private trouble, but when the result is costly damage to other tenants' property, then it is a collective affair. c) The mobilization of resources—residents take steps toward organizing and networking to gain access to key people and critical resources, including jobs, goods and services. Community empowerment is about organizing community-conscious residents to draw attention to their neighborhood problems and to seek both private and public assistance to address them.

In this book, empowerment is conceptualized as a *process of becoming* empowered in all three spheres: social, political, and economic. The empowerment process, then, begins when a group of concerned residents becomes aware of the need to alter their state of affairs (e.g. organize to get rid of the drug dealers, demand swift

housing maintenance from management, petition the police chief for
more police presence, etc.). Once citizens are aware, social action
ensues: tenant organizations are formed to approach the appropriate
public agents and agencies, both in writing and in person, with specific
demands and expectations on how to deal effectively with
neighborhood problems.

The effectiveness of tenant empowerment rests largely on the
shoulders of the tenant organization and its leaders. Tenants are
expected to change the behaviors which contribute to the problems in
the neighborhood. Through their organization, there is the potential for
tenants to become confident and to find a voice. This confidence, for
instance, reinforces their demand that the police respond in a timely
fashion to their service-calls and awakens the management to their
complaints about shoddy workmanship and to their concerns about
drug dealing neighbors.

This book examines the purposive actions of people, their strategic
behavior in collaboration, in conflict, and in response to the actions of
private and public organizations. However, as will be discussed later,
efforts to empower tenants may be well-intentioned but constrained by
structural conditions which perpetuate impoverishment in these
communities. For example, while a tenant group is able to pressure the
local police department to assist the community in ridding it of drug
dealers, the unemployment, lack of quality education and low wages
which make drug dealing attractive to some of the residents are scarcely
addressed. With a significant number of residents lacking adequate and
quality education and marketable skills, and young men stigmatized by
their drug-related incarceration and unable to find entry-level jobs, the
likelihood of the illicit drug trade remains. The context in which to
comprehend the ghetto, I suggest, lies not in some esoteric culture of
poverty, but the very market culture in which the pursuit of private
gains, legal or illegal, has become the pervasive organizing principle of
all social life.[19]

The first contribution of this book is the attempt to explain,
systematically, how a community which was home to reputable middle
and working class blacks between the 1950s and 1960s was
transformed into a crime-ridden, impoverished neighborhood of
predominantly low-income people. Subsequently, the impoverished
conditions—lack of maintenance, trash collection, neglect by the
owner, the fiscal crisis of the city—all contributed to making the
community vulnerable to drug dealers from other parts of the country.

The result was the transformation of Sun-Hope neighborhood community into one of the largest open-air drug markets in Washington, D.C. Significant, too, are the efforts some residents made to regain control of their community from the criminals and drug dealers.

The second significant contribution of this research to the literature is the attempt to use the sociological imagination as the primary analytical tool. The significance of the sociological imagination is that it provides an elaborate, panoramic framework by which to illuminate the intricate relationship among individuals, social institutions, social structures and ideologies.

The third significant contribution of this book is its effort to situate a case study within a national context. The study of Sun-Hope reveals not just the decay and decline of a once-prominent community, but also the impact that national policies, such as desegregation in schooling, housing, economic change, and the war on drugs, had on people at the neighborhood community level.

RETROSPECTIVE OVERVIEW

This study was conceived in the midst of highly publicized problems of crime, homicides, police raids of crack kitchens and the 24-hour drug market in the housing projects of Moon Crescent and the twin apartment complexes of Hope Mansions and Sunrise Apartments (hereafter Sun-Hope). All proper names used in this book, with the exception of persons who are well-known elites, are replaced by pseudonyms. Similarly, the names of people interviewed, places, organizations, streets and neighborhoods have been altered.[20]

By 1985, the residents of Moon Crescent public housing, being the first to experience disorder and drug-related crime, started mobilizing to counter the drug dealers.[21] As a result, the tenants forced the drug dealers and the criminals to relocate in the Sun-Hope community. Also, in 1985 the FCC, the owner of Sun-Hope apartments, sold the property. Gail Peterson, the president and founder of Shelter Incorporated (SI)— a housing development enterprise based in Washington, D.C.— acquired Hope Mansions. Jason Saunders, a former board member of the Faith Church, and other partners purchased Sunrise Apartments.

In September 1990, I sought and was granted the permission by Gail Peterson to attend resident meetings at Hope Mansions. The first meeting I attended was held in response to a homicide which took place in the community. At this meeting, there were about 50 adults and 10 children present that evening. On one of the walls hung a life-size glossy poster of the anatomical system of a human being, detailing the deleterious effect of narcotics on the liver, the brain, the heart, the spleen, the kidney and other organs. On the exterior walls of the buildings were spray-painted warnings for the living: "You might not make it. Crack kills. Who's next?" Another stated: "Serpo is gone. Stop drugs." Strolling to the subway station after the meeting, a young woman introduced herself and asked if she could join me. When I inquired how she and her three children liked the community, she responded: "It's a trap. It's a trap."

Ms. Peterson introduced me to her staff members, Patricia Mason, the executive director of the People's Advocacy Corporation (PA). People's Advocacy is an organization retained by the residents' group to mobilize and empower residents to become cooperative owners of Hope Mansions apartments after the rehabilitation was completed. I was also introduced to Betty Singer, president of the Resident Council (which was later renamed the Hope Mansions Cooperative) and a few other residents. I took the opportunity to gather phone numbers of some of the key persons at the meeting and ask for the date and time of the next scheduled meeting, which was in September, 1990.

I continued to attend the weekly meetings. Although Ms. Mason had introduced me several times as a graduate student from George Washington University doing research on the community, many of the residents thought of me as "the man from the *Washington Post*." This perception of me was helpful in that it legitimized my constant note-taking at the meetings. Moreover, since the neighborhood had been a continuous focus of the media, it as was not unusual that the residents thought of me as "the guy from the *Post*."[22] I determined that being the "man from the *Post*" was helpful in that the residents saw the free publicity as helping their cause. From the perspective of the residents, the more their plight got good press, the more likely it was that public officials and the new owners would improve the quality of life in the community and increase police patrols to deal with the drug problems facing the community.

Inquiries, such as "Why do you come to the meetings all the time?" enabled me to explain my academic interest and to ask the inquirer for an interview. Unlike many suggestions in the literature about "going native," I presented myself as graduate student studying the history and people of the community. I did not find it necessary to move into the neighborhood.[23] Instead, I spent an average of 12 hours per week there engaged in various activities.

Being a young black male, and a college student with a foreign accent, was very helpful for several reasons.[24] First, the meetings and many of the community activities were dominated by women. Many of the women were single heads of households. Some of the women often expressed how delighted they were to see men at the meetings. The leaders of the group often went to great lengths to entice any man who made it to the meeting to join one of the subcommittees. More often than not, the men declined with an excuse that they were too busy to take on any responsibilities. Second, given the prevalence of illegal drugs, the memory of Jamaicans and all kinds of strangers coming into the neighborhood, residents were often apprehensive about me. However, once I explained that I came from Ghana, my accent and country of origin often served as a topic of conversation. This enabled me to ask for interviews at the opportune time.

During the meetings, I took notes on the concerns residents expressed—drugs, verbal abuse, apathy of other residents, latch-key children, abusive teenagers, fear of certain neighbors, loud stereo systems, graffiti, abusive parents, the persistence of the drug trade, poor maintenance, abusive personnel in the management office, and many more. The fact that I was a stranger recording these concerns seemed to have empowered some residents to speak their mind. Because of their prolonged neglect by the owner, management and the police, the tenants had come to rely on the press to make their plight known. In fact, they documented their plight themselves in their monthly newsletter, *The Hope Mansions News*, produced by the Resident Cooperative. The newsletter was initiated by the board of directors as a way to keep residents informed about the developments in their neighborhood. The newsletter became the medium to appreciate individual and group accomplishments, to enable residents to voice their concerns about their neighborhood, and to record the issues raised at the meetings.

For four months, I regularly attended the meetings, and established a rapport with both children and adults. More often than not, after the meetings, Ms. Mason gave me a ride to downtown Washington, D.C. This gave me the opportunity to ask numerous questions about the plight of the residents, why the meetings were attended predominantly by women and their children, why men did not attend, and whether Housing Secretary Jack Kemp's proposed Home Ownership for People

Everywhere (HOPE II) initiative might complicate or aid low-income residents. And also, I asked what it would take for the homeownership prospect to "sink in" with the average resident with less than a ninth-grade education, a resident who is without credit and/or a bank account, and who, for multiples of reasons, does not see the value of active participation in the nascent resident cooperative effort. The answers to these questions comprise the focus of this research.

In addition, attending the resident council meetings gave me a sense of some of the administrative needs of the residents. While the meetings enabled residents to articulate their concerns, they also served as a teaching mechanism for residents on how to conduct meetings. What became obvious to me was that residents rarely discussed what was to be done to deal with the numerous problems that they confronted. I volunteered my services to work with any of the committees—fundraising, grounds—but they declined my offer each time. The reason was that the residents felt they had to "learn by doing" for themselves. I later realized the focus of the empowerment agenda was the tenants themselves. They realized that if they were to form a viable organization with the goal of purchasing and managing Hope Mansions as a cooperative, they must invest in their own human resources. This included tolerating a secretary who had a poor writing and reading skills and struggled to write the minutes as well as read them for their approval.

Six months into my research, I asked and obtained the approval of some of the residents to tape-record their deliberations. Many of them agreed because they "got nothing to hide." However, whenever I sensed that a resident was apprehensive in speaking her/his mind, I turned off the tape recorder and resorted to taking notes. I recorded over 60 hours of deliberations and took copious notes. The cooperative president legitimized my use of the tape recorder when she asked me to share my transcribed notes with the board. During the first year of attending the resident meetings, the resident council had problems retaining a secretary to take minutes of their proceedings.

After three months of attending the weekly meetings, I asked Ms. Patricia Mason if there was anything I could do to help the residents so that I could gain deeper insight into their grassroots organizing. In January 1991, Ms. Mason offered me an internship position in her office to file all the background documents on the Hope Mansions Cooperative and gave me permission to make use of any information I found relevant to my dissertation. Among my finds were the resident survey conducted in 1987.

Another opportunity which enabled me to interact with residents directly was the Hope Mansions Energy Conservation Training Project. The purpose of the project was to teach residents to utilize gas wisely and thereby minimize their gas expenditures. Ms. Mason asked for my assistance in working with the residents on the energy conservation project. I became the project manager, responsible for writing the monthly reports. This role proved to be one of the most important means by which I gained access to individual residents.

The following year, I assisted the residents in writing and submitting a proposal for $25,000 to Washington Gas Light to expand the community-based energy conservation training program. The grant was awarded and I was tasked with the implementation of the grant proposal. This gave me the chance to visit individual households to encourage residents to participate in the program. This activity enabled me to get firsthand knowledge of various household situations. I also participated in scheduled tenant association meetings, signed up for neighborhood watch and the community after-school tutoring program. All of these activities were essential avenues by which to gather useful data.

By participating in community activities, I identified over a dozen tenants actively involved in the cooperative efforts. They served as a snowball sample. In addition, the PA had three field managers who had an office in one of the apartment complexes. I had the opportunity to schedule interviews with each one of them. Some of the individuals working in the field office were also residents who assisted me in getting interviews with other residents. Using a semi-structured questionnaire, I interviewed about thirty current and former tenants. I developed a strategy of taking with me newspaper articles dating back to the late 1940s whenever I went to interview a respondent. By showing residents some of the news stories, they were able to recall events and experiences with ease, and to speak about them with more certainty. Frequently, the respondents telephoned neighbors to ask them what they recalled about the news report.

The newspapers articles provided me with the names of potential respondents—former or current residents—whom I could call to interview. The articles also served as cross-references to events narrated by tenants. These in-depth interviews provided insight into tenants' perceptions and the realities of their neighborhood community, the management, the police, the drug problem and their current effort in cooperative endeavor.

My internship with the People's Advocacy also reinforced my access to the employees of Shelter Incorporated. Joe Jackson, Shelter Incorporated field manager, provided me with volumes of information—official information, newspaper articles and introductions to other individuals I should interview. One of the most important documents made available to me was the transcript of the *Hope Mansions Community Focus Group* (1987). Shelter Incorporated commissioned the focus group and it was conducted by a research agency. The focus group was conducted as a gesture to include tenants in their community's affairs by gathering information about their concerns, while providing Shelter Incorporated the necessary information on how to proceed with the neighborhood rejuvenation.

The participants of the focus group were drawn from both Sunrise and Hope Mansions and spanned different age groups, income levels, and employment statuses. A separate session was held for teachers from the schools in the neighborhood. The focus group sessions revealed that the drug problem and associated violence provided a common challenge to all the residents, and that the socioeconomic status which once had differentiated the two apartment complexes was no longer evident.

The PA staff, in general, were supportive of my research and often introduced me to various people as someone "writing about the history of Shelter's low-income housing project." From time to time, while writing the newsletter, Mr. Jackson also solicited information from me. On other occasions, he consulted with me to get a sense of why the residents were resistant to Shelter Incorporated's implementation plans and what approaches could be considered.

In 1987 the Nation of Islam/The Fruit of Islam (NOI/FOI) came to Hope Mansions and Sunrise Apartments by invitation to deal with the drug trade.[25] The Sunrise management invited the FOI to patrol and clear the grounds of the drug dealers and addicts who threatened the residents. The FOI's actions in Sunrise, in part, led to the flight of the drug dealers and buyers out of the apartment complexes and into Hope Mansions.

The Hope Mansions resident cooperative promptly asked Gail Peterson to take the necessary steps to retain the FOI to do for Hope Mansions what they had done for Sunrise. The FOI established a permanent presence in Hope Mansions and thereby facilitated the departure of the drug dealers from the area. In the course of my field research, I got acquainted with a few of the FOI members, and some gladly granted me interviews. I also gathered ample data about the FOI neighborhood activism from various newspaper sources.

Despite concerns about the increasing lawlessness, during the course of the research, the community's residents consistently complained that whenever they had called the police for assistance, the agency was unresponsive. The pervasive assumption held by many residents was that the police did not care about the ordinary citizens living in the neighborhood. As a result, very few residents saw the police as helpful government agents. I tried to verify this allegation. Under the Freedom of Information Act, I requested and obtained police-call-for-service records between 1985 and 1990 for analysis. The police data, as I will discuss later, enabled me to sort out the realities from tenants' perceptions of how they viewed the police and policing in their community.

Other data, such as Mayor Marion Barry's speeches and letters about Sun-Hope, were obtained in the District of Columbia Archives. After several failed attempts, I had the opportunity to interview one narcotic agent. In 1988, she worked in Sun-Hope as an undercover agent purchasing illegal drugs as part of the police's law enforcement techniques in an effort to apprehend drug dealers. Her insights into policing drug-plagued communities were essential in understanding both the tenants' distrust of officers, and in turn, some officers' resistance to enter such areas.

The use of various sources of data helped to lend credence or validity to the data. Conducted by an independent agency, the focus group sessions yielded invaluable data about the attitudes and opinions of residents of different age groups (teenagers, young parents, and seniors) about management, neighbors, the school system and the police. Also documented were tenants' future aspirations and expectations about the impending neighborhood rejuvenation. Participating in events myself enabled me to formulate interview questions, identify active members of the neighborhood for interviews, cross check their opinions and observations with those reported in the dailies, memos and the focus group transcript.

All the information gathered combined to provide ample data for analysis. The data is analyzed thematically, focusing on significant events, tenants' interpretation of those events, and the actions of a host of people and organizations which had ramifications for the community. The following chapters are attempt to tell the story of Sun-Hope neighborhood community.

NOTES

1. Richard J. Meister, *The Black Ghetto: Promise Land or Colony?* (Lexington: D.C. Heath and Company, 1972).
2. See Douglass S. Massey and Nancy A. Denton, *American Apartheid: Segregation and the Making of the Underclass* (Cambridge: Harvard University Press, 1993).
3. Meister, *The Black Ghetto,* vii.
4. For detailed examination of the topic, see John Kain's anthology, *Race and Poverty: The Economics of Discrimination* (Englewood Cliffs: Printice-Hall, 1969).
5. For a more detail analysis, see Douglas Massaey and Nancy Denton, *American Apartheid: Segregation and the Making of the Underclass* (Cambridge: Harvard University Press, 1993).
6. Harold X. Connolly, "Black Movement into Suburbs: Suburbs Doubling Their Black Populations during the 1960s," *Urban Affairs Quarterly* 9 (1973):91-111; Reynold Farley, "The Changing Distribution of Negroes within Metropolitan Areas: The Emergence of Black Suburbs," *American Journal of Sociology* 75 (1970):512-29.
7. For the purpose of consistency, I have adopted Massey and Denton's definition: "a ghetto is a set of neighborhoods that are exclusively inhabited by members of one group, within which virtually all members of that group live." See *American Apartheid.* "Of all poor black people," noted Jacqueline Jones, "six out of ten lived in central cities, but only one out of three poor whites lived in these areas." See Jacqueline Jones, *The Dispossessed: America's Underclass from the Civil War to the Present* (New York: BasicBooks, 1992), 270. Consequently, the black ghetto will remain a fixture in urban America unless there is a major policy to reduce poverty, and to deconcentrate the population of poor people in these areas.
8. Elijah Anderson, *Streetwise: Race, Class and Change in an Urban Community* (Chicago: University of Chicago Press, 1990).
9. Alex Kotlowitz, *There Are No Children Here: The Story of Two Boys Growing Up in the Other America* (New York: Doubleday, 1991).
10. Nicholas Lehman, *The Promised Land: The Great Black Migration and How It Changed America* (New York: Knopf, 1991).
11. See works by Ken Auletta, *The Underclass* (New York: Vintage Books, 1983), Julius William Wilson, *The Truly Disadvantaged: The Inner*

City, The Underclass, and Public Policy (Chicago: University of Chicago Press, 1987), and Jacqueline Jones, *The Dispossessed: America's Underclass from the Civil War to the Present* (New York: BasicBooks, 1992).

12. Patrick D. Moynihan, *The Negro Family: The Case for National Action* (Washington, D.C.: U.S. Department of Labor, 1965).

13. Oscar Lewis, "The Culture of Poverty." *Scientific American* 215 (1966): 19-25.

14. Gary S. Becker, *Human Capital* (New York: Columbia University Press, 1964.)

15. Lawrence Mead, *The New Politics of Poverty: The Nonworking Poor in America* (New York: The Free Press, 1992).

16. Anthony Giddens, *Central Problems in Social Theory, Action, Structure and Contradictions in Social Analysis* (Berkeley: University of California Press, 1986).

17. C. Wright Mills, *The Sociological Imagination* (New York: Oxford University Press, 1959).

18. Rachel G. Bratt, "Mutual Housing: Community-Based Empowerment," *Journal of Housing* 41 (1991):4.

19. Elliot Currie, "The Market Society," *Dissent* (Spring, 1991):255-58.

20. This format conforms to the ethics of ethnographic research. See Elliot Liewbow, *Talley's Corner: A Study of Negro Streetcorner Men* (Boston: Little Brown 1967). Also, Elijah Anderson, *Streetwise: Race, Class and Change in an Urban Community* (Chicago: University of Chicago Press, 1990). This strategy was necessary to protect me from risks (legal and otherwise), to protect individuals who may have made self-incriminating statements in the course of interviews, to protect individuals from possible retaliation, and to minimize conflicts which may subsequently erupt as a result of making public the contents of confidential memos, project reports, and letters used in this book.

21. David Osborne, "They Can't Stop Us Now," *The Washington Post Magazine,* 30 July 1989.

22. Others discretely referred to me as "the *Washington Post* Man." Some thought I was "a new resident" who had "he moved in not long ago".

23. Many residents understood what a school project was all about because their past school experiences. Whenever I had mentioned I was doing "dissertation research," however, my inquirers often wanted an explanation of it.

24. In one of the meetings for which there were two other teenage boys present, the local minister acknowledge us by saying "it is so nice to see some of young boys here this evening." Some of the women who knew me looked at

me bewilded. Later, a resident informed me that I looked like a teenager because I had shaved my beard and had my hair cut very short.

25. The NOI is the umbrella organization, and the FOI is a subsidiary organization which provides security services.

CHAPTER 2

Racial Segregation and Rise of Sun-Hope Neighborhood Community

In the 1950s, the newspaper accounts celebrated Sun-Hope as an impressive stable family community. This image counters the intense open-air 24-hour drug trade, crimes and homicides of the 1980s. The interplay of factors which gave rise to Sun-Hope's emergence and transformation will be examined.

During the depths of the 1930s depression, a "negro" evangelist by the name Father Jonas arrived in the District of Columbia and established his Faith Church of Christ (FCC). Through his "Happy Am I" daily radio program, Father Jonas gained a considerable number of followers. He became one of the most influential black persons in the city. Although racial segregation was the norm, Father Jona's radio program drew listeners across the racial divide. Among some of his listeners were the white "movers and shakers" in the nation's capital. On his list of honorary deacons were District Commissioner George E. Allen, Major Dwight D. Eisenhower, as well as the President's secretary "Steve" Early, Clark Griffith, principal owner of Washington's baseball team, and Harry Butcher, vice president of the Columbian Broadcasting Company.[1] Father Jonas, however, was more than a "prophet of God," as he liked to refer to himself; he was also a self-made businessman.[2]

Father Jonas made things happen. In 1940, he persuaded the District of Columbia Commissioner George Allen that gambling on horses displeased God. As a result, the Commissioner sold his horse and dropped the bill he was sponsoring to decriminalize horse racing in the District. In 1941, Father Jonas, in partnership with George Allen and with the financial support of his congregation, acquired the Lenning Street horse racing track where he built homes to meet the growing housing needs of middle- and working-class blacks the city.[3] Later, the notable Davis College architect professor Keaton Jones also joined the partnership.[4]

Father Jonas' mission was to "form his congregation into a self-sufficient unit and to help other dispossessed people beyond his church."[5] While other black churches and movements were fighting racism and segregation, Father Jonas and his Faith Church directed their efforts toward the black community itself. The church set up a soup kitchen to feed the unemployed and, in turn, solicited their labor to upgrade two apartment buildings for homeless people.[6]

With the assistance of First Lady Eleanor Roosevelt and other networks in President Roosevelt's administration, Father Jonas obtained the first Federal Housing Administration loan of $3 million to complete the housing project. At a time when discriminatory practices against blacks were the norm, Father Jonas managed to call upon Mrs. Roosevelt to intervene whenever the real estate project was faced with possible foreclosure. What emerged from the former race track were two apartment complexes: Sunrise Apartments, in 1946, and Hope Mansions open to let in 1960.

These apartment buildings were the first of their kind in the nation in that they were architecturally designed, built and managed by black enterprenuers. In response to the discriminatory ordinances barring blacks access to decent and affordable rental units, Sunrise Apartments provided housing for some of the black elite. Similarly, Hope Mansions offered inexpensive and affordable accommodations for low-income and working-class residents. Predating Sunrise Apartments and Hope Mansions in the same neighborhood were Eden Estates and the Park Dwellings housing project. Families living in Eden Estates owned their homes, while the families in Park Dwellings Public Housing were renters. All various housing combined, the area became a community of mixed-income black residents.

THE COMMUNITY AND SUNRISE-PARK DWELLINGS CIVIC ASSOCIATION

In 1960, a group of residents formed Sunrise-Park-Hope Civic Association in response to what they felt was a social class antagonism between them and the homeowners of Eden Estates. (Hope Mansions was fully completed in 1960). This association, however, was troubled from the start. The Eden Estates group cited the Sunrise-Park-Hope group as an "illegal body" and a "splinter organization which was operating without legal sanction."[7] Although Sunrise and Park Dwellings residents sought to forge their own association and identity, their organization also was plagued with social class antagonism. The residents in Sunrise Apartments, were predominantly middle-class professionals, and those in Park Dwellings, a delapidating public housing, were working-class and poor.

Park Dwellings Housing Project Residents

In 1943, the Park Dwellings housing project was built to offer low-income affordable homes under the federal low-income housing program. According to a former resident and president of the Sunrise-Park Dwellings Civic Association:

> Park Dwellings was built as a temporary facility during World War II. It was a framed structure with no design. It was only built to temporarily house poor people. That was what it was built for. After the war it was supposed to be torn down.[8]

But several years after the war, the buildings continued to house large and impoverished families. The construction of public housing such as the Park Dwellings was seen as "merely substituting new Negro ghettos for old."[9] A former resident who spent part of his childhood years in Park Dwellings stated:

> [Park Dwellings] was one of the first public housing development the in city. As you know or you might not know, around 1939, whites, particularly in Georgetown and in southwest Washington areas, started displacing black folks because they wanted those areas that were older areas to be developed for their use. . . . I lived and was born in the neighborhood. We moved out of Georgetown in 1942. We then moved to Park Dwellings which was developed for indigent

folks with large families. When we moved into Park Dwellings, we didn't have paved streets, and we didn't have all the [street] lights.[10]

Although in 1948, the Supreme Court "reversed the ruling of the lower courts on the legal enforceability of restrictive housing covenants," landlords still covertly discriminated against blacks:

> Voluntary adherents to housing covenants, though no longer enforceable in the courts, still severely limited the areas into which Negro families could move, and, quite apart from restrictive agreements, the prices of real estate in Georgetown virtually completed the decoloration of that section.[11]

The discriminatory housing practices not only led to the formation of mixed-class black neighborhoods, but they also led to the concentration of many poor people in various sections of the city. Residents in Park Dwellings, in particular, moved into the housing project largely because the alternative was to be homeless. The result was that "you had a tremendous mixture of folk and they had . . . to develop coping skills to get along with each other, and that was called 'the projects' at the time."[12] In other words, because of the culture of segregation in housing, both poor and nonpoor blacks lived in close proximity.

Many of the Park Dwellings residents were working poor. For these households, their meager wages could not support their large family sizes. Many residents, however, saw their situation as a stepping stone to someday buying single family homes. This view was engendered by the government's intimations that living in subsidized housing would enable residents to save more of their salaries so that they could buy and own homes later. However, the problem many residents in Park Dwellings experienced was that their rent subsidies were directly tied to income levels:

> Because [Park Dwellings] was controlled and built by the government, everytime you got let's say a 5 percent raise, [the public housing authority] went up 4 percent on your rent so you were never ever able to accumulate anything to get out of the project.[13]

The intent of the housing policy was incongruent with the economic reality of some of the residents.

Responding to their financial constraints, some of the residents adopted innovative techniques to facilitate their escape from the housing project.[14] Families of four or more moved out of two or three bedrooms into in one bedroom apartments renting for less money. On the one hand, this strategy enabled some residents to save money in the long-term. On the other hand, the consequences were overcrowded apartments and a densely populated neighborhood.

Other residents who did not have enough income "hustled" to supplement their wages. One former resident presents the following portrait of Park Dwellings denizens:

> You've got to realize that in those kinds of settings there were people who did all kinds of things. There were not many job openings. People, they did a little bit of bootlegging; people wrote numbers; people did a lot of non-violent illegal activities, but a lot of illegal activities as the government defined it.[15]

Faced with poverty, some felt justified in engaging in various deviant behaviors to support their families. One resident explained, "my hustle was we just strip the refrigerator of the copper and brass" at the D.C. garbage dump and then sold the metals to local dealers. Although those who hustled were mocked, they were respected nonetheless for making a living independently:

> I worked in the Montgomery County school system. I was a custodian. I worked in the evening. I'd wake up early in the morning and go over there [the D.C. garbage dump] and make 20, 25 dollars and give it to my wife to get on the bus go to work everyday to get ahead. People used to laugh and make fun at me, but I didn't care about that; I was taking care of my family.[16]

When unemployed adults were not "hustling," they sometimes sought public assistance. However, receiving public assistance carried a social stigma:

> In a lot of instances, you begin to see, at that time, they did not call it welfare—they called it relief—and a lot of people living in [Park Dwellings] didn't want their neighbors to know they were receiving relief because at that time it was kind of a shameful thing to be getting relief. So you tried to stay away from that. But you will see

them go away the first of the month and coming with groceries and I
guess they will get their little small checks in the mail, you know, and
around the first of each month they had more capital than some of the
other folks.[17]

The social stigma attached to public assistance made it embarassing,
and for many, less desirable than hustling. These adaptations, ranging
from relocation to "hustling" to receiving public assistance, show that
contrary to the claims of the conservative behavioralists, the ghetto is
not essentially the product of pathological behavior. Rather, the
strategies adopted by various families and individuals develop in
response to both the financial and housing constraints.

The constraints faced by these families invariably affected life
chances of their children too. Children in the area became a part of the
discordant relationship between privileged and underpriviledged
residents. Security guards in Sunrise enforced the segregation of
children in Park Dwellings from those in Sunrise. A former resident
who grew up in Park Dwellings recalled the experience of being denied
access to the playground in Sunrise: "We were not allowed. We went
over there to play, but they had a man by the name of [Agent Jackson].
He was the security force and he will run us out. But we played all
kinds of tricks on Agent Jackson."[18]

The security guards in Sunrise did not merely protect property:
they enforced the class separation between the children from Park
Dwellings and Sunrise. Likewise, the middle-class residents of Sunrise
used the neighborhood children to reinforce their social and economic
status:

It was a class situation. Most of the folks who lived in [Sunrise] were
of light complexion. Most of the people living in the projects [Park
Dwellings] for the most part were of dark complexion. After
becoming adults I saw what all of that was about this time. Being a
child, one thing that happened, the kids there were told not to
associate with the kids in the project. But we went to school
together—[JFK school]. Even though the parents told the kids not to,
kids will wanna come together.[19]

Similarly, the swimming pool in Sunrise was out of bounds to
children (and adults) from Park Dwellings. Whenever the Park

Dwellings children failed to evade the Sunrise security guards, they resorted to the creek:

> When we want to have some fun, we will—we will be about 10 of us—go over there. But usually, we had to go through [Sunrise] to get to our swimming hole, okay. We had a creek we swim in okay. In fact, the creek run along there [pointing to the creek] right now. That's the creek we swarm in. During that time that water run about 4 or 5 or 6 feet deep and especially after it rained everybody went swimming. While it was raining we will go swimming in the creek.[20]

Over time, the playground and the swimming pool became sources of frequent conflict among the children of the two apartment complexes. As a result of the fights, the management closed both recreation areas.

However, Sunrise was more than a playground for some of Park Dwellings' impoverished children. The children of Park Dwellings witnessed a way of life toward which they could aspire. Articulating this aspiration, another resident who was raised in Park Dwellings and later lived in Sunrise as a working adult expressed his attraction to Sunrise this way:

> When they built [Sunrise]—because they had it so immaculate, people in [Sunrise] were really what you called middle- and upper-class kind of black folks as we knew them at that time—the desire of a lot of kids like myself in [Park Dwellings] was to eventually to move to [Sunrise]. That was a stepping stone up."[21]

Although residents in Park Dwellings were generally poor, former residents recalled the community being neighborly and relatively free of criminal activity. Expressing the nostalgia for "the way things were" in Park Dwellings, one former resident stated:

> One of the unique things was that all the families that lived there— there was camraderie, there was a family atmosphere—meaning every father was my father. Every mother was my mother. Every child was my brother and sister. And that attitude was fostered throughout the community. When one hungered, he was fed or she was fed.[22]

The "camraderie" mentioned by this respondent suggests that poverty at the time engendered far fewer hostilities than it does today. The community was enriched by human compassion. As one Sunrise resident noted: "We knew that the people were mostly families and some of them grew up to be very successful. So far as I know there were no problems in the late 40s and early 50s in Park Dwellings."[23]

That the Park Dwellings Apartments residents were poor but lived in relative peace had to do with the wholesome living environment the tenants created for themselves during the 1950s and 60s. There were informal social controls to thwart undesirable behaviors which threatened neighborhood order:

> My thought now about the community is that the socialization in the community was second to none as opposed to the way it is today. A winehead who everybody knew was a drinker, we didn't call them winehead because we respected everyone: that individual will make you go to school. That individual had the respect of everybody in the community. No child heard an adult use profanity. That's how it was.[24]

In addition to its healthy neighborhood relations, the housing project was well-maintained and inspected by the National Capital Housing:

> One of the things that made Park Dwellings unique was the management, National Capital Housing management. Every home had to have green grass; it had to be cut and manicured. That was one of the rules for being on the property. They had regular inspections of your home to ensure that there were no adverse damages; children, if a child broke a window. They were rules that were really needed. It was a form of discipline . . . everyone accepted.[25]

The regular inspections of homes also generated a form of peer pressure among families and households. The residents competed for the best-kept lawn and flower gardens and awards were given. Although Park Dwellings residents were working-poor people, they took pride in "their" housing project. As one former resident recalled, Park Dwellings was "a neighborhood where we cared about the property, cared about other people."[26] The result was a clean, safe environment for the residents.

But beyond the pride and poverty, many adults and children were hopeful about their future prospects; they looked forward to the day when they, too, would be able to own their own home or live in a nice apartment complex like Sunrise Apartments.

Sunrise Apartments

Reminiscing about the earlier days, a former resident says: "I could use all the superlatives in the world talking about Sunrise. . . . If you go back in time, Sunrise Apartments was the best place in America for middle-income and upper-income blacks to live."[27] Considering that it was an era when blacks were denied housing overtly in certain sections of the city, even when they could afford it, Sunrise "attracted a cross-section of doctors, university professors, lawyers, school teachers, social workers and businessmen."[28] This recollection is confirmed by a tenant who, unlike her cohorts who moved to suburbia in the 60s and 70s, has lived through all the upheavals and changes in Sunrise. She recalled prominent persons such as Dr. Robert Cephas, an historian, and Mr. Keaton Jones, an architect and professor, and a prominent Congressman from New York as her neighbors.[29]

Indisputably, Sunrise Apartments complex was an enclave for reputable black people. Up until "596 well-to-do Negro families moved in 1954, . . . virtually no comfortable living units were available to self-respecting Negroes."[30] When Sunrise opened its doors, it was estimated that 5,000 people were on the waiting list.[31] Prospective applicants were screened to ensure that they held steady jobs with salaries to afford the rent. In addition, an applicant needed to submit letters of recommendation from his/her previous rental agent or an honorable public official in order to be considered for tenancy. Not only were middle-class families attracted to the neighborhood, but their influence ensured that the community received the necessary public services.

The often-cited reason why Sunrise attracted so many prominent people is that it was beautiful. The grounds were kept clean and the lawns were green and well-maintained. To ensure that the Sunrise Apartments grounds were kept up were two resident managers and a staff of twenty, including engineers, electricians, and maintenance men. One older resident recalled the scenery:

> At the time when I first came there in 1950 . . . we had a crab apple, we had dogwood, forsythia, azaleas, other small plants or shrubs . . .

in front of our unit. We had a wading pool for the little people and I think that impressed me. I love to see green grass or just grass, and there wasn't a bare spot to be seen, and it was clean. The people that lived here at the time took pride in their surroundings so therefore everyone in the complex took pride.[32]

To prevent and deter vandalism and crime, the management hired security guards to patrol the grounds and to protect the property. He spoke to children to find out if they were behaving themselves— attending school regularly and refraining from trouble. One resident, Mr. Bobson, appointed himself a truancy officer. He also was known to peek through residents' windows to ensure that they maintained the interiors of their apartments.[33] "The people that lived there at that time," says one resident, "took pride in their surroundings so, therefore, everyone in the complex took pride."[34] The pride came with the collective energy residents invested in the community through Sunrise-Park Dwellings Civic Association.

In addition to maintaining a respectable community externally, Father Jonas Jones, founder of Sunrise Apartments, attempted to maintain a wholesome moral community among Sun-Hope residents. The social events held by the Sun-Hope Civic Association excluded dancing, bingo, card playing or any recreational gambling. The sale and consumption of liquor were prohibited on the premises. Father Jonas considered all of these activities works of the devil, destructive not only to the Church but the black community at large.[35] Many adults, perhaps, disregarded these prohibitions. But to the extent that they kept these behaviors indoors, the community was kept free of loitering, trash, and public disturbances. It remained relatively stable.

Hope Mansions

Father Jonas and his Faith Church completed the construction of Hope Mansions in 1960. Hope Mansions was an extension of Sunrise; however, the 600 units were designed to offer affordable rental housing to predominantly working-class black families. Hope Mansions residents were inducted into the Civic Association which was renamed Sun-Park-Hope Civic Association. However, the residents' participation in the Civic Association was short-lived.

The Fall of Sun-Park-Hope Civic Association

By early 1960s, the Civic Association disbanded. One key member explained the organization's emergent problems as a combination of ineffective leadership and the departure of influential members:

> Our civic association was known as [Sunrise-Park Dwellings Civic Association]. Later it was expanded to be [Sun-Park-Hope] Civic Association. [Mr. Sam Banc] was the next to the last president to the Civic Association. The Civic Association lasted for a long time but the president following Mr. Banc [laughing] did not function and the organization came to a grinding halt. At the same time the tenant council was established which meant that tenants had two meetings to go and I advised against it.[36]

A number of reasons accounted for the loss of power of the Civic Association, but for the most part, its demise reflected a certain class tension. Hope Mansions was adjoined to Sunrise Apartments, and both were owned by the Faith Church. However, Hope Mansions, similar to Park Dwellings Public Housing Project, was designed for working-class black families. The status of Hope residents in the Civic Association was the same as that of the Park Dwellings residents: neither resident groups felt at home at the meetings.

The socioeconomic difference among between Sunrise, Hope Mansions and Park Dwellings residents was vast. Although the residents of the three apartments did function together under the banner of the Sun-Park-Hope Civic Association, ordinary, everyday interactions between residents were limited because of the social class difference between the two communities. Although they did encounter each other through the [Sun-Park] Civic Association, the membership dues deterred the working-class families from full and equal participation in deliberation and decision-making. The Sun-Park-Hope Civic Association was under the leadership of Sunrise's mostly educated, professional and dues-paying members. Park Dwellings residents were encouraged to attend the meetings, but their concerns were not given much attention:

> The people in [Sunrise] wanted the people in [Park Dwellings] to come [to the meetings], but they didn't want [Park Dwellings] to develop its own agenda. *They* wanted to set the agenda for [Park

Dwellings]. But they were critical of [Eden Estates] who had the civic association charter for the area, previously, to do the same thing for them, so eventually Sunrise did get its own and recognized by the Federation of Civic Associations. . . . But the Civic Association fought so much among itself that it was very difficult to get things done.[37]

Regardless of the social class division among members, the Civic Association provided a forum for identifying and dealing with neighborhood problems.

Residents, however, were paying more attention to their separate Tenant Councils. In their initial stages, the Tenant Councils appealed to residents for two main reasons. First, the discrete councils implicitly resolved the antagonism between the two social classes. The less privileged project residents felt their dignity restored, not having to subordinate themselves under the leadership of the middle class in Sunrise Mansions. Secondly, each Tenant Council could focus on issues concerning its immediate housing areas.

In the mid-1960s, the disintegration of the community-wide mediating institution marked the beginning of the community's decline. Similar to the Civic Association before them, the Tenant Councils of all the three housing areas progressively unraveled. Community-wide problems could not be addressed effectively because the residents had disbanded their community-wide mediating institution. Because they lacked the resources and know-how, the leaders, as I will discuss later, were unable to meet the needs of tenants. They, in turn, grew increasingly apathetic and powerless.

In addition, the community experienced dramatic demographic changes. There is inverse relation between the community's decay and decline and the steady out-migration of its "movers and shakers." Not only were the incoming residents poorer, but they lacked the sense of "ownership" and committment of those who had come before them. Moreover, they arrived in a community without an active mediating institution. To boot, the FCC was itself faced with a leadership in crisis. In the ensuing chapters I will discuss the details of the external and internal problems leading to the gradual decline of Sun-Hope community.

SUN-HOPE COMMUNITY DURING THE STUDY

My first visit to Sun-Hope community was in September 1989. Gail Peterson, the president of Shelter Incorporated, had scheduled a general meeting with the tenants because there was a "shooting over the weekend" and one person was reported killed. The meeting was convened so that the residents could discuss with the owner how to get the drug dealers out of the neighborhood, curb the violence and make tenants feel safe. The violence had grown pervasive as the drug syndicates fought each other for the neighborhood market share. The open-air drug trade resulted in several drug-related homicides in the Sun-Hope community between 1983 and 1990. The details of this matter will be discussed later.

In addition to the fact that they were poorly managed, the location of the twin housing complexes along a major highway proved to be strategic to drug dealers. The main transportation systems for those without cars were the Metrorail and the bus line stationed across the highway from the apartment buildings. Not far away were Amtrak and Metrorail stations. Residents crossed the highway via an overpass leading to the public transportation systems. The twin apartment complexes spanned a one mile radius and were bound by Sunset Lane and Rust Place. These were continuous one-way streets which met to form a horse shoe shape. Every fifteen minutes a bus departed from the Metrorail/bus station to drop off residents at the various stops around the complexes. These neighborhood features, as I will discuss later, facilitated the drug trade and made policing problematic.

Dating from the purchases of Sunrise and Hope Mansions by separate investors in the 1980s, Sunrise Apartments has been separated from Hope Mansions by a high steel fence. Sunrise residents drove through electronic gates leading to the various parking lots or entered through miniature gates leading to all the walkways for the residents. To a visitor, the fence symbolized the separate ownership of the apartment complexes. To those in the know, it underscored the historical continuation of separate class consciousness between the two resident groups; however, in reality the majority of the residents shared the same socioeconomic strata—lower income.[38]

As a result of the drinking prohibition, management prohibited Sunrise residents from drinking openly in the courtyards. The enforcement of this tenancy regulation accounted for confines of Sunrise being clean. Over the duration of my field work, I noticed maintenance workers regularly tending the grounds. Sunrise Apartments looked newer and well-lit at night-fall. This was the result of of the 1.2 million dollar renovation undertaken by Jason Saunders and other investors who bought the property from the FCC.

One of the frequent scenes I noticed with time was the men from Sunrise Apartments who gathered in evenings in clusters underneath the large trees shades along Rust Place during the summer months, sharing alcoholic beverages, cigarettes, jokes and laughter.[39] The frequency of the drinking ritual explained the accumulated trash— empty alcoholic beverage bottles, shattered glasses, candy wraps, aluminum cans, cigarette containers and butts—along the curb and sidewalk across the street from Sunrise Apartments. For the most part, the men were able to carry on their social activities without sanctions. Lacking legitimate power, the typical tenant did not have the audacity to break up the party; only the police could have interrupted them.[40]

Within a quarter of a mile of Sunrise Apartments' main entrance was Hope Mansions. Unlike Sunrise Apartments, Hope Mansions lacked fences and gates, thereby allowing unrestricted access. Nearly 50 percent of the buildings were boarded up and others had their glass windows broken. The common entrance doors to many of the apartment buildings were either torn off or the locks were severely damaged. Some of the structural damage to the buildings looked intentional. I observed that many of the steel doors were indented, some of the glass windows had been shattered by projectiles and left to collapse, and some of the walls had bullet holes in them. The cement holding the bricks in place in some of the buildings was eroded severely as a result of the weather. Some of the buildings had signs warning residents to stay away from structures for fear of unanticipated collapse.

Unlike Sunrise, there were weeds growing around the abandoned buildings. The breezeway walls were lined with graffiti in honor of dead individuals and warnings to the living. Other graffiti, I learned later, were "signs" or signatures of youth gangs who sold drugs in the community. The parking lots and streets were strewn with abandoned cars, vandalized or stripped of any saleable parts. The remains of these cars served as receptacles for disposed furniture, clothes and other debris. All the fifteen apartment buildings of Hope Mansions looked similar. Each of the buildings was numbered, but these numbers were hardly visible at night because of inadequate lighting.

On my first visit to the community, I became aware that many of the residents, especially the women, lived in fear. The first woman I queried about the location of Building 6 hurried away from me saying, "I don't know." The tenant meeting I was attending drew about fifty residents. Among the people present were Gail Peterson, the president of Shelter Incorporated, four staff members, the board members of the resident council, and Patricia Mason of the People's Advocacy. Also present was Beacher Bronze. He owned and operated a neighborhood "store-on-wheels," and was highly regarded by the tenants. Because Bronze worked outdoors and interacted with the residents—drug dealers and ordinary tenants alike—six days a week, he witnessed a significant amount of vagrancy, drug dealing, and police activity in the community.

The first order of business was that the individuals involved in the "shootings"—victim and armed man—were not Hope Mansions residents, at least they were not legally listed as tenants on any household lease. This seemed to satisfy most tenants present, so they moved onto other issues, still related to lawfulness.

The residents took turns speaking about how unsafe the neighborhood was. As one tenant stated: "the kids are still dealing in drugs late in the night when the police are long gone." Resident complainants spoke at length about the loud music, the going and coming of people in certain apartments all night, and how the owner should intervene to either evict unlawful residents or maintain order. The complainants, however, when asked to identify the unlawful and disorderly residents, refused to do so. A typical response was: "I ain't gonna be a snitch but I want to have my peace." The tenants' attitude did not provide the owner with many options. In response, Peterson stated: "then there is nothing I could do about it."

A former resident who was well-known and respected by many of the residents addressed the attendants. He argued his point that the prevalence of misbehaving teenagers was because parents were abdicating their responsibility within the community:

> If you parents are not going to deal with your kids, how could you expect to have a peaceful neighborhood? The drug dealing continues because there are no mothers to speak to the children about the problem.[41]

After the meeting, this man revealed to me that some of the parents living in Hope Mansions would not intervene in their children's "business" because many of the families lived off the money that their children made selling drugs. "Many of the kids give their parents money every week—say $200, $500 or more. The mothers don't ask their kids where the money is coming from because they—the mothers—need the money."[42]

As a consolation, Peterson advised the residents present at the meeting to inform the Fruit of Islam (FOI) members who patrolled the property 24-hours a day to police for drug dealers and buyers. As will be discussed later, Shelter Incorporated retained the Nation of Islam to protect the property from vandals and drug dealers. Other residents at the meeting barraged Gail Peterson for the delay in relocating them into the newly renovated apartments in Hope Mansions. She assured them of the expeditious work being done to complete the renovations on time.

After the meeting, I observed women asking a few of the men present to walk them to their respective apartments. Women living in the same apartment buildings sought each other out to walk together. Even women whose buildings were nearest to the meeting place asked those in groups to "watch my back" while they raced across the bear courtyard to their apartment buildings. The common determinant of the women's behavior was fear, both percieved and real. They were reacting to the random "shootings" or "muggings" by people who might be hiding in the dark and obscured areas of the buildings. Although the change in ownership from the Church to the new investors (Shelter Incorporated acquired Hope Mansions, and Jason Saunders and his associates, Sunrise Apartments) generated excitement about the improvements underway, many of the residents considered Sun-Hope community a dangerous place to live.

SUMMARY

This chapter explains the historical development of Sun-Hope community: the situation of owners, the waxing and waning of their civic associations, social class antagonism, the exodus of the middle class, and tenants' concern for their safety as a result of the violence associated with the neighborhood drug dealing. This kind of analysis detailing the genesis of neighborhood poverty is often overlooked by subcultural theorists. Their primary focus, more often than not, is on individual abberant individual behaviors detrimental to family stability and community order.

The Sun-Hope community is a product of racial housing segregation facilitated largely by restrictive housing covenants and a shortage of housing for blacks. The declining use of restrictive housing covenant later in the 1960s, however, caused significant changes in the demography of the Sun-Hope community and led to its subsequent destabilization. In addition, the internal struggle for power within the Church, management's poor screening of prospective tenants, underfunding and inadequate supervision of the property, and inadequate public services in the area contributed to the demise of the community, as the following chapter shows.

NOTES

1. Constance Green, *Secret City: History of Race Relations in the Nation's Capital* (New Jersey: Princeton University Press, 1976).

2. For a biography of Father Jonas, see Lillian A. Poe, (Ph.D. diss., College of William and Mary, Williamsburg, Virginia, 1975).

3. Green, *Secret City*, 1976.

4. The partnership fell apart in the 1960s after a long legal battle between Father Jonas and Keaton Jones.

5. Poe, diss., 144.

6. A sample census survey conducted in 1947 revealed that "a Negro family is two and a half times as likely as a white family to live in a dwelling containing six or more persons. A Negro family is also:

> 9 times as likely to live in a house needing structural repair
> 4 times a likely to lack a private flush toilet
> 10 times as likely to lack central heating
> 11 times as likely to lack running water
> 8 times as likely to lack electric lights.

Bureau of the Census, *Current Population Reports, Housing*, July 1947. Cited in Kenesaw M. Landis, *Segregation in Washington: A Report of The National Committee on Segregation in The Nation's Capital* (1948), 26.

7. *The Washington Post*, 25 June 1960.

8. Former Tenant, personal interview, 18 May 1992.

9. Green, *The Secret City*, 283.

10. Former tenant and President of Sun-Hope Civic Association, personal interview, 13 September 1991.

11. Green, *The Secret City*, 283-284.
12. Ibid.
13. Ibid.
14. Robert Merton, *Social Structure and Social Theory* (New York: The Free Press, 1968).
15. Former tenant, personal interview, 13 September 1991.
16. Clergyman, born and raised in the neighborhood, personal interview, 25 March 1992.
17. Former tenant, personal interview, 13 September 1991.
18. Clergyman, personal interview, 25 March 1992.
19. Ibid. Among African Americans, skin complexion and social status continue to be a source of contention about access to privilege in a racialized society. For more detailed discussion, see Gregory Howard Williams, *Life on the Color Line*, (New York: PLUME/Penguin, 1996), Kathy Russel et. al, *The Color Complex: The Politics of Skin Color Among African Americans* (New York: Harcourt Brace Jovanovich Publishers, 1992), Jame E. Blackwell, *The Black Community: Diversity and Unity* (New York: HarperCollins Publishers Inc., 1991).
20. Ibid.
21. Former tenant, personal interview, 13 September 1991.
22. Clergyman, personal interview, 25 March 1992.
23. Tenant and former secretary of the Hope-Sun Civic Association in the 1960s, personal interview, 25 October 1991.
24. Clergyman, personal interview, 25 March 1992.
25. Ibid.
26. *The Washington Times*, 23 April 1990.
27. Former tenant, telephone interview, 23 May 1991.
28. Ibid.
29. Tenant, personal interview, 11 March 1992.
30. Green, *The Secret City*, 262.
31. Al Sweeney, *The Washington Afro-American*, 24 July 1982.
32. *Focus Group*, May 1987, 33.
33. Former tenant, personal interview, 13 September 1991.
34. *Focus Group*, May 1987, 38.
35. This elderly tenant noted, however, that alcohol was used by several residents, albeit indoors. Similarly, a former tenant also confirmed that while illicit drug use was not common, once in a while there was the odd person using a reefer.
36. Tenant, personal interview, 25 October 1991.
37. Former tenant, personal interview, 13 September 1991.

38. In 1980, the median household income for Ward 7, where Sun-Hope community is located, was $14,470. This was below the city-wide household income of $16,200.

39. In 1993, Shelter Incorporated cut down the trees as part of an area Redevelopment Plan leading to the abatement of the curbside drinking parties.

40. For more elaborate analysis of how police control neighborhood disorder such as public drinking, see James Q. Wilson and G. Kelling, "Broken Windows: Police and Neighborhood Safety," *Atlantic Monthly* 249 (March, 1983):29-38.

41. Former resident and now a neighborhood vendor, personal interview, 18 November 1989.

42. Ibid.

CHAPTER 3
Social Class Segregation and Fall of the Sun-Hope Community

Internal and external events drive neighborhood change. These events are empirically interrelated but analytically distinguishable. Changes from within the community might occur due to community members' tolerance of deviant behaviors, residents' varying vested interests in the community, people's social mobility, management's efficiency, and other demographic variables (income, family size, marital and employment status). External factors affecting the community include legal changes, public policies, the transfer of real estates, and the response of various public agencies, most notably the police, to events in the community. Equally significant is the traffic of people with varying interests into the community. These factors will be examined in the context of Sun-Hope community.

As already mentioned, the main external factor that facilitated the flight of the black elite from Sunrise Apartments and Hope Mansions to predominantly affluent neighborhoods and even the suburbs dates back the 1948 Supreme Court decision rendering the restrictive housing covenant illegal. The legislation of the Civil Rights Act of 1964 expanded the civil rights of minorities to pursue equal access to employment, better education, bank loans, etc. More specifically, the 1968 Fair Housing Act set the stage for well-to-do Black Americans to buy homes in neighborhoods previously closed to them. Prior to this legal change, many African Americans of various socioeconomic backgrounds lived in segregated neighborhoods.

When [Sunrise Apartments] was built in 1945, there was so much
discrimination in housing that blacks did not have avenues to go live
in certain places that were restricted to them. Once that restriction
was lifted, then [Sunrise] no longer attracted that type of persons they
had attracted in 1945.[1]

The type of persons whose influence and presence made the community
reputable and stable were the same persons who were financially
prepared to take advantage of the opportunities created by the Supreme
Court's ruling. The first to leave the community were those in
professional occupations. The in-coming residents did not have same
occupational caliber and influence. Inadvertently, the lifting of the
restrictive covenants initiated the destabilization of the Sun-Hope
community.

However, not all residents could or desired to leave their
community. One of the original tenants who remained in Sunrise stated:

It was in the 60s, late 60s. Many people bought homes in nearby
Maryland and thought they wanted to be in the suburbs. But some of
us thought we should stay in Washington and why be pushed into the
suburbs. . . . It's a mess and many of these places don't have bus
services on Sundays.[2]

The original residents who stayed in the community were
predominantly single, widowed and/or elderly women. The majority of
these people lacked the means to afford homes in the suburbs.

You got to realize, once the 1954 decision was made, what you
call *affluent* blacks moved out. Then you had some old people that
stayed there, like Naomi Crantz . . . what's the other lady's name?
Miss Mable Talker? Chilsom Bobson. Bobson and a few of them
stayed there.[3]

These "old people" constituted the remaining group of residents who
were the first to live in Sunrise Apartments and Hope Mansions since
their opening.[4] At writing, there were also several single tenants,
mostly women with children, who were born and raised in the
community. Some of these women residents moved to Sunrise or Hope
Mansions from Park Dwellings Public Housing when the city
government declared their decayed apartment buildings unsafe.

While racial integration at various levels alleviated some of the economic and social barriers experienced by American blacks, it had the unanticipated effect of widening social class and neighborhood gaps between the haves and the have-nots. In Sun-Hope, as the middle class and educated blacks left their segregated neighborhood, the area became depleted of vital human resources—leadership and political clout. A clergyman raised in the community explained:

> People began to move out of the District into the suburbs. During that time segregation/integration was beginning to raise its ugly head. *Integration was the worse thing to have ever happened to African Americans to my estimation because it isolated us from one another.* We began to think that we were better than one another, because integration said that you now could go anywhere you want to go, and the counter began to open up; you could go to the movie houses. But a big migration took place. Not only were African Americans moving out but the Caucasians were moving out as well.[5]

Here, the clergyman illustrates one of the most frequently mentioned reasons for the decline of Sun-Hope. Raced-based housing segregation forced the formation of relatively stable mixed-class black neighborhoods. On the one hand, housing desegregation facilitated equal access to housing based on income, regardless of race/ethnicity. On the other hand, desegregation caused the dissolution of stable and mixed-income urban black communities such as Sun-Hope.

From the accounts of a few former residents and newspaper articles analyzed in later chapters, it appears that the nonpoor were not the only ones who left Sun-Hope. By the 1980s, the working poor followed, leaving behind new residents who were even poorer.[6] The out-migration of the nonpoor led to an emergent community of concentrated poverty.

Aside from desegregation, another factor which led to the departure of many of the residents from the community was that Sun-Hope apartments and surroundings were no longer as attractive as they once were. The pride many people had felt living in Sun-Hope was gradually fading as management failed to live up to their expectations, and as the buildings fell into disrepair. Unlike many of the new apartments being built in other areas of the city, Sun-Hope's apartments were not equipped with modern amenities, such as air conditioners. The laundry facilities did not meet the needs of the scores of households living in the community—not to mention the frequent wear, tear and delays in getting the washers and dryers fixed. A social service worker who managed activity programs for senior citizens stated:

> [Sun-Hope] started loosing some of its glitter. . . . It didn't have the attraction to the same caliber of people. And then, you may also have some people in the neighborhood who grew up in the neighborhood. Some get out, some don't. Then those who stay tend to take the place for granted. You see some people take projects or apartments as: "well it is not mine." So they don't have the same regard they will have if they were buying it. And even though "it was mine"—in the sense that if I live there and this is the place I am raising a family—it is not the same sense of permanence.[7]

The exodus of many resourceful people had another effect on the community. The community became vulnerable to new problems. The incoming residents were not of the same socioeconomic status as those who preceded them. The community was becoming a ghetto.

GHETTOIZATION OF SUN-HOPE NEIGHBORHOOD COMMUNITY

Specifically, Sun-Hope managements (still under the FCC) were allowing the community to become a ghetto. Declining organization, accountability and funds led to physical deterioration, lagging security measures and an increase in squatters and drug dealers, at the same time that the middle-class exodus deprived the neighborhood of leadership and resources. The departure of the black middle class made room for those without adequate housing to find suitable and affordable housing in Sunrise and Hope Mansions. In contrast to the tenants of Sun-Hope before the 1970s, the incoming tenants were primarily wage earners, dependent on Section 8 rent subsidies, and single parent households on welfare.[8] A former resident who lived in Sunrise between 1977 and 1981 said he moved there:

> 'cause rent was cheap and I could get in on the Section 8. You make so much money and your rent don't be so high. When I first moved out there I was paying about $155 a month for one bedroom. And I was not a person with money.[9]

The upward mobility of many black families and their consequent flight from Sunrise Apartments and Hope Mansions presented the Faith Church with the task of filling up the vacant apartment units.

By the late 1970s, the community was attracting mostly unemployed, undereducated, single, unwed teen-mothers largely because the management company was under pressure to fill the vacant apartments. These teenage mothers, with their government rent subsidies, provided a steady flow of rent money to the landlord. Even Sunrise Apartments, which was originally occupied by predominantly middle-class families paying rent comparatively higher than tenants in Hope Mansions, soon became a home of many single-parent families without steady incomes. One of the residents who has been living in Sunrise Apartments for most of her adult life explained that:

> Most of the people in the 1950s and 1960s . . . so far as I know most of the residents in Sunrise were paying fair market rent. Only a few of us are paying market rent now. Last year [1991] there were only 15 families paying market rent out of 560 apartments, maybe a few more this year.[10]

The shift in the socioeconomic status of residents has been dramatic. Even the number of families with blue-collar jobs and steady sources of income has declined. The majority of the residents in the neighborhood community have become economically dependent on array of federal and local government entitlement programs.

In view of this, the tenancy standards were lowered to accommodate many of the apartment seekers. During the heydays of both Sunrise Apartment and Hope Mansions, a potential applicant had to obtain recommendations from respectable persons in the community before he/she was considered for an apartment. The former president of the Civic Association—who was also raised in the community—moved out from Sunrise largely because, in his judgement, the management company was allowing unqualified residents into Sunrise:

> They don't do the same kind of . . . screening that you need to make sure the applicants are people who pay the rent, keep the apartment up and things like that. I stayed there for 25 years and I moved out because [Sunrise] had become a slum. I moved out in 1981.[11]

Blaming the declining living conditions in Sunrise on the building management, he stated:

> They [management] did not screen the applicants. Your residents is what keeps the properties up, if they behave themselves and do right. In the early 70s most of the people that were there were about something—and this is no disrespect to the people in there at Sunrise—but the people that were there [when he left] did not have the same zeal or zest for keeping up Sunrise. A lot of those people were behind in their rent.[12]

Another resident who moved to Sunrise in 1978 found that the requirement to get an apartment was rather easy. This resident had moved from another state to Washington in search of a job. Although he had no source of steady income,

> it was easy to move out here because at that time all you had to have was money to get an apartment and I think all [the management] wanted was money. I don't think they did too much of credit checks. I know when I moved out here I got an apartment in three days time and the rent was $205.00 for one-bedroom. When people moved into the neighborhood, what usually attracts them is the cheap rent.[13]

Although the rent was cheap, some tenants had the tendency to default on their rent because they lacked a regular source of income. It appeared their earnings were insufficient to support themselves and their families. Some residents, too, knowingly defaulted on their rents without fear of eviction because of the inefficiency of the management staff. Investigating the conditions of Hope Mansions, a HUD inspector reported:

> There is a major problem in tenant rental collection. In some cases tenants have not paid their portion of their rent for months and have been allowed to continue their residence despite efforts made to evict them[14]

The portion of the rent mentioned refers to the payments a subsidized renter makes to complement HUD's Section 8 rent subsidy. Some tenants ceased paying rent because they were able to bribe someone at the main office. Others held up their rents in protest of having to live with inadequate amenities.

The source of the inadequacies the tenants faced was, of course, the management, whose deteriorating organization, accountability, commitment and funds yielded degeneration. It was evident that the management was inept or lacked control over the property and residents. There were some people living in the buildings for whom management could not account. This made it difficult to control the disorderly behavior in the community. For instance, many women or teenage girls dependent on AFDC (Aid to Families with Dependent Children) and Section 8 housing subsidy shared their apartments with unauthorized adults. Against federal rules, some women shared their apartments with boyfriends or nonrelatives in exchange for cash or companionship:

> There was like, as you know, most of the women was on welfare. Most of the guys worked. That's the way it was. But it was a lot of guys that didn't work. They stayed with the women that was on welfare. Everybody in my building worked. I was in Building 7, 3590. Everybody in my building worked.[15]

> You know there is this underground system where some men stayed with women on welfare—and they were not suppose to do that. We had one man, anytime a notice goes out that the inspectors were coming out here, he will get all his belongings and put them in his car. Sometimes he'll do this all week because nobody knows the exact date the inspectors are gonna show up. The last time I asked him why he was moving out he said he was going to do his laundry.[16]

The problems of maintaining the property were compounded by the fact that not only did the Faith Church disinvest in the community, but the management company made little effort to collect overdue rent. The ineffectiveness and deficiencies of the previous owner/management were revealed after the Shelter Incorporated acquired Hope Mansions. Upon auditing a random sample of tenants' files and apartment units, the Housing and Urban Development inspectors discovered the following:

- Tenant A - 3542 #302
  1) Missing security deposit receipt and unit inspection reports

    2)   Application for rental incomplete.
- Tenant B - 3676 #202
    1)   Missing security deposit receipt and unit inspection reports.
- Tenant C - 3679 #101
    1)   Unit inspection report missing.
- Tenant D - 3680 # 201
    1)   Security deposit receipt mission
    2)   Statement from unemployment needs to be updated.
- Tenant E - 3693 #103
    Model lease and security deposit receipt missing.[17]

The problem in all of these cases was the incomplete documentation of the tenants living in Hope Mansions. There is ample evidence to suggest that the previous management was not only ineffective, but also deliberately accepted prospective tenants without fully gathering all the necessary tenancy documentation.

The previous management could not deal with the periodic recertification of tenants to ensure that they were deserving of the Section 8 rent subsidy. When Shelter Incorporated acquired Hope mansions, the new management was saddled with the task of reviewing and updating tenants' records. In 1988, HUD auditors stated that:

> Management is to be commended for bringing recertification up to date, developing proper tenant application screening procedures and adequately managing the Section 8 subsidy since their inception. They have had to overcome many obstacles such as poor record keeping by the former agent. It is anticipated that the present agent will continue to improve in this area and the rating can be raised in the future if [tenancy] policies and plans . . . are implemented and enforced.[18]

In the 1970s, in the midst of the FCC's declining commitment, the death of Father Jonas sealed the degeneration of the real estates and the decline of the community. His death resulted in a sort of chaos. The trustee charged with the administration of the real estate was faced with dwindling funds. Whatever funds were derived from the tenants were divested out of the community. The Faith Church of Christ neglected the upkeep of the property: the Church became a slumlord. The real estate which was to have been the basis for economic strength of the

Church became a burden. This affected both the management and the maintenance of the property:

> Father Jonas died. When he died the vision was not the same. Within the Faith Church, I don't think you had the same *zeal* about coming out, checking the property, making sure everything was going right. Once in awhile, at least, [Father Jonas] would come out there.[19]

A youth activist in the community who "saw the rise and fall of Sun-Hope" added that:

> After Father Jonas died there was a power struggle and less attention and other things that may be defined as selfishness, some say greed. And these typical quarrels that you find not just among blacks. And unfortunately it was never resolved. What you have now is only a ghost or phantom of what the man [Father Jonas] was talking about. And one of the reasons some people are talking about is that he did not prepare his cadre.[20]

The poor management of the property left the Faith Church in debt. Not only did FCC fail to reinvest the property; they also failed to pay their utility bills. An investigative report on the financial condition of Hope Mansions stated that:

> Historically, the accounts receivable and payable have been very high for this project. . . . Tenant Accounts Receivable for the month of December 1987 totaled $73,580.25. Accounts Payable totaled $1,076,812.08. Of this amount, $256,481.67 was owed to the Washington Gas Company and $701,044.64 for past due water and sewer bills.[21]

In addition:

> Accounts with the District of Columbia Department of Public Works for water and sewer services provided to Hope Mansions are delinquent in the amount of at least $675,000.[22]

The financial problems and the schism within the Church shaped the caliber of the various management teams retained by the Faith Church to maintain the property. As a result of underfunding, there was a high turn-over rate of management companies and maintenance staffs, ultimately resulting in dilapidation and deteriorating safety:

> First of all, the management. That has the major affect on every thing that happens. They change so often and they don't do what they are supposed to do. If I call, especially in [Hope Mansions], if I call for a problem it takes them awhile. Emergencies? You can forget it.[23]

Furthermore, many residents complained about not knowing "who is in charge" at the management office. In reaction to the situation, some of the residents knowingly refused to give their consent to allow maintenance workers into their apartments in their absence. The frequent reason tenants gave were that "they don't know" or "they don't trust" the maintenance workers. Other tenants were peeved by the fact the maintainance workers were poorly trained and performed shoddy work. As one older resident stated:

> Oh listen. One of the reasons most of the tenants were assigned to bad maintenance was for the fact that [the maintenance crew] come from the Lorton Reformatory, escapee [laughter] or dismissed people from Lorton. And they come here and get a job or Sunrise goes and gets them and gives them a job. They are poor workers.[24]

As a result of the underfunding, the management was engaged in cost-cutting measures, and hence the reason for hiring unskilled workers. The awareness that they had ex-convicts as maintenance workers, who were poorly supervised, made many of residents uneasy. The elderly people were especially concerned for their safety:

> There were a few fears. Some people may have been a little distrustful of younger maintenance guys. They kind of want to know a little bit more about them. Older people tend to fear the younger men. There is the fear that you don't know what they may do. There is the potential that they may grab your purse. There is the potential of somebody, perhaps, trying to hurt you physically. There is the thing of better not say anything to them because you don't know what they will do to you.[25]

In addition, the majority of the maintenance crew were thought to be inexperienced and unprofessional. They had poor working habits and often left a trail of poor workmanship and wasted resources:

> One man in particular felt that the help was not adequate. Shoddy workmanship. One of the maintenance men felt that they will do better with older people [older and experienced maintenance crew] because the older people were more reliable; they took their work seriously. What happens with some of the younger workers, especially in places like Sunrise and [Hope Mansions], young guys get work in the neighborhood, they get friendly with some of the girls [Section 8 teenage residents] and they are hiding out most of the day in their apartments. You see by then [the young workers] have established relationship with the young ladies, you know. As the place gets older, it takes more work but if you have younger workers who are not doing what they are suppose to do, you know, it doesn't help.[26]

The intention of using inexperienced maintenance workers might be considered a community service in that the management created employment. Unfortunately, the workers were unreliable and often left the job before the tenants trusted them enough to allow them in their homes alone.

The property was decaying too rapidly for the few inexperienced maintenance workers. To compound this problem, the owner ceased to reinvest money in the property. With the decaying of both the interior and exterior of the buildings, many of the residents found themselves living in affordable but indecent housing. Using their influence—albeit waning—the remaining "old people" pressured the management to maintain the standards they had known in the past. Their efforts were fruitless:

> A Colonel Holland, and some of these people, John Holland, I think his name was, *really* worked to try to get management to keep the place up. You got to realize management did not put money back into the place. That's what caused it to deteriorate.[27]

By the 1980s, Sun-Hope apartment complexes had deteriorated to an extreme condition. One resident summarized the indecent conditions this way:

We have a problem with our sewage out in Sunrise because I live on
the first floor right, and regardless of whether it rains, snows, sleets or
hails our floor is covered up. It is so bad in order for us to get the
odor out of your house [apartment unit] and get your floors fixed, you
probably would have to leave out of your apartment for a few weeks
or something like that so they can come there and get that stuff. When
it's time for you to pay rent again and it's more money and that
shouldn't be because all that should be combined in your rent.
Because you're paying extra for something that should already have
been done.[28]

Another resident complained:

The need to remodel the apartments, right. And they need Johnny B
Quick, right. They need security locks. Real bars on the windows
where people been breaking in. You need to clean that whole area up
around there. They need to get to work on that. A lot of little things
they need to do around there.[29]

Not only did management fail to address issues of decay and
safety, but mismanagement led to further security problems. Poor
security at the management office in Sunrise resulted in the theft of a
master key and consequent thefts of property in various apartment
units:

Somebody stole the pass [master] key to the entire apartment
complex. Seven apartments were broken into but mostly what was
stolen were teenagers clothes and children clothes. This happened in
February this year [1992]. But no big things like TV or anything like
that. [Mrs. Bradford] said it was probable some tenants being careless
with a house key when it first started. Letting a teenager have a house
key and the teenager passed it around to their friend. But when it
happened after seven times they decided somebody must have the
pass keys and so they asked everybody to change their locks.[30]

The residents who could assume the cost changed their locks to ensure
their own safety. The others who could not afford new locks continued
to live in fear for their lives and/or that their apartments might be
burglarized.

While replacing door locks alleviated the security concerns of the residents, it was now impossible for the management to conduct inspections, not to mention to respond to emergencies. For example, during a Housing and Urban Department investigation in Hope Mansions, the investigators noted:

> Management has not been able to gain access to individual units as they should in order to follow-up on work orders, provide extermination for roaches and mice and check for tenant housekeeping problems. Many of the tenants have dead bolted their doors and have not supplied management with keys. In other instances management will not attempt to enter a unit for safety reasons.[31]

One resident stated:

> This management doesn't give a heck. I can move out, you take over my apartment, you don't know me. As long as the neighbors in the building do not complain, nothing is going to get done; management does not care.[32]

Finally, the same carelessness that yielded physical dilapidation and failing security facilitated squatting in the apartment complex:

> There's an apartment where I live, right? Somebody moves out of that apartment, right? I mean they've been out for about 8 or 9 months now. That's vagrancy. All through the night you hear a whole lot of banging and doors closing and stuff. The other day I went up there and the sink was burned up and everything. I guess they were free basing or whatever you call it. I called management and they said they couldn't do nothing about it. I mean they could put a lock on the door. They told me to call the police, right? The police said what good is it for us to come over there. We keep on putting them out and management will not put a lock on the door that they cannot break open. They're still doing it.[33]

In addition to squatting and generally taking advantage of an inefficient management team, some residents engaged in full-scale illicit drug distribution and trade. The neighborhood drug trade, as I will argue, thrived in an environment where all mediating institutions were dormant or nonexistent. I will explore this in detail in the next chapter. In a nonrandom tenant survey conducted by Shelter Incorporated in Hope Mansions, many of the residents identified their concerns as "management and drugs:"

> As much rent as we pay, we shouldn't have to make but one phone call to management and they should be there. The rent in Sunrise goes up every six months or something like that. The money that we pay could be money towards a house. But when you can't find that house at your income, what do you do? You have to stick with the management.[34]

The transformation of Hope Mansions and Sunrise Apartments from a middle- and working-class neighborhood to one of predominantly impoverished residents living in substandard conditions is attributed to a combination of structural change, primarily desegregation, and the mismanagement of the property. There is, however, another factor to be considered: the human factor. As already mentioned, just the fact that Sun-Hope attracted mostly the working poor and chronically jobless people does not necessarily mean that these residents were prone to criminal activities. The tendency toward criminal and other deviant activities in the community stemmed from patterns of behavior associated with neighborhood disorganization and decline. This encouraged the typical resident's disregard for disorder and diminished interest in the community. Many residents saw no need to defend the community and property, except their own private spaces.

NEIGHBORHOOD DISORGANIZATION (1970-1990)

It has been established that the situation in Sun-Hope was not desirable. Several buildings and apartment units were boarded up. Residents who moved out of apartment units left behind broken furniture, cooking appliances which leaked gas, leaking faucets, holes in the drywall, blue molded refrigerators, dirty carpets, rodents and cockroaches. However, these empty, boarded up apartment buildings were liveable for squatters and "zombies," drug addicts and derelicts who roamed the property. These empty apartments also served as brothels for some of the women who traded sex for crack cocaine and/or money. Drug dealers were able to process crack cocaine in some of the boarded up buildings without being noticed by the management because the buildings were master metered for gas and electric.

The buildings that were habitable and occupied by some of the respectable residents in the community were not secure. The security doors were, in many cases, ripped off their frames, hanging loosely on hinges. In many cases, it was the residents, their acquaintances or relatives themselves who vandalized the security doors. Some residents vandalized because they could not get into their apartments due to management not replacing their lost security door keys. Others vandalized out of passion. In cases where men were barred access by their partners, they did not hesitate to break the lock to gain entrance. Some tenants, simply due to laziness, damaged the locks so that friends could get easy entry when the buzzers in the apartments were ineffective.

With the exception of residents who could not afford an extra lock, most the residents had their doors deadbolted. They feared that "drug crazed" criminals would break into their apartments while they were asleep or out:

> The first things you do when you get in your house is you start putting on those fifteen locks. And I have some friends who have fifteen locks. I have one lousy one. But they do because of something that happened a few years back. A lot of people, especially where I live, have these grillwork on the inside of their door. And I got angry when I looked at the $150 bucks I paid some guy because some clown wanted to get into my house and get something I don't even have. But what I'm saying, you end up investing in all of these things and it's really to protect yourself so you don't feel threatened.[35]

As evening approached, residents had the tendency to act with trepidation at the sight of another fellow human being or at the sound of any noise in the dark. An elderly resident lucidly stated:

> You don't feel that you can just walk out on a summer's evening without perhaps somebody running you down with a moped or anything like that. Not that it happens that often, but it does. Like you want to take a stroll after dinner in the summer. It's a warm evening and I've decided to walk my dinner down. I'll walk around to Phyllis' or I'll walk around to her apartment, or I'll walk down over to the park or something. Unless you've got a neat little 45 tucked up

underneath your arm, and you're not afraid to plug a hole in
somebody, you'll find yourself constantly harassed.[36]

Unlike this individual, the majority of residents in Sun-Hope
community did not have the nerve to carry a concealed weapon in order
to feel secure. The only sense of security residents felt was within the
confines of their own apartments. But, even then, some residents
cultivated the habit of closing their curtains day and night. With the
buzzers to the apartment units damaged beyond repair, residents
responded to a knock on their doors with trepidation.

According to Hope Mansions' residents and Shelter Incorporated
staff, life in Sun-Hope was analogous to life in "a penitentiary." The
threat of violence was imminent. Many parents did not allow their
children to play by themselves outside the confines of their apartments
for fear of compromising their children's safety. Those residents who
had established friendships over the years, talked to each other on the
phone to "find out how they were doing." Others developed strategies
to ensure each others' safety by exchanging extra keys to their
respective apartments:

> I have keys to three of my neighbors' apartments. In one apartment if
> I do not hear the water running I know there is something wrong and
> I start asking questions and we all do this. And it's very important. I
> mean it doesn't have everything that we would like. I think all of us
> would like to be in better surroundings. But when you go to bed at
> night there is peace in knowing that you are surrounded by your
> friends if you cannot get out of bed in the morning and I have had this
> to happen. I used to suffer headaches, sinus headaches and I could not
> get up. And I had another neighbor and they had keys to come in to
> see about me. This is very important.[37]

This sense of "neighborliness" or "community" explained by this
resident was shared by a group of "older residents." There was,
however, also a group of young residents who joined forces with the
older residents to "turn the community around."

The majority of the residents wanted a stable community free of
litter, bags of trash, drugs and crime, but they did not actively
participate in efforts to keep the property viable. The inactivity of a
large number of residents, combined with an inefficient

owner/management, led to the continued physical decay of the property and an escalation in disorderly behavior in the neighborhood:

> Any community is upheld by the residents if the residents want to keep the community up and keep the community clean. When you find a resident that is destructive you go to management and say "Hey, this won't work." If you are in your apartment minding your business, and this person is in his apartment minding his business, and another lady with her kids down there letting them destroy it then that's just the way it is. When Sunrise was first built, the kids did not go outdoors and dig up the grass. After awhile the kids are out there digging up the grass and their parents didn't say nothing about it. See, a lot of things that happen with any property—even if you own a house—if you let your kids be destructive in your house, your house is not going to last long. But if you make your kids act in a responsible way, not to tear up, not to dig up—and if you dig up, you replace the dirt—then you are going to have nice properties. *People make things deteriorate.*[38]

In fact, tenants who confronted children about their destructive behaviors often risked antagonism from their parents:

> You see the tree sitting out there? Couple of weeks ago I've been looking out at the window and a little boy had a rope with something tied on it pulling them down. So I said let me take a look at it. So I said: "hey little boy get off that tree. You tearing the tree down . . . people put that stuff out there to grow to make it better out here." He was pulling it down. And, I did not know that his mother was sitting out there. He says: "Mamma, this man . . ." I says: "Is that your son?' She says: "yeah." I say: "you seeing that boy doing that and you didn't say a damn thing." "Well he's playing." I walked in into the house. I got a lot of temper I can't stand that junk man. She's standing right down the step looking at him, boy. I'm looking through my window and he's pulling them limbs down. Someday it could benefit some of the trees, you know. And he is calling his mamma. I couldn't believe her sitting right there.[39]

Another tenant stated:

I can't say just children because there are unruly adults. They have no respect for themselves, so therefore they do not have respect for others. Now I want to differentiate and draw a line there. There is an element that does not have respect for themselves or others, and then of course you have an element that has respect for themselves and respects the property and tries to help maintain it. I think if those things were corrected it would not look the way that it does because we compare notes on a daily basis.[40]

While one cannot deny individual behaviors, it is crucial to understand the social dynamics which shape, if not determine, a community's behavior towards its members and its surroundings.

As mentioned above, property managers who repeatedly fail to maintain their property eventually destroy their relationship with their residents. Unable to move because of their economic circumstances or due to shortages of affordable housing, residents are likely to become disgruntled with their living conditions. It was obvious that the building management was blatantly ignoring the dignity of the residents of its community. To retaliate, some residents did not pay rent or clandestinely "sublet" their apartments to "outsiders" to conduct illegal activities in the community (i.e., drug processing and distribution, and prostitution).

In Building 2 you've got all these women out there serving men who come in all day and night. You go to bed at night and all I hear is door banging all the time. They run up and down the stairs making noise that keep you awake all the time.

Given the owner/management's disregard of the deteriorating condition of the property, many residents did not see the need to make any effort to keep up the very surroundings in which they lived.

The decaying buildings and the litter strewn around the property revealed more than mismanagement: they emphasized the lack of ownership and control. Without hesitation, many of the residents littered the grounds especially in the area where the vending van was stationed. Although the vendor provided a receptacle for trash, some of the residents instead chose to litter their own community.

I don't understand why they behave that way. Sometimes I intentionally don't give them a paper bag but then they ask me to put their stuff in a bag for them. They will then turn around and take the ice cream out of the paper bag and leave it on the ground. They never use the bucket I hang on the van to throw their thrash in. So every evening, before I leave this place, I go around all over there and pick up the trash on the ground so that this place will be clean.[41]

Ironically, while the property was strewn with trash, the only area which looked clean surrounded the vendor's van; every evening before closing shop, he collected the trash strewn around the area.

The colder months made things worse. Some tenants left their bags of garbage in the hallways, stairways, breezeways and in the front of the buildings. Although there was a centrally located container for tenants to dump their bags of garbage, many tenants left them just anywhere:

One other thing I want to add is the trash. We have trash containers and I'm sure everyone here has seen a person get out of their car, dump their trash on the curb or if they are on the playground or whatever, we have little baskets for them to put their trash in. They can be standing as close to it as the end of this table and they will invariably put it on the ground. I think if those things could be remedied it would look much better than it does at the present time.[42]

Another manifestation of the decline of the community was evident through residents' (most often young men) public drinking. In the summer months, men and women lined the sidewalk across the street from Sunrise sharing cans of beer, gin, and cigarettes. Although the alcoholic drinks were often concealed in brown paper bags from passers-by and police, it was obvious what was going on. One could not help noticing the broken bottles, cigarette butts, and the foul smell of urine on the overhead walkway leading to the apartment buildings from the Metrorail/Bus station. Similar gatherings took place in Hope Mansions near the huge garbage container behind Building 7. Although participants appeared convivial, the persistence of these gatherings amplified the preexisting conditions of neighborhood disorganization, escalating disorderly behaviors.

The drinking parties usually did not end on the sidewalks or behind the garbage container. Other residents continued partying indoors. Although indoor parties were out of sight of uninvited residents, the consequences were usually felt by the neighbors. The loud music and "the comings and goings of folks all night" kept neighbors awake. Under normal conditions, it would be considered neighborly simply to inform the partying households to tune down the noise. But, given the prevalent use of drugs and alcohol, and the quick use of guns to settle disputes, residents disturbed by loud partying were forced to endure their sleepless nights in fear and in silence.

Many of the residents also felt that it was the responsibility of the management to deal with such disturbances on the property. However, the management staff did not reside on the property. In absence of a central, neutral authority to deal with this type of problem, many residents learned to "live with it." As one resident explained, many residents do not respond,

> because they are numb. They've seen it so much and so often it's not foreign. Even though it is wrong—it is so everyday for them. They don't think it's wrong. They think loitering, drinking and music playing loud—they think that is okay, everyday, party time. I don't want to see that. That is just my personal opinion, if I can help it. It's okay during a holiday or something when you have your own space to do that. But we live in apartments and it's not built that way.[43]

Even in situations where residents anonymously called the police about disturbances, the tenants involved seldom were concerned about the repercussions stemming from their behavior. The police, if they did respond to the call, often only gave warnings to the residents involved. The concerned residents did not report incidents to the management office because they believed management did not care about the tenants:

> For instance the building over here 3757, I guess it is where Mrs. Bobson and Mrs. Sanford used to live, they had a nice clean building, very quiet. But right next to them on either side is these pokies—all kinds of carrying on and the police coming and so forth and so on. So when you have that kind of situation occurring no nice people are going to move in.[44]

Sometimes residents disregarded the disturbances, afraid to call the police, because they were afraid the culprits might retaliate:

The other thing that would hinder [the tenants] is fear for their lives. They may have been threatened before by somebody. "If you call I'm going to do this, that and the other to you and your family." Or they are in it themselves—so no they ain't going to call. They are getting paid. The favorite word around here would be a snitch. Someone who calls the police and suppose to be a fellow neighbor even though that neighbor is doing something that can take us all down, can destroy your family, your child, but continues to do it because he's suppose to be your neighbor. No, I don't agree with that.[45]

Most residents resigned themselves to the fact that the management would not be able to restore relative order on the premises, and the police would only come if one called about a high-risk priority incident: a man with a gun or a homicide.

These problems were reminders of the management's neglect of the residents and in turn, some residents' disregard for the property. Assessing the community decay and breakdown of civility, one tenant who grew up in the community and was a former Hope Mansions Cooperative president stated:

Breakdown? It's a number of things. A few things that I can see is . . . I don't know really how to answer it and be honest about it. I mean the quality of the people, the education, the family structure. People not being able to find jobs, unemployment, public assistance—the whole nine yards. It's people that have allowed different management companies to come in and not be the type, the caring and sensitive type they could have been a little more with the people. The screening of the people. I think it's a lot of things.[46]

SUMMARY

This chapter analyzes some of the factors which led to the decline of Sun-Hope community starting in the 1960s. While urban decay is attributed largely to deindustrialization and withdrawal of businesses, it is argued here that a well-meaning social policy can have a similar effect, too.[47] One of the significant factors in the decline of Sun-Hope community was the dismantling of discriminatory housing practices which previously had segregated and isolated blacks. *De jure* desegregation and subsequent federal housing policies promoting access to bank loans and better housing for the black middle class encouraged their exodus from predominantly black neighborhoods. The policy of racial integration in housing overlooked a related problem, namely, social class segregation. Sun-Hope was, over the years, depleted of mediating institutions and resourceful people whose influence made the community stable. Their exit left tenants who lacked adequate education, who were often single heads of households, and youth and young adults who were chronically jobless. Residential segregation, therefore, remains a significant factor in the making of the black underclass in the urban impoverished neighborhood.[48] In Sun-Hope community, and many urban areas like it, housing desegregation led to both intra-racial and inter-class segregation.

The social and economic decline of Sun-Hope, due in part to its mismanagement, provided a conducive environment for the drug dealers who emerged in the community during the 1980s. Lacking leadership and political clout, law-abidding residents in depressed neighborhoods had limited avenues with which to confront the disorderliness and lawlessness in their community. Thus, Sun-Hope community became entrenched in crime and violence. The consequences of the low socioeconomic status of the residents and weakening of the neighborhood community civil society are the focus of the next chapter.

NOTES

    1. Former tenant, personal interview, 16 July 1992.
    2. Tenant, interview, March 11, 1992. Writing in 1957, Marvin B. Susman predicted the impending "black flight" from the inner-city to the suburbs as a result of the potential for improved educational, economic conditions and diminishing white racism. Susman argued that in segregated black neighborhoods, "members who can now afford to own one-family home are most likely to lead such a migration, and even to pioneer by moving into secluded white suburbs." See Marvin B. Susman, "The Role of Neighborhood Associations in Private Housing for Racial Minorities, *The Journal of Social Issues* XIII (1957):31-37.
    3. Tenant, personal interview, 16 September 1991.
    4. The concept "old people" is comparable to the Elijah Anderson's use of the term "old heads." These are residents who can give complete history of the neighborhood, know most of the residents, are trusted and respected by

other residents, and the most influential in the neighborhood. See Elijah Anderson. *Streetwise.*

5. Clergyman, personal interview, 25 March 1992. (Emphasis mine).

6. In his book, *Disorder and Decline* (1990:12), Wesley Skogan observed that: "even in places which on the surface appear tranquil, families move away, building age, and macro-economic forces continually affect the price of housing. However, if approximately the same number of people move in as move out, and if the new arrivals resemble those who left, the area can be counted as stable. . . . Stability means that the neighborhood reproduces itself as a social system."

7. Geriatric Social Worker serving senior citizens in the Sun-Hope community, personal interview, 14 April 1992.

8. Section 8 Certificate is a rent subsidy voucher issued by the government. "It ensures that income-eligible households pay no more than 30 percent of their income for rent. The difference between that rental payment and the fair market rent established by the federal Department of Housing and Urban Development is paid throug the Section 8 program." See the Indices: A Statistical Index to District of Columbia Services, August 1991, 211.

9. Former tenant, interview, 15 May 1991.

10. Tenant, personal interview, 12 March 1992.

11. Former tenant, personal interview, 13 September 1991.

12. Ibid.

13. Tenant and Fruit of Islam member, personal interview, 16 April 1992.

14. Quoted from a Management Review Report about the conditions of Hope Mansions, written by William Hill, Chief, Loan Management Branch, Housing and Urban Development, Washington DC, 20 January 1988.

15. Former tenant, personal interview, 15 May 1991.

16. Tenant, personal interview, 27 August 1993.

17. William Hill, letter to Gail Peterson, 20 June 1988, Shelter Incorporated files, Washington, D.C.

18. Ibid.

19. Former tenant, personal interview, 13 September 1991.

20. A former neighborhood youth activist, personal interview, 4 March 1992.

21. William Hill, U. S. Department of Housing and Urban Development, Washington D.C. Field Office, Region III, a letter to Gail Peterson, Shelter Incorporated, Washington, D.C. 20 June 1988.

22. Paradise Manor Cooperative Agreement, 28 October 1987:15.

23. *Focus Group*, 1988, 8.

24. Tenant, personal interview, 25 October 1991.

25. Geriatric Social Worker, personal interview, 14 April 1992.
26. Ibid.
27. Former tenant, personal interview, 16 September 1991.
28. *Focus Group*, May 1988, 26.
29. *Focus Group*, May 1987, 34.
30. Tenant, personal interview, 25 October 1991.
31. William Hill, U. S. Department of Housing and Urban Development, Washington D.C. Field Office, Region III, a letter to Gail Peterson, Shelter Incorporated, 20 June 1988.
32. *Focus Group*, May 1987, 10.
33. *Focus Group*, May 1987, 11
34. *Focus Group*, May 1987, 26.
35. *Focus Group*, May 1988, 41.
36. *Focus Group*, May 1988, 41. The teenage drug couriers used mopeds to distribute drugs to buyers and users who did not want to risk arrest by coming into Sun-Hope community. A moped is also relatively cost efficient and effective way to avoid detection by the police: the police are more likely to stop and search a teenager driving an expensive car. Moreover, the age requirement makes it impossible for many youth to obtain a drivers' license.
37. *Focus Group*, May 1988, 39.
38. Former tenant, personal interview, 16 September 1991.
39. Tenant, personal interview, 1 June 1992.
40. *Focus Group*, May 1987, 44.
41. Former tenant and neighborhood vendor, personal interview, 19 November, 1991.
42. *Focus Group*, May 1987, 44.
43. Tenant, personal interview, 16 June 1992.
44. Tenant, personal interview, 25 October, 1991.
45. Tenant, personal interview, 16 June 1992.
46. Ibid.
47. William Julius Wilson, *The Truly Disadvantaged: The Inner City, the Underclass, and Public Policy* (Chicago: The University of Chicago Press, 1987).
48. For a quantitative analysis of how racial and housing segregation concentrates poverty among urban blacks, see Douglas S. Massey, "American Apartheid: Segregation and the Making of the Underclass," *American Journal of Sociology* 96 (1990): 329-57.

CHAPTER 4

The Making of an Open-Air Drug Market

Father Jonas and his associates built Sun Rise Apartments and Hope Mansions on Judeo-Christian conviction. They sought to form a community where residents' lifestyles would emulate biblical teachings: a wholesome community free from alcohol, drugs, prostitution, self-hate and foul language.[1] At least for the first 10 years from its inception, the community lived up to founders' ideals. Because some of the devout members of the Faith Christ Church monitored the management staff of the property, public drinking, drug sales and use, and loitering were minimal and infrequent.

But the people living in Father Jonas' community were not all saints. As one elderly resident stated, "[s]ome of them [drug users and dealers] were home grown. Don't let anybody tell you that it was something that was happening five or eight years ago. It's been happening for twenty, twenty-five years."[2] Illicit drug users and dealers, if any, coexisted covertly with ordinary residents during the earlier years of the community. Retropsectively, many residents hardly recalled there being widespread and open drug use or dealing even during the 1970s, on the heels the community being transformed into a low-income area. This former tenant's observation concurred with a few others regarding the situation then:

> I ain't seen nothing out there at the time, but some reefer. Might have been some 'bone' out there—some heroin. There was some guys I used to see nodding and scratching. I don't think they were selling it. I think they was just going up somewhere and coming back with it.

But there might have been someone out there selling it, but I doubt it.[3]

There were no accounts of overt conflict in the neighborhood because there were no competing gangs settling their turf disputes through the barrel of the gun. Deviant behaviors such as public drinking were kept discrete in the community.

As the composition of Sun-Hope neighborhood changed from mixed income to predominantly low income residents, however, the Church members' efforts to uphold the teachings and expectations of Father Jonas fell on deaf ears. The incoming tenants did not share the same sentiments of the "older tenants" about what the community "used to be" and why their disregard for the tidiness and upkeep of the community contributed to the community's "going down." As one stated:

> I think it's bad because I've been here for so long. How basically it used to be a long time ago I think [it] was real nice. You could practically sleep outside, you know, relax. You wouldn't have to worry about anything. But [Sun-Hope] did go down in such a bad manner all 'cause of drugs and killings and things like that.[4]

The widely shared attitude that the community had "gone down" led residents to resign themselves to the fact that nothing could be done about neighborhood situation. For example, the physical disorder, namely the poorly maintained building, the broken lights, and trash-filled grounds, rodent-infested apartments and broken glass-windows were to the tenants, an on-going reminder that the management and the landlord was not interested in their well-being. The physical disorder was inextricably linked to the social disorder—an array of disparaging behaviors such as sexual harassment, graffiti, vandalism, drinking, insults and disrepect of others.

The combination of both the physical and social disorders undermining the quality of life in the community were evident in the self-hatred among residents. For example, in response to the physical disorder, some tenants saw nothing wrong in leaving empty beverage containers in the courtyards after partying or in disposing of their trash improperly. For the older tenants who were concerned and felt trapped in the community, they looked upon their neighbors with scorn, racial deprecation, and exasperation about "black folks." There prevailed a form of antagonism between residents who wished for a better civil community and those who saw no need to be emotionally invested in the community. This impasse escalated and entrenched the disorganization within the community. The internal disorganization of the community made it possible for invasion by a host of miscreants. The deteriorated relationship among residents, the management and the police made the neighborhood community accessible the drug dealers evading formal and informal controls, squatters seeking decaying and boarded-up buildings, crack prostitutes seeking money and drugs, and some law enforcement agents who took advantage of the situation to enrich themselves through corruption in the community. Sun-Hope community, then, was a conducive area for the crack cocaine trade upon its advent in 1983. The illicit drug business correlated with gang conflicts, homicides, intimidation of residents, and traffic of buyers and dealers to the area from elsewhere.

Inadvertently, the architectural design of Hope Mansions and Sun Rise Apartments, aimed to provide residents maximum comfort and mobility, also facilitated the drug trade. The Apartments' design included a network of pedestrian walkways connecting the four playgrounds, the apartment buildings and parking lots. The high curbs along the edges of the parking lots prevented anyone from driving into the interior part of the property. The courtyards consisted of alternating pedestrian walkways and large open spaces. Also, the courtyards and parking lots were linked by breezeways on the ground level either at the end or the center of the buildings. The drug dealers took advantage of the layout of the apartment complexes, transforming it into a business setting, presenting the police with an occupational nightmare, and a terrifying living situation for the legitimate residents.

The barrack-like design of the buildings offered the drug dealers a clear view of the activities in the parking lot, the courtyard and segments of Sunset Lane and Rust Place. Having taken over the breezeways, the drug dealers deliberately destroyed the lights to enable them gain control over the area. Operating in unlit breezeways enabled the drug dealers to identify potential clients, foes and law enforcement agents from the courtyards and walkways, while remaining invisible. By adopting this strategy, the drug dealers made it difficult, if not dangerous, for law enforcement agents to operate effectively. Knowing the detailed outlay of the apartment complexes gave the drug dealers an advantage over the police. A former youth organizer explained the feasibility of the drug enterprise in the community:

> Look at its configuration. You have a horseshoe shape. Over here you have barren land. Not necessarily barren land, but you can hide in it. Not cultivated land. Over here you had a park . . . [Eden Estates]. The highway. And you've got a number of options to escape. Now, you had two-way traffic. So you can come in here any way you want to come in here, get your product and keep pushing. That's what was happening. The clients were coming into this area to buy. And this is where the mixing houses were. This is where the chemistry labs were—see what I'm saying? The distributors. The youth and everything else that was involved. It was perfect in terms of all the elements you need to have a complete unit. And if you had dominant control over this particular facility, then you can run Washington.[5]

As one local news reporter observed, for the drug enterprise:

> Not just any street setting will do. Dealers avoid places where property owners have the resources and energy to persistently fight their presence. Dealers like locations with plenty of garbage, places where they can throw on heavily littered ground and claim it is not theirs.[6]

Thus, the Sun-Hope community became a conducive environment for the drug trade. Although it was located at the margin and isolated from the city core, the community was easily accessible by way of a major highway. This highway offered easy access for the drug buyers from both the nearby Maryland suburbs and from distant cities such as New York City, Philadelphia and Miami. Both apartment complexes were also accessible by public transportation. The Sun-Hope community was within walking distance from the Metro/Bus Station and a mile away from the Amtrak/Metro Station. These were also convenient options for drug dealers and couriers from New York and Philadelphia. The Amtrak/Metro station, in particular, offered drug dealers a strategic point to evade the tight police scrutiny in force at the downtown Union Station.[7] Such infrastructure provided the security needed by drug buyers avoiding possible encounters with the police and residents who might be taking note of their license plate numbers.

INNER-CITY POVERTY, THE DRUG TRADE AND GANGS

In the 1988 survey of Hope Mansions residents, persons under 20 years old constituted 52 percent of the households. Of the 197 males identified in the household survey, 25 percent were between the ages of eleven and twenty. The survey also confirmed the extent of poverty in the community. Of the 152 households who responded to the question about their earnings, 44 percent (67) reported earning under $6,000 per year, 36 percent (54) up to $12,000, 10 percent up to $18,000 and the remaining 10 percent earning more. Regarding employment, 66 percent of household members (above eighteen years of age) were unemployed. And of this, 18 percent of the respondents stated that at least two adult members were unemployed in their households. Although similar data for Sun Rise Apartments was unavailable, its demographics were far from dissimilar. The concentration of youth, impoverished households and jobless adults in a community which was experiencing physical and social disorder provided some of the key ingredients for the establishment of the drug trade.

It must be made clear that the drug dealers were not attracted to Sun-Hope community and other similar areas in the city because the residents were the main buyers and consumers of cocaine. To the contrary, the drug dealers were attracted to Sun-Hope because it was a depressed and a defenseless neighborhood community: a socially disorganized area without mediating institutions, where law enforcement was infrequent and where potential buyers and users could buy drugs discretely. And it was a neighborhood where many of the residents were too impoverished to resist the drug dealers' overtures for money in exchange for use of their apartments for illegal activities. One of the few residents who had a Master's Degree, and who had lived in the community for 35 years, stated lucidly:

> Now the newspaper gave a lot of sympathy for [Sun-Hope] people that they were deluged by dope dealers, and that dope dealers were terrible, and the druggies and the addicts and the junkies were persecuting Sun-Hope residents. But Sun-Hope was responsible for the situation to some extent. The tenants in Sun-Hope were responsible for the situation because they were the friends, and relatives—mothers, fathers, and cousins—of the drug people. And they were the ones allowing them to come in their buildings and apartments.[8]

Moreover, the fact that Sun-Hope was a conducive area to trade in illicit drugs was not the main attraction to the drug dealers: the attractions included the metropolitan area's middle-class drug culture, and the area's exorbitant prices due to high demand and limited supply of illicit drugs. The drug traffickers brought their commodities to Washington, D.C. because the profit margin was comparatively higher than it was in Philadelphia or New York. According to Attorney John F. Finnegan: "Because of the availability of cocaine and crack in New York, a port city, prices are low there. . . . In Washington, dealers can get $30 for what sells at $15 in New York."[9] Competition for market share and for profit maximization led to the formation of syndicates and rivalries among the drug dealers. In the Sun-Hope area, drug trade police estimated there were 100 drug syndicates competing for market shares. By 1987 the out-of-town drug dealers, particularly the Jamaican "posses," became noticeable.[10] They came to Sun-Hope to overthrow the pre-existing drug dealers violently and to control the market there. Also vying for a share in the drug market were the Miami Boys, the New York Boys, the Rayful Edmond Boys and other independent dealers.[11] The antagonism among these gangs in Sun-Hope and other neighborhood drug markets escalated the overall rate of drug-related violence and homicides.[12]

Assisting some of the drug lords in Sun-Hope were the teenage and adolescent males who lived with families, relatives or friends in the community. Many were high school drop-outs, lacked marketable skills and were chronically unemployed. The alternative to making a living was by participating in the drug trade. For many of the youth participating in the drug trade, risking arrest was not an unfamiliar experience. A considerable number of them were graduates of the District of Columbia's reformatories and Detention Homes. These seasoned juvenile delinquents, therefore, were prepared to take risks in the hope of making fast money. Lamenting over what some of the area youth had to do to make money, a former youth organizer stated:

> This is the place where the distribution, the processing, the production [took place] and you have money in that. What you have here is young kids—twelve, thirteen, fourteen years old—getting $400, $500 a weekend just for standing on the corner watching [looking out for] for cops.[13]

As gangs competed for a larger share of the drug market, open violence became inevitable. One Hope Mansions resident who sold drugs in 1983 to supplement his income said:

> Everybody in the neighborhood knew each other. So if anybody from another area was to come here, the dealers here will jump on him and start beating him. . . . I've noticed that there will always be that conflict. They will never let anybody stay on their turf. I never claimed any turf to myself but meanwhile I tried to make some money on the side.[14]

One of the notorious "home-grown" youth drug gangs was the Committee.[15] The members were subsequently arrested and charged for drug-related homicide. Led by Big Alonzo and Mister Dealer, they were responsible for finding and purchasing cocaine, weapons and hiring needed workers. Jordan and Tracy K. Tree ("Kaytree") managed the money. Franco M. Tilton (Big Til) was an "enforcer" and supervised the preparation of crack cocaine for the market. Given the high risk of being robbed by rival drug dealers or "stick-up boys," the youth were armed at all times. "After I got robbed," Big Til stated in an interview, "I figured, well, I got to give me something to protect myself. I don't want to keep letting [robbers] take my money."[16]

Turf battles were the primary sources of violence in the community beginning with the Jamaican Posses. Later, in Hope Mansions, the violence escalated between two gangs, namely, the Miami Boys and the New York Boys. Incidents leading to homicides and arrrests also revealed the backgrounds some of the drug dealers in the area:

> Police and prosecutors said the mayhem at [Sun-Hope] reflects the first major influx of drug dealers from cities such as New York and Miami who are lured here by the high prices that cocaine and its potent derivative "crack" bring in this area.[17]

For some of the single heads of households, predominantly teens and young adult women, the lure of the drug dealers' cash in exchange for sex or use of the apartment units as a staging ground for packaging and distribution of drugs was especially strong. Invariably, a few "crack houses" or "stash houses" sprung up in the community. One of the first crack houses the police raided was operated by a 31-year old Nawla (Big) Crank. Asked in court about the reasons for her involvement in the drug trade, Crank cited both the fear that if she had denied the drug-dealing youth the use of her apartment they might have harmed her, and also her financial needs made her vulnerable: "Sometimes I would get money . . . Sometimes it would be drugs and money."[18] Her apartment also served as a brothel for the youth and their "rock prostitutes."[19]

YOUTH AS "LITTLE SOLDIERS"

Because of their financial needs, some residents, especially the male youth, were attracted to the drug trade by the chance for quick profits. Vulnerable youth in Sun-Hope community became the "little soldiers," or agent for gangs retailing crack cocaine in the neighborhood streets.[20] The suppliers were adults and other youth from outside the community. The common knowledge held throughout the community that the drug dealers, mostly from outside Sun-Hope, "have frequently hired children from the community to carry out the actual transactions."[21] The youth operated,

> like a cell, with a core of six to 10 regulars, highly organized and "integrated" in the business sense, controlling its product from start to finish, processing, keeping track of sales with an electronic money counter. It was lean and mean—armed with .38s—and businesslike: no colorful bandannas to aid police in identifying the members.[22]

The children served as a "front" to shield the adult drug dealers: when arrested, these children were prosecuted as juveniles and received only a few months incarceration in detention centers. Moreover, juveniles were not fearful of having a criminal record: delinquency records were expunged when at age eighteen.[23] "The juveniles don't have to pay a price," Chief Isacc Fullwood lamented. "The kids don't have to worry about retribution in the system."[24]

TEEN MOTHERS AS ACCESSORIES TO THE DRUG TRADE

The illicit drug network also included unmarried teenage mothers with no long-term vested interest in the community in which they live. They were the objects of contempt from the standpoint of the concerned residents. As one adult resident remarked, "these girls have no business having babies. They are kid raising kids and they get to have their own apartments, too." This residents observation epitomizes the scornful opinions of many of the concerned residents:

They got young parents out here now. They are all on Section 8 [rent subsidy] or whatever, public assistance. . . . Young age is any age where they can start having babies. I wouldn't be surprised if we got couple of fifteen years olds with babies living out here. . . . Their kids are about four or five years old. They are on Section 8; government is paying half of their rent. The little bit they pay, they don't care about where they live, how they live. They're too busy running around here finding out what Peter [a lover] they could catch. . . That is the way it is. Look around you. What do you see?[25]

The pervasive complaints of the older tenants was that the apartment units of the teen mothers served as "stash houses" and relatively safe havens for their drug-dealing boyfriends or companions.

In a focus group discussion, there was a general consensus among participants that the drug dealer preyed upon the vulnerable, unwed teen parents:

Some of the people that live out there do sell drugs. It is my suggestion that management needs to get rid of those people. If my 11 year old son selling drugs, get rid of him and me both, and that way you're going to get rid of somebody. But they got Jamaicans; they done come out there and took over. They pay these young gals $1,000 for their apartment. And me, myself, I'm not letting anybody take over. I wouldn't let any man take over.[26]

Another tenant stated:

Mr. Bailey, he said Sun Rise is very remiss in allowing the apartments, especially the one-bedrooms to be rented by the teenage mothers. He says they make very poor tenants, and not only are they noisy, but they are dirty and allow people to congregate in their apartments. They are suspected in being in league with the drug dealers and so forth and so on. But that is something recent. Their use of unwed mothers started I guess more in the 70s and 80s.[27]

As I have indicated previously, these unwed teenage mothers allowed young men to assume informal tenancy in the apartment complexes in a subletting arrangement. By one estimate, a disproportinate number of the neighborhood drug dealers came from other states.

I will say 50 percent of them live here and 50 percent of them don't.
Yes, a lot of them do live here and some of them are from the outside
of [Hope Mansions]. Some are rent-paying tenants. A lot of them are
kids of the young men that live here.[28]

Another tenant concurred:

I think you had a mixture of both. You had some set-ups, where you
had, unfortunately, single parent . . . women, who were being used for
their homes and their time and their kids and whatever . . . which is
unfortunate. (sigh) It can get real sticky.[29]

Like the big dealers, the young parents also used their children as
accessories in the drug trade. With the knowledge of their parents, the
kids served as lookouts for police, delivered, or sold drugs to customers
in the streets. One tenant lamented:

Not only are the young kids that's out there doing this crap, but it's
the parents too. How can you guide a child if you're out there doing it
too. That goes right back to the parents. Some of them are role
models and some of them just need to be thrown away. Or just kept
away from the kids. Because they are the ones who make the kids
bad. The kid will only learn as much as we let them learn.[30]

Since many of them operated under the direction of their parents, these
neighborhood youth feared no reprisal for their behavior.[31] In some
instances, the dealing drugs was a family business: the kids sold drugs
with impunity.

THE OUTSIDERS: THE JAMAICAN POSSES

In a focus group, a tenant responded in agreement with others when she
stated the things she disliked least in the community as: "The property,
the dirt, the Jamaicans, the drugs and the shooting cause you don't
know when the bullets are going to fly."[32] Although there were other
drug syndicates operating the community, the Jamaicans stood out in
contrast to the ethnic homogeneity of the community. Many of the
residents interviewed consistently claimed knowing the Jamaicans by
"their clothes," "their appearance" and "their accent."

They lived right down from me and everybody knows they were Jamaicans. Jamaicans have a language different than Americans. A lot of them had braids, the big hats to hold the braids, and a lot of them smoked ganji or reefer. They did not smoke it in public, but they weren't ashamed to let you know what they was about. I knew one person personally who use to stand out in the front of the apartment all day long and he would, and he told me, he was happy because he makes about $2,000 a week. And, around that time I had started using drugs myself. I had started selling reefer myself.[33]

Given the ethnic homogeneity of the community, the Jamaicans inevitably became the focus of attention. Like the other drug syndicates, the Jamaicans drug dealers moved to Sun-Hope community to take advantage of the community's disorganization: infrequent policing, inefficient management, and a lucrative market of middle-class consumers in the District, Virginia and Maryland.[34] Among the newcomers, most heavily armed, and reputably violent, were the Jamaican gang.[35] One resident who lived in the community intermittently explained the changes he noticed in the neighborhood after he had returned from college:

I left in 1976 to go to school and came back in October 1980. I noticed they had started having drugs. In 1981, I noticed there was some Jamaicans that had moved in here, and the drugs started speeding up. In 1976, everything seemed peaceful. People were friendly. I had about three friends and they were people that lived in the community. . . . In 1980, I met a young lady and we got married so we moved into our own apartment right by the ice cream truck. And, at that point I noticed the crack people had started hanging out more late at night. I noticed where the Jamaicans were at is the apartment that people were tracking in and out. So I noticed the crowd of people started to increase.[36]

The Jamaican dealers also were blamed for introducing crack and for attracting multitudes of strangers into the neighborhood:

Yeah, it's bad around there but it's mainly because of the Jamaicans or something. They came out here in [Hope Mansions] and just came up with something new called crack. And that took over [Hope Mansions]. And now the junkies are worse. They'd be shooting up right in the hallways in front of anybody. They don't care. The shoot up in the hallways.[37]

The Jamaican gang members were able to rent apartments because management did not conduct background checks. Once settled, the Jamaicans, just like other traffickers, were able to deal narcotics freely because, simply, they were never forced to stop:

> Once they were able to get the community to know there was reefer around, they were in business. There is always one Jamaican posted out front [the apartment building entrance]. If there was somebody coming to get [buy] reefer, the Jamaican himself will go into the apartment and get the reefer and bring it back out and go around the corner and make the sale or in the hall way and make the sale out of the public [view]. Then it got to a point where traffic was coming so regularly that he almost couldn't come outside. He almost had to stay inside to sell it right at the door. But what they will do on the inside, if some body ever got the chance to go inside, they will take a big block and nail a piece of block on the floor and put a big block in front of the one that is nailed in the floor so that if somebody tried to come through the door, it will jam the door. And, when he got ready to go out, he will move the block and somebody will put the block back again after they leave. I had a chance go into their apartment and that's why I saw it. And they will have a certain knock that they will give when it is [one of] them.[38]

The Jamaican gang proved their business adeptness by their benevolence to some of the residents. As one elderly women testified: "At Christmas time everyone exchanges gifts. You know we've got this Jamaican and she done got to be just like us."[39] Without question, the Jamaican gang was just one of many groups operating in the community. Their pursuit for the chance to get rich by selling drugs, coupled with the demands by users of various backgrounds, all contributed to the sustained decline of the community.

CONSEQUENCES OF THE COMMUNITY DRUG MARKET

Upon the advent of crack cocaine in 1983, a 24-hour, open-air drug market emerged and engendered violence, death and destruction in Sun-Hope. A community which some earlier residents had considered a sprawling suburb within the city was now experiencing an unusual volume of traffic in strangers and cars, frequent gunshots, drug addicted derelicts and prostitutes roaming about, and weary residents afraid of taking walks in their own neighborhood.

The Sun Rise-Hope open-air drug market provided buyers and sellers a relatively safe environment in which to conduct their business. In a neighborhood which older tenants recalled being so tranquil and safe in the evenings, such that in the summer some residents slept outside, the drug trade generated considerable commotion and trepidation. One resident who witnessed the rapid growth of the drug market stated:

> 1984, my first year here was really [bad], people were in and out of here. It was madness, chaotic. Lot of traffic, lot of tension. You could see it, you could feel it. People were afraid. Worked, the ones that worked. The ones that loitered and did the drug trafficking were out there day and night. It didn't matter.[40]

Another added:

> The busiest days of the drug trade were Fridays and Saturdays. That was the busiest days because there was so many people outside like flies all night long. You will think you were living in New York [City].[41]

Many people were drawn to Sun-Hope community because the drug dealers marketed assortments of drugs: cocaine, crack cocaine, LSD, PCP, and marijuana. The drug culture was also such that besides word-of-mouth, any press report helped in advertising the open-air drug market in Sun-Hope.

Given the *de facto* racial and class segregation of Sun-Hope community, the white people who ventured the area were placed promptly into one of two categories: drug buyers or undercover police officers buying drugs as part of the law enforcement process. Although their drug dealing in the community was infrequent but swift, the white drug buyers were valued clients to the neighborhood youth dealers. Members of the Committee, for instance, singled them out as "special customers" who had plenty of money and who bought powder cocaine in unusual quantity. In an interview with a reporter, one member of the Committee stated that they packed the drugs in $50 quantities for

their white clientel. The middle-class clients who did not want to risk
the possibility of arrest in the Sun-Hope area could contact the dealers
by phone and have drug couriers deliver the goods. It was because of
the middle-class clientel that several of the kids carried beepers,
cordless phones, and had mopeds standing by.

Some older residents talked with contempt about the white people
who came to the community to buy drugs. From the point of view of
some residents, these outsiders were contributing to the demise of the
community by patronizing the informal drug economy. They resented
the fact that when caught, the police treated the white drug consumers
leniently:

> You know, they really blame black people for using a lot of drugs . . .
> buying a lot of drugs. Black folk, if you look at it, are in the process
> of trying to sell some drugs to some people. But if you look at the
> kind of cash that's involved in drug raids where you got millions and
> hundreds of millions of dollars, black folk don't control that kind of
> money. See, they need to focus their thrust on the middle-class, upper
> middle-class whites that walk around with hundreds of dollars in their
> pockets and that can afford to buy drugs.[42]

> Sometimes they'd be in cars, in Virginia cars, including white people
> all the way down from the second bus stop on Sunset Lane all the
> way down to [Hope Mansions]. Virginian tags. There used to be a
> telephone booth in [Hope Mansions] near the bus stop. That is where
> the cars [buyers] will be and I have seen white people in their cars,
> too.[43]

The phone booth which was installed for the use by residents who
could not afford services became the domain of drug dealers and
addicts. Other people also sought to break into the pay phone unit for
what ever money they could find so often that the phone company
ceased to make the services available. Invariably, the lawful residents
had to bear the brunt of this collective punishment.

At sundown, both Hope Mansions and the Sun Rise Apartments
become a point of convergence for all the various people connected to
the drug trade. While ordinary residents barricaded themselves behind
closed doors, the dimely lit courtyards, the basketball court, breezeways
and the parking lots drew clusters of people. One resident explained a

typical evening. From the vantage point of her apartment window, she saw groups of people of varying ages:

> Anywhere from 15 to 35 . . . it would be a mixture. A lot of cars riding in and out of the driveways at record speed . . . that didn't need to be there. You knew they didn't need to be there, didn't live here, a lot of them. We had a lot of transient New Yorker, Jamaican-speaking people. A lot of traffic. Gun shots ringing out in the night. Not so much during the day, because I was at work during the day and away, but during the night . . . the ambulances, the sirens. The lights would wake you up out of your sleep.[44]

By 1986, gunshots were a routine occurrence in the community. Although the shots were often pranks, each gunshot struck terror in the hearts of the residents. Other times, people were wounded or killed. On such occasions, residents tried to recall which of the array of gun shots they had heard the previous night actually might have caused the injuries or deaths. In a six-week period during the fall of 1986, three men and one woman were found shot to death in Hope Mansions. (See Chart 9.1, Violent Crime Statistics).

Nearly everyone in the community knew or had heard of a neighbor who had died because of drug-related violence or overdose. The intensity of the drug trade and attendant violence in the community elicited the following editorial:

> Day and night, New York-based drug traffickers vied with local dealers for control of the streets and the courtyards. Buyers placed their orders at one end of the complex and picked them up on the opposite side. In one year alone, 12 people died from gunshot wounds or drug overdoses. As one resident put it, "You didn't go out at night. You stayed away from windows. Sometimes, you were even afraid to send you kids out to school."[45]

Pondering the number of deaths during her ten years residency in Hope Mansions, one tenant stated: "I have to say about 30 dead . . . to *my* knowledge. It could be more."[46] Another tenant, who had been an independent drug dealer in the neighborhood, said:

> I had a friend, her name was [Marsh]. She got strung out on crack and she had witnessed a lot of killing. She had gone to a rehab and come

out. Some of the people who knew what was going on actually gave her the cocaine either with some rat poison [adulterated] or some kind of poison and when she smoked it that gagged her. That was to shut her up from talking. I know a lot of people lost their lives out here but I don't know them. I know of three other people who died but I did not know them personally.[47]

An elderly resident recalled two families that suffered drug-related deaths:

The husband worked in the State Department . . . [and the wife] she had a nice home, very nice children and all but one died last year. [They died of] narcotics and AIDS and everything all mixed up. So that family disintegrated.[48]

About another family, the tenant stated: "Mrs. Danson's daughter used drugs quite a bit. She worked for Pepco. Evidently she was stoned and died on the job."[49]

The local minister who, at the invitation of a group of concerned residents, assisted with the moral rejuvenation of the community recounted the scene in the community during his earlier days in Hope Mansions:

There was shootings. In the evening we will come out and run revivals. . . . The scene of crack cocaine. This was in 1983/84. At that time, a request came—because our church was affiliated with this property—and they wanted a minister to come out and see what he can do. It was brought to my attention and I said that I will come out.[50]

The impact of the drug trade was felt in virtually every sphere of the community. Most tenants agreed something needed to be done, but only a few were prepared to organize and publicly counter the drug dealers, elicit the help of management and/or and the police for fear of retaliation.

One of the visible signs of a 24-hour open-air cocaine market is the constant presence of young men, "hanging out" in clusters in various parts of the property, waiting to approach just about any adult person to make a sale. Equally visible are the derelicts and drug addicts. These are men and women who are willing to do anything—steal money or give sex in exchange—for drugs. Frequently, they are known to scrounge the area where the drug dealers discard crack cocaine when police officers are in pursuit of them.

Residents referred to the drug addicts as "zombies," and encounters with these loitering strangers became an inescapable part of life in the community. This concern was expressed by many of the residents:

> Sometimes I come in the basement way and sometimes I come in the front door. And when you come in the basement there are I don't know how many in their basement—all these strange fellows and they are in their 20's and some of them may be a little younger and this everyday. And they play the boom box enough to be tired when they leave. But my basement is a regular hangout for drugs and what have you.[51]

> Say you go down maybe to get your car or to the bus. And you want to empty your trash on your way out so you go out the back door. My god, you walk down the steps and there's some guy and it's frightening.[52]

> But I just would like to see the people educated and not so much loitering. . . . There are so many people that are not working and a lot of them don't even live in there and just hang around all day long. You know, just idle. I'd like just to be able to walk down and not have to say excuse me stepping over somebody that's in the way. Cause we don't hardly have any lights at night. It's just a few light spaces on the top of the building and some places it's really, really dark out there.[53]

> No [security] doors, people loitering in the halls. You don't know who they are. In and out, in and out. So far, no one has bothered me but you have apprehension when you open your apartment door because you don't know who is out there. So I am striving to get into a decent place.[54]

> You wake in the morning, get ready to go to work. You open your door and a person sleeping behind your door falls into your room. One woman, she was so afraid, she wouldn't even come out from her apartment unless to go to work. Other than that she'd stay in all the time.[55]

Patricia Mason, the President of the People's Advocacy, upon her initial visit, expressed similar concerns about the community's parasites:

> Well, you get the feeling that you were in a penitentiary when you walked out there because a lot of the units were vacant, and the people who were outside didn't seem to be residents. And, there were people who were definitely addicted to substances who were outside transacting with other people. It wasn't safe. That was an obvious challenge.[56]

The drug trade also gave rise to prostitution in the community. Some teenage girls and young adult women who lived in the neighborhood used prostitution as a means to earn money, or in some cases simply traded sex for drugs:

> You find a lot of cars come from Maryland, Virginia—some with prostitutes. Prostitutes thrive not on the black guys that buy them, but on white men that come around and buy the black prostitutes. The same thing with drugs. Cars from Maryland, Virginia, though sometimes they might have a black guy driving in there to pick up the stuff, but some white person sent them to get it 'cause they got the cash, they can afford it.[57]

The teenage girls were also lured by the symbols of success flaunted by the drug dealers.[58] This resident lamented the vulnerable position in which many girls find themselves:

> I think they are too materialistic. I see teenagers and one is associated with the other. There are a lot of BMW's and a lot of Mercedes around there and with our social economic background we can't afford those things. So it has to be associated with something that you are doing wrong. Whatever, ok? I see a lot of girls, they're starting to get into prostitution. Ok? Because they want these materialistic things. Ok? And if I had a chance I would make a change in that. Because we teach our kids to be like the Joneses, ok? And try to keep them up with this economic thing that we can't afford to do. And it puts a strain on us and this is what cause the drug problems. Because when they can't pay their bills then they want to take the scapegoat. So, because they want to live like the Jones.[59]

Not only were residents forced to witness prostitutes turning tricks; they were also forced to avoid certain public areas. Non-resident prostitutes who came to Sun-Hope in search of business turned the two laundry facilities into brothels.

The drug trade corrupted the neighborhood youth and engendered hostilities between neighbors. And, except in cases in which parents were accomplice, the drug trade created an intense intergenerational antagonism. The elderly and respected residents often felt the kids derided and disregarded them for trying to "talk some sense into the kids." Some the elderly people reported that it was not unusual to have some young parents yell abusive remarks at them for reprimanding their kids. So relentless were the kids to peddle their drugs that they barely took notice of the people with whom they dealt. According to an elderly man (and one of the few remaining tenants from the 1960s), "One evening I heard this young boy calling, 'Mister, are you looking?' I turned around and he looked at me and said, 'Oh, Mr. King. Is that you?' And I said, 'What difference does it make? You're trying to sell me drugs just the same. Ain't you?'" For many of the elderly people, there was a sense that they have lost their place in the community.

Of all the problems that confronted the ordinary residents in Sun-Hope, none was more threatening to their lives than the violence associated with the drug trade:

> The environment. The people are bad. They're doing wrong things and that ain't good. Out there selling drugs and stuff that ain't good. People getting shot and stuff and its not safe around there. [Hope Mansions] is bad. You can't go no where. If they ain't shooting I don't know what they are doing.[60]

This prevailing sense of imminent danger underscored the distrust residents harbored for any individual not familiar to them but with whom they had to share public spaces. Residents claimed to particularly fear young black males.

The insecurity many residents experienced was a product of the neighborhood disorganization. The open air sale and use of drugs in the community and the attendant violence among sellers and users reminded residents of the unpredictable conditions in which they lived:

> The second thing, as every one else has said, is drugs. The drug atmosphere out there is humongous. It's a serious problem. And it's

to the point where people are afraid. I mean the ones that want to do it right or the ones that are thinking positive, they are actually afraid to come out to go visit other people because you have so much drug traffic in the area. You don't know when this person might pull out a gun and shoot at the person and you may be walking and don't even know what's taking place.[61]

The aberrant behaviors of some of the drug addicts and the youth were the focus of concern for the tenants:

The fear of these young people is that people are afraid they may be under the influence of drugs which causes bizarre behaviors. So again you go back to the drugs. Before it used to be younger people, again a different breed, used to have respect for the older people. You wouldn't think of looking at older person funny. "You know this person may know my grandmother or something." But now it looks like the children are more brazen. The value of the human life isn't the same. Some of these kids would shoot you and they wouldn't even think about it.[62]

The drug dealers saw each person in and around their "turf" as a potential customer: they do not discriminate among tenants, buyers and, for that matter, possible undercover police officers. The shared experience of many of the residents was one of consistently being approached to buy drugs. "You can be going to visit somebody and go through the apartment building and somebody will come up to you and say, 'I have something, you know.'"[63] Other drug dealers would hawk their commodity to anyone they encountered in the pedestrian walkways and parking lots announcing: "two for five, two for five." "Are you looking?":

If you was to go out in the neighborhood you see people hanging out and if you come they would say "man, are you looking?" They would say "Are you looking?" to keep them from convicting themselves. "Are you looking?" means are you looking for drugs? Everybody knew that language. They would also say something like "I got it." And by them [youngsters] staying out and seeing this, they go out and tell their people [in other neighborhoods] come in [into Hope Mansions] and set up shop.[64]

During inclement whether, drug dealers privileged to have a crack house moved their retail business indoors. The buyers drove up into the parking lots, leaving their car engines running while an associate dashed into the building to make the purchase. For tenants who shared hallways with crack houses, privacy even behind closed doors was an illusion. One youth explained the experience this way:

> And every night the doors would be slamming and all different peoples running in the hallway. We didn't know what was going on. It was bad. My mother was ready to get away from around there.[65]

The sporadic gun conflicts between rival gangs had profound effect on innocent children. For fear of compromising their children's safety, many parents forbade their children to play outdoors after school:

> One of the unique things is I did not see a lot of children. When I first came out all I saw was adults okay? And I attribute that to the shootings that took place, shootings of police officers, and there have been times I've been out here and there have been shootings all around.[66]

Some children were allowed to play outside, but were called in by 3:00 or 4:00 p.m. when the drug business started to convene and areas such as the playgrounds and the basketball courts were overrun by dealers. As one resident explained,

> [drug dealers] would start moving in on the basketball court and maneuver the kids back to the buildings. . . . If the police came, they would pick up the ball and pretend they were playing.[67]

This power play signifies not only the dominance of the drug dealers in the community; it marked the powerlessness of the ordinary families living there.

The general reactions of the parents to the drug dealers and the violence accounted for the seeming absence of pre-teen children playing outdoors. As one parent and former President of the Tenant Council stated:

> It was a bad situation. Literally, you didn't want to come outside. The kids didn't come out. And my daughter has seen some things and

she's ten years old. And she wasn't ten then—she was a little
younger. She would say, "I saw a bag of something outside" or "I
saw a syringe." Kids don't have any business being exposed to that,
but those are some of the things that they saw.[68]

Every school-age child in Sun Rise Apartments and Hope
Mansions was aware of the drug trade, the violence associated with it,
and the safety problems were forced to confront daily. Some the youth
expressed their concerns and dislikes about their community:

"I hate the drugs and the way they're messing up other people."

"The drugs and the fighting."

"The drugs and some of the people. You know, as you walk down the
street they approach you with drugs and I don't like that."

"Drugs and housing—the whole place."[69]

In an essay contest, 11-year old Sabrina Ford wrote:

In my community, all you see is drug addicts, pushers, and police. It
scares me because I know that I can't do too much about this
problem, except say no to drugs. . . . I will not be influenced by my
classmates, friends or anyone to use drugs. I feel as if I am strong
enough to remain drug free.[70]

Parents of daughters had additional fears: some young girls were
raped and others assaulted by men roaming the neighborhood:

Yeah. My daughter, man, the girl upstairs right now, her and her
buddy was playing one day, little girl, she was semi-retarded . . . and
a guy picked her up. I used to always tell my daughter, "don't never
go nowhere with nobody, don't accept no money," so they was
playing, but I watch 'em. They was playing on the swings and then
they went up front. I said, "y'all come on back here." But in the
meantime I seen 'em talking. My daughter came back there, the other
little girl didn't. About two minutes later, man, somebody picked her
up and raped her.[71]

For parents raising children, the negative influence of the drug dealers in the community presented a constant source of challenge:

> We have killings, rapings, robbing, muggings, things like that. You have to set an example for a younger persons so they can strive. So they won't go the wrong way or make the wrong turn. But if you don't, you see one person out there selling drugs to someone and you have a younger child standing right there while you're doing it or while they're transacting their business. So later, two weeks, two days, two months, you might see that same young child out there doing the same thing. So you have to set an example.[72]

The Influence of the Drug Pushers on Pupils

In any impoverished community, as in Sun-Hope, the neighborhood schools are rarely unaffected by the drug trade and drug-related violence. Parents, teachers, and other social control agents must compete constantly with drug pushers for the attention of community's children. Given that the drug dealers in these communities had something—cash, status symbols and peer admiration—to offer the school children that many teachers and parents did not, the influence of the drug dealers became a menace. The testimonies of some of the concerned teachers point to the fact that even the elementary school children were not secured from the influences of the drug dealers:

> I was talking to a student about a former student one day and the student pointed out that a particular student was now a lieutenant. And I said did he graduate that long ago? I though it was just a few years ago? And he said, not in the Army, he's selling drugs. They see how [the drug dealers] have succeeded, their "definition" of success and they have not followed what we are suggesting that they do and we are communicating a message that is conflicting with what they see operating and succeeding everyday.[73]

The negative pressures from drug-dealing peers were felt at school. By flaunting the material wealth gained through the sale of drugs, drug dealers got the attention of their classmates without saying much. One teacher noted:

Before the crackdown and arrest of student drug pushers, some of
them wore silk shirts and gold chains, drove Mercedes and BMW's
and had beepers which would go off in the classroom, so they would
ask to be excused and everyone knew why they were really asking to
leave the classroom.[74]

Even the deaths of some of these youth became an advertising
medium. To honor their dead "little soldiers," some druglords paid
funeral expenses and distributed gifts to the youth present:

[Samson] was a 16-year-old student who dropped out of school, but
who came to school dressed sharply and who wore a lot of gold
chains. He got killed and the drug overlords dressed him in real fancy
clothes, gave him a big funeral and the next day the kids came to
school in T-Shirts that said, "We love you, [Samson]."[75]

TENANTS' REACTION TO THE NEIGHBORHOOD DRUG DEALERS

In any community where a full-fledge open-air market takes root, there
is certainty that there are no mediating institutions, absentee landlord
and/or strained relationship between residents and management, and
poor police-community relations. Under such conditions, drug dealers
and buyers go about their business with considerable freedom and with
little concern for the law. Characteristic of poor communities faced
with the drug problem is that residents are unable to act collectively and
decisively to counter the drug dealers because they lack mediating
institutions:

I think [the residents'] concern is whatever happens happens. They
don't want to come out of their houses and do anything about it. But
when they see something happening and it is not the way they want it
to happen, then they are quick to judge but they are slow to help, and
that is what has been the problems of most neighborhoods, not just
[Hope Mansions]. In most neighborhoods, most of the people like to
sit in their houses and not do anything. And the ones that are doing
something are the ones that are making the change.[76]

The few people who elect to act against lawlessness are often overwhelmed and outnumbered. Although it was not the primary cause of the decay and decline of Sun-Hope, the drug trade escalated it. Faced with a flourishing drug trade and violence, tenants who otherwise could have been encouraged to be active in their community found "legitimate" reasons for not participating in any community endeavors. Defining the drug-plagued community as hopeless, some residents saw no reason to invest their energies in ways to rid the area of the drug trade.

SUMMARY

The low socioeconomic status of the residents has rendered them powerless. The drug dealers were aware of the fact that many of the residents were unwilling to testify in court against them. For many residents in entry-level jobs, taking a day off to testify in court could be costly: an employer was not going to pay a laborer or a temporary worker for days taken off to be in court. What many middle-class residents regard as a civic duty is for many low-income residents an economic burden. As I will discuss later, there is no economic or social incentive for many low-income residents to appreciate the usefulness of civil duty, especially when they percieve the justice system has failed them.

The sense of powerlessness stems from the tenants' collective inability to alter their state of affairs: management is ineffective in ensuring the safety of the residents, they cannot rely on the police to rid the area of deviants and violence, and as a group experiencing varying degrees of poverty, tenants lack collective consciousness and resources to maintain the bear minimum of informal social control. The attitude of this resident echoes many others in the community:

> I'm in [Sun Rise] and they're selling it and then they're in my basement using it. And my apartment areas is the regular hangout so that's why I am disgruntled. Because there is nothing I can say because I don't want to get hurt and I don't see the situation getting any better. The police come but they have people that look out for the police.[77]

Residents seldom called the police for fear of compromising their safety. There was a widespread belief among residents that the drug dealers had connections with some police officers who supplied them with the telephone numbers of the "snitches" in the neighborhood.[78] Some who did call the police were frustrated by the response:

> When you done call the police, all they been doing is asking so many questions like "is he black?" "You see him carrying a gun?" "What kinda clothes he's wearing?" They even try to trick you to tell them your name. They are not suppose to ask for names.[79]

One retired senior citizen and a Hope Mansions resident for 20 years, recalled that: "I made one or two calls . . . when I was over there [in Building 1]." But in each case, he refused to identify himself:

> No sir. I just say such and such is happening but don't give my name. No sir. You'll get killed man. No. I don't know any body who would give their names. Folks over there are just like me. They know better than that.[80]

Although there is no evidence of anyone being threatened for assisting the police in apprehending drug dealers and murderers, a rumor mill of drug dealers making threats to kill "snitches" made residents extremely fearful of retaliation. On the occasion police attended to a situation, residents refused to come outdoors to help the police with their investigation. In the charged atmosphere of drugs and guns, residents feared that being seen speaking to a uniformed officer for an extended period of time could invoke retaliation:

> No, unless you want to get killed. Once somebody knows you're the one who called [the police], you gonna get killed. . . . You'd be surprised how those racketeers were. People would put you to sleep. They ain't playing with you.[81]

A few residents initiated a petition to pressure the management/owner to evict residents known to be operating crack and whore houses. However, fear of retaliation from the druglords reigned:

> We have been petitioned and petitioned and a lot of us have gotten together. But people don't want their name to be called out and you don't want to be pointed out.[82]

In addition, many of the residents were of the opinion that the persistence of the drug trade in the neighborhood indicated that the apartment managers were themselves afraid to confront tenants who were dealing in drugs, or were accomplice to the drug dealers:

> The tenants can pull together and help management. And management is waiting now for the tenant council to try to bust the people for drugs. But I feel the [tenant] council is not going to do it because they live out here. This is management's job. Just like management do not have nothing to do with calling the police. They will not call. They will not just tell [on] certain people.[83]

The drug dealers controlled the residents by mere intimidation:

> The drug dealers have completely intimidated us. I've seen them carrying guns I've never seen in the Marines. When people see that, they run inside, lock their doors, and they're not going to call the police for anything. People are afraid of retaliation.[84]

Sun-Hope became destabilized as a result of its transformation from a mixed-income and stable community into a neighborhood community of predominantly low-income, welfare-dependent and broken families. The poverty of the residents, coupled with the failure of the landlord to reinvest in the property and the management's inability to control recalcitrant residents, contributed to the disorganization of the community. This made the community easy target for invasion by drug dealers. The 24-hour open-air drug trade and struggle for turfs ushered in a seemingly protracted violence and lawlessness in the community. The situation engendered hostilities between neighbors, between them and the management, and distrust between powerless residents and the police. The drug trade wreaked havoc on poor communities like Sun-Hope, such that the federal government proposed a "War on Drugs" policy to be waged by local enforcement agencies. To this issue we turn in chapter five.

NOTES

1. Lillian A. Poe, *[Father Jonas]: His Social and Political Interests and Influence*, (Ph.D. diss., College of William and Mary, Williamsburg, Virginia, 1975).

2. Tenant, personal interview, 11 March 1992.

3. Former tenant. personal interview, 15 May 1991.

4. *Focus Group*, 1987, 26.

5. Former neighborhood youth organizer, personal interview, 4 March 1992.

6. Joel Garreau, "The Invisible Hand Guides D.C.'s Visible Menace: Street-Corner Drug Trade Provides a Model of Capitalism, Say Economists, Police," *The Washington Post* 29 December 1988, A1, A14.

7. The D.C. Police officers' frequent stops and searches of "suspicious" African American and Hispanic men for drugs at the Union Station generated heated debates in the city. The first case ended up in the U.S. Court of Appeals in Washington in 1991. See Michael York, "D.C. Search Upheld in Drug Case," *The Washington Post,* 12 May 1993.

8. Tenant, personal interview, 16 July 1992.

9. Nancy Lewis, "Out-of-Town Drug Dealers Invade Area," *The Washington Post*, 18 July 1987, A1.

10. Ibid.

11. See Clarence Lusane, *Pipe Dream Blues: Racism and the War on Drugs* (Boston: South End Press, 1991).

12. Alexander Cockburn, "From Andes to Inner Cities, Cocaine Is a Good Career Choice," *The Wall Street Journal*, 7 September 1989, A15.

13. Former neighborhood youth organizer, personal interview, 4 March 1992.

14. Tenant and FOI member, personal interview, 6 April 1992.

15. The police dubbed the group Committee. The shooting death of one member as a result of intragroup conflict led to the arrest and conviction of 4 gang members in 1988. Even after arresting the gang members, the police were unable to determine where the group obtained its cocaine supply. During my field research, one respondent informed me that the group was also know as the "Rayful Boys." In his book, *Pipe Dream Blues: Racism and the War on Drugs* (Boston: South End Press, 1991), Clarence Lusane described Rayful Edmond III as "the most renowned and notorious drug kingpin in the history of Washington, D.C." (173).

16. Sari Horwitz, "A Drug-Selling Machine That Was All Business." *The Washington Post,* 24 April 1988, A1.

17. Victoria Churchville, "NE Tenants Hope to Outlast Siege of Drug Violence," *The Washington Post*, 2 August 1987.

18. Ibid.

19. Prostitution follows the drug trade. Either because of the addictive nature or the cash value of crack cocaine, some poor women (and men) engage

in various "sex-for-crack exchanges." See Mitchell S. Ratner's *Crack Pipe as Pimp: An Ethnographic Investigation of Sex-for-Crack Exchanges* (Lexingon Books: New York, 1993).

20. This observation is consistent with the situation in other neighborhoods. See Terry Williams, *The Cocaine Kids: The Inside Story of a Teenage Drug Ring* (Reading, MA: Addison-Wesley, 1989).

21. *The Washington Post,* 13 April 1988.

22. Sari Horwitz, "A Drug-Selling Machine That Was All Business," *The Washington Post,* 24 April 1988, A1.

23. As one reporter noted, "In the street-level operations, the 'little soldiers,' teenagers . . . are crucial. They were put on the front lines to insulate the adults from arrest. Adults go to prison. Juveniles, generally treated leniently for drug violations, can be back on the streets quickly." See Sari Horwitz, "A Drug-Selling Machine That Was All Business." *The Washington Post,* 24 April 1988, A16.

24. Ibid, A16.

25. Tenant, personal interview, 23 July 1993.

26. *Focus Group,* May 1987, 10.

27. Tenant, personal interview, 25 October 1991.

28. Tenant, personal interview, 16 June 1993.

29. Tenant, personal interview, 19 June 1991.

30. *Focus Group,* May 1987, 30.

31. This observation departs from Hirschi's social control theory where family is construed as inducing conformity. See Travis Hirschi, *Causes of Delinquency* (Berkeley: University of California Press, 1969). Faced with economic hardships, some parents do not hesitate from encouraging their children to engage in petty crimes.

32. *Focus Group,* May 1987, 18.

33. Ibid.

34. By all accounts "[c]rack and Washington were a natural combination. With a per capital buying income of $16,908, far above the national average and higher than that in New York, Los Angeles or Chicago, Washington offers a lucrative market. Indeed, the crack that sells for $5.00 in New York runs $25 here. Buyers include suburbanites from nearby Virginia and Maryland." See David Shribman and Jore Davidson, *The Wall Street Journal,* 14 April 1989.

35. For a full account of the convergence of many of the various drug syndicates in in the city, see "Nancy Lewis, "Out-of Town Drug Dealers Invade Area," Washington Post, 28 July 1987, A1.

36. Tenant and FOI member, personal interview, 6 April 1992.

37. *Focus Group,* May 1987, 26.

38. Tenant and FOI member, personal interview, 16 April 1992.

39. Focus Group, May 1987.

40. Tenant, and LJTP staff member, personal interview, 16 June 1992.

41. Tenant and FOI member, personal interview, 6 April 1992.

42. Former Tenant and president of Sun-Hope Civic Association, personal interview, 16 September 1991.

43. Tenant, personal interview, 14 November 1991.

44. Tenant, personal interview, 19 June 1992.

45. Editorial, *The Washington Post,* 29 June 1991, A22.

46. Tenant and LJTP staff member, personal interview, 16 June 1992.

47. Tenant and FOI member, personal interview, 16 April 1992.

48. Tenant, personal interview, 15 October 1991.

49. Ibid.

50. Clergyman, personal interview, 25 March 1992.

51. *Focus Group,* May 1987, 40.

52. Ibid.

53. Ibid., 43.

54. Ibid.

55. Tenant, personal interview, 24 November 1993.

56. Patricia Mason, Former CEO of the People's Advocacy, personal interview, 2 March 1993.

57. Former Tenant, personal interview, 3 September 1991.

58. The symbols of success derived from the drug trade are the same everywhere. Drug dealers with profitable gains tend to flaunt their wealth by buying and driving expensive cars, adorning themselves with expensive clothes and jewelry, and dating several girls. See Terry William's *Cocaine Kids: Inside Story of a Teenage Drug Ring* (Reading, MA: Addison-Wesley, 1989), and Elijah Anderson's *Streetwise,* 100.

59. *Focus Group,* May, 1987, 31.

60. Ibid., 24.

61. Ibid., 30.

62. Former geriatric social worker, personal interview, 14 April 1992.

63. *Focus Group,* May 1987, 25.

64. Tenant and FOI member, personal interview, 6 April 1992.

65. *Focus Group,* May 1987, 25.

66. Clergyman, personal interview, 25 March 1992.

67. Sari Horwitz and James Rupert, "Calm Returns as Police, Muslims Patrol in NE," *The Washington Post,* 20 April 1988, A16.

68. Tenant, personal interview, 19 June 1991.

69. *Focus Group,* May 1987, 7.

70. Lawrence Feinberg, "In My Community, 'All You See is Drug Addicts, Pushers and Police,'" *The Washington Post*, 30 April 1988, B4.

71. Former tenant, personal interview, 15 May 1991.

72. *Focus Group*, 1987, 24.

73. Ibid., 59.

74. Ibid.

75. Ibid.

76. Tenant and Fruit of Islam (FOI) member, personal interview, 6 April 1992.

77. *Focus Group*, 1987, 40.

78. Similar concerns about D.C.'s 911 were expressed by Dorothy Brazill, the president of Columbia Heights Neighborhood Coalition, and candidate for the D.C. Council's Ward 1 seat. See Patrick Symmes, "Good Cop, Bad Cop," *The Washington City Paper*, 19-25 August 1994, 18-26.

79. Fieldnotes, 6 March 1991.

80. Tenant, personal interview, 1 June 1992.

81. Ibid.

82. *Focus Group*, May 1987, 10.

83. Ibid., 10.

84. Sari Horwitz and James Rupert, "Calm Returns as Police, Muslims Patrol in NE." *The Washington Post*, 20 April 1988, A16.

CHAPTER 5
Policing a Neighborhood Community Open-Air Drug Market, 1987-1988[1]

During the later part of the 1980s, officers of the Sixth District in Ward 7, where Sunrise-Hope is located, referred to the neighborhood as "Hell's Horseshoe" or "Little Beirut."[2] These labels denote not only the disdain and resignation police officers had for the community, but also the heightened danger—real or perceived—awaiting them.

This sense of imminent danger in the Sun-Hope neighborhood became a factor in officers' response to calls. Each police officer determined the level of risk involved in a situation before responding to any assignment. As one anonymous police officer pointed out, "You can listen to the dispatcher at night, reading out call after call, begging, 'Any unit, please respond.' And you won't hear any answer."[3] In the minds of some of the patrol officers in the area, Sun-Hope spelled danger. It must be avoided. As one detective stated:

> Just like citizens don't want to be hurt, police don't want to be hurt either. It's foolish to put themselves in a position where they could be. . . . It would be foolish for a person, especially in a place like [Sunrise-Hope Mansions], that has all those breezeways, for an officer that's by themselves to go. If you don't have a backup, you're supposed to wait. If you have an assignment, and you can't find someone to go with you, you're not supposed to go without a backup. The only time you ever go anywhere is to take a written report on a burglary that's already happened.[4]

97

Previous negative experiences also reinforced the caution with which officers responded to calls for service in Sun-Hope. For example, the fatal shooting of a police officer and a detective in 1980 and 1985, respectively, provided police officers with legitimate reasons for reluctance in responding to residents' call-for-service in the Sun-Hope neighborhood. A detective recalled her experience in one of the incidents:

> [Officer Luke] was with us and still they shot him. The [drug dealers] knew he was the police, and I was there. When things like that happen, it only serves to make you more cautious. The citizens need help, but we are not going to go in and get ourselves killed either.[5]

She added:

> I worked with someone who was out there the other night and got shot there. Personally, I wouldn't do it. You'd never get me to go in there by myself. I did it when I was buying drugs because I had to. But, at that point in time, you have a little bit of an edge because they're not sure that you're the police. So they are less likely to do something that would threaten you. I know it sounds bizarre, but criminals, drug dealers, are more apt to test a police officer if they know they are police and they are by themselves. One single person going in there that might be the police, but more likely is just a drug user. So I would go in there by myself and buy drugs but once I stopped buying drugs and I started arresting them, I wouldn't go by myself.[6]

The conscious decisions by individual officers to delay or not respond alone to calls for service in Sun-Hope community were often interpreted by residents as a cold and calculated racial and class bias toward them.

This interpretation was inaccurate. The actions of the police officers must be evaluated in within a broader framework. The reality in Sun-Hope community was that police officers had a definate reason to be apprehensive: officers were more apt to encounter individuals who were bearing loaded guns and would not hesistate to exchange fire with them. During the peak of the drug trade between 1983 and 1987, gunshots were frequent. Bullet holes in walls of some the buildings were testaments to the precarious situation in the community. Secondly, the discretion of the officers must be understood in terms of the city-wide police understaffing. This problem was particularly acute in the Sixth District.[7] So intense was that drug trade that any coordinated effort to bust drug dealers required that the Metropolitan Police Department (MPD) deploy all its officers and even those of other districts (including those off-duty) to one neighborhood. According to Gary Hankins, chairman of the Fraternal Order of Police (FOP):

> Some nights that we have studied, we had eight officers and occasionally half a dozen officers working the evening shift for the full district [D.C.]. In order to make one drug arrest, we need a team of eight to ten people: two undercover officers to make the purchase, one officer working as backup to observe from a distance, and another four to six to make the actual arrest.[8]

The combination of perceived heightened danger and understaffing led to longer response time for call-for-service from the Sun-Hope neighborhood.

Lacking a clear understanding of the forces which shaped the police's ability to respond promptly to their calls, residents defined the situation as blatant disinterest in their plight. Many of the residents perceived themselves as stigmatized by the police for living in a low-income black neighborhood with serious drug problems. The police officers, residents argued, approached them with derision. One of the tenant leaders expressed the frustration of many residents this way:

> Our relationship with Sixth District—over there on Minnesota Avenue ten minutes away—was not a good one. *Ten minutes . . .* Right there. Ten minutes. [The police] would take their time getting here, have an attitude when they got here. You know, so people said, "Hey, why call? They're looking at me like I'm the one, I'm the perpetrator." As opposed to, "we need your assistance." But then again, I don't know what kind of attitudes the police dealt with from people out here. Were they getting cold calls? Were they getting calls that didn't mean nothing when they got here?[9]

Another resident explained:

> The police were present a lot but it was always after the fact. And I don't remember they ever came when they could make an arrest.

They came after someone had told them they've seen something and they are getting information.[10]

More frequently than not, the callers were not on the scene to assist the police. Consequently, arrests were rare. Comparison of data from two neighborhoods with varying socioeconomic backgrounds and community-police relations illustrates the point.

TABLE 5.1
Police Service-Calls in 2 Neighborhoods
(January 1, 1990 - August 30, 1991)[11]

Item	Sun-Hope (Renters)	Bragg Road (Owners)
Number of cases where a citizen met and gave report to police	109 (21%)	65 (34%)
Number of cases where no citizen met and gave report to police	350 (69%)	88 (45%)
Number of arrests made by police on or near the scene	49 (9%)	40 (21%)
Total Police calls-for-service	508	193

Of the 508 and 193 calls-for-service made in Sun-Hope and Bragg Road neighborhoods respectively, 21 percent of Sun-Hope callers compared to 34 percent in Bragg Road met with and provided the necessary information to police officers. Thus, the arrests made by the police in Sun-Hope and Bragg Road were 9 and 21 percent, respectively. As the data shows, there is a positive relationship between effective arrests and assistance by neighborhood residents. Thus, what made it problematic for the police handling the situation in Sun-Hope was that more often than not, the callers and witnesses were unwilling to assist the police in doing their job: this was situation in 69 percent of the cases in Sun-Hope.

In response to Sun-Hope residents' complaints about the police, one detective responded:

> [Residents] need to realize that in order to get the help that they
> need, they have to give [the police] help. [To] call up and tell the
> police there are people out on the corner selling drugs and hang up is

not going to help. When [residents] call, they need to be as explicit about what the problem is as they can—descriptions, locations—and to stay on the phone with the dispatcher so that they can tell the dispatcher, "okay these people have now moved to another block" or "they went in this house," so the police can come and the dispatcher can tell them: "that person is no longer on the corner. You need to look for them at such-and-such a house, or such-and-such a car, or at a different location" because these people don't stand still. So, the police come and they don't do anything because this is where they have been told to go. They don't know what is happening and they don't know where those people went to.[12]

In any neighborhood where the drug trade and violent crimes seem protracted, tenants have the tendency to deride the efforts of the police. Residents develop deep-seated resentment and distrust of the police. As expected, Sun-Hope residents became suspicious of the police as being part of the problem. A Nation of Islam convert who was a former drug dealer and user stated: "I had some friends living in one of the apartments over there. One of the guys who used to come over to do drugs there was a cop. In broad daylight, and he'd be there. Sometimes in uniform and all."[13]

A series of scandals involving some MPD officers confirmed what some residents had suspected all along and gave others more reason to distrust the officers in their local police district. Corrupt police officers sold protection and classified police information to the very drug dealers they were mandated to apprehend.[14] Other police officers confiscated drugs and money from drug dealers for their own use or for reinvestment in illicit drug businesses elsewhere.[15]

According to a former tenant, his close friend who was a police officer became wealthy off the drug trade in the 1980s. He was adamant that, like his police friend, some officers were drug dealers themselves:

What they'd do with the drugs? You think they report all those drugs? Hell no. They might say: "We took such and such." They be keeping some of the drugs. They're making money themselves, or whatever else they want.[16]

A vendor in the neighborhood also recalled that on several occasions one or two police officers confiscated money from drug dealers known as the New York Boys and the Miami Boys, but made no arrests.[17]

Recalling the situation with resignation, a senior citizen and a long-time resident, who, in 1996, managed the refurbished Hope Mansions Community Center, stated:

> That was a joke. A joke. Running people back and forth. Running the sellers, they catch'em, take 'em up the streets and the next hour they're back again. Whatever was happening they weren't getting locked up, some of them. Eventually they took all the police they were using in this area and transferred them to another area. They put a brand new police officers in this area and that is when things began to clean up.[18]

"Things began to clean up" because of the "War on Drugs" policy. Predominantly urban low-income neighborhoods such as Sun-Hope became targets for aggressive policing in the cause of waging the war on drugs.

THE MAYOR'S "OPERATION CLEAN SWEEP"

In the 1980s, the Reagan Administration instituted its "War on Drugs" policy. On August 31, 1986, this federal policy was instituted at the local level by Mayor Marion Barry's administration in Washington, D.C. as "Operation Clean Sweep." Defining this law enforcement concept, Mayor Barry stated:

> It literally means what the title implies; sweep the streets clean of trash, drugs, abandoned property and anything that contributed to blight and decay of our neighborhoods.[19]

The ensuing intensive and highly visible policing in Sun-Hope, and many low-income neighborhoods like it, resulted in the arrests of several hundreds of drug dealers, buyers, users, and the seizure and forfeiture of narcotics, weapons and vehicles. "Operation Clean Sweep," however, did not result in sweeping the streets of "trash, drugs, abandoned property and anything that contributed to blight and decay," as declared.

One of the initiatives by concerned residents and the owners of the Sunrise Apartments and Hope Mansions was a formal request to meet with Jammie Wilson, Deputy Chief of the Sixth District, in which Sun-Hope is located. Reiterating the concerns and interests of the owners and residents, Peterson wrote:

> As we discussed, the community is in the grip of drug dealers, drug buyers and drug users. Development of this community as a safe and attractive environment for the decent families who live there will not be able to proceed until this grip is broken. This can only be brought about by the concentrated police action you promised. Belief in this promise was reinforced by finding that foot patrols had been assigned to the [Sun-Hope] area on the evening of June 3 [1987]. It made an enormous difference to the safety of the community and we all hope that this will continue. You and your officers impressed us with your dedication and professionalism which we now have reason to believe will be brought to bear in the community.[20]

This letter, while appreciating the police presence following the tenant-police meeting, also asked the police department to live up to its promise in delivering swift services. As a result, the Sixth District employed multiple strategies, which included tips from concerned residents, undercover officers, foot patrol by uniformed officers, and a surveillance trailer used to monitor the activities of suspected drug dealers. From here, the police planned roadblocks to intercept drugs and arms traffickers, served court-issued search and/or arrest warrants, and orchestrated "crack house" raids.

The first significant act of the police was the arrest of eleven men and one woman a week after the above letter was sent to the police department. On June 16th,

> police broke open a crack ring. . . . The seizure netted $5,274 in cash, two stolen automobiles, 10 assorted guns and 109 rounds of ammunition, 10 lids of PCP with street value of $6,340 and 233 vials of crack with a street value of $5,825.[21]

This raid was conducted within eight hours after complaints were made by residents and observations of the drug dealers were made by undercover police officers. Commenting on the significance of the raid, a police spokesman stated:

When you take into consideration the small concentrated area, 12 people locked up in an eight-hour period, the quantity of narcotics seized coupled with the number of weapons taken, it's a very significant operation.[22]

On the same day, a group of police officers raided the apartment of an elderly tenant. The 64-year-old man was charged with the possession of a firearm and possession of drugs—cocaine, PCP and marijuana—with a value estimated at $1.5 million. The police also confiscated a handgun and a 1980 Toyota in which they found a stash of marijuana.[23]

Between August 28 and 29, the police mounted a succession of surprise raids in Sun-Hope. The eleven-hour "Operation Clean Sweep" employed more than 150 uniformed and undercover officers. The result was the arrest of 72 individuals, the seizure of cocaine, PCP and marijuana valued at $13,000, two motor vehicles and a handgun.[24]

The intensive police surveillance in Sun-Hope between June and August 1987 became the centerpiece of Mayor Marion Barry's press conference. Using Sun-Hope as a backdrop, Barry summarized to the press and residents his administration's accomplishment in dealing with the neighborhood drug problems:

19 juveniles and 427 adults have been arrested and of those arrests; 13 of the juveniles and 121 of the adults were charged with drug offenses; $15,849 in U.S. currency has been seized in connection with the distribution of illegal drugs. A total of 23 weapons have been confiscated; and eight (8) D.C. Superior Court narcotics-related search warrants have been executed.[25]

Such intensified police efforts to overwhelm neighborhood drug dealers were sporadic. The lack of sustained police presence, however, did not stop the law enforcement officials from declaring victory whenever they confiscated drugs and drug-related assets valued at several hundreds of dollars. In a post-raid press conference, Deputy Chief Jimmy L. Wilson of the Sixth District stated:

[The raid] disrupted the drug traffic in the high narcotics areas of the Sixth District . . . and pretty much shut it down. This was Operation Clean Sweep with a twist. Once we chased [dealers] out of a [drug trafficking area], we anticipated their movement. When they arrived [at a new location] we were already there. We were waiting for them. That's what made this particular operation unique.[26]

The police operation may have been unique, but it by no means deterred the drug dealers or created a safe community. In the evening of December 1, 1987, plain-clothes officer Herman J. Keels was shot and killed as he was purchasing drugs as part of a police investigation. The culprit, 17-year-old Antoine Warren of New York City, shot Keels when he identified himself as a law enforcement agent.[27]

The lack of deterrent effects of the police raids in Sun-Hope had to do with the fact that for many drug dealers, the gains outweighed the risks. The monetary gains to be made, coupled with the users' demand for crack cocaine, provided ample incentives for the drug dealers to resume business as soon as police teams left the area.[28] Lured by the chance for quick profit, new drug dealers filled the void created through police drug raids and arrests. The result was an overwhelmed police force faced with seemingly intractable problem. As one detective observed: "We used to work in groups of ten, fifteen, twenty, thirty people, and still that wasn't enough".[29] A long-time resident agreed: "You know, I think if they take five [drug dealers] away, ten come back. [The police] don't catch the right ones.[30]

While the drug raids disrupted the drug trade for short periods of time, they were not enough to drive the drug dealers out of the neighborhood. This led Gail Peterson and a few of the residents to ask for more drastic measures, namely, police blockades.

THE POLICE BLOCKADES

In addition to their request for the presence of uniformed and plain-clothes officers, the Hope Mansions Resident Council and the owners:

> discussed [with the police] the feasibility and possible benefits of changing the . . . thoroughfare surrounding [Sunrise and Hope Mansions] into a one-way street.[31]

In a letter to Deputy Chief Jimmie Wilson, the property manager wrote:

> The general consensus at the meeting was that this change would restrict the easy ingress and egress of those persons involved in illegal activities in the area thus aiding the Police Department in their

efforts to identify and discourage the obvious drug trafficking. Please accept this correspondence as our request of you to pursue whatever avenues and/or processes required to obtain permission to bring about this change.[32]

The residents' demand to convert the adjoining streets into a one-way street was promptly implemented by the Department of Public Works. This enabled the police to stop and search cars, seize and arrest individuals transporting illegal narcotics and firearms. In order to prevent individuals from evading the police blockade, some officers were also stationed at the point of entry. Being a one-way street, drivers evading police search by driving in the opposite direction were then stopped, searched for drugs, firearms, and charged accordingly. The police blockades were effective temporarily, until the drug buyers and dealers gained knowledge of the operation.

In order to evade police blockades, many of the drug buyers resorted to parking their cars at the parking lot of a nearby convenience store. As a justification for parking, the individual(s) would make a small purchase in the store and then wonder off into the Sun-Hope area to buy drugs.[33] Other buyers and users devised different schemes to purchase drugs. Some parked their cars in nearby neighborhoods, then walked past the roadblocks to purchase drugs. As a consequence, residents in those areas complained of not being able to find parking spaces near their homes.[34]

The outcome of Operation Clean Sweep engendered debates from many quaters of the city. On the one hand, the police were quick to release accounts of their neighborhood drug raid. On the other hand, residents in these neighborhoods continued to complain about their neighborhoods not being safe because the police were unable to eradicate the drug trade. The situation was the same around the various housing projects experiencing the impact of the drug trade. Joining the fray were affected landlords, some members of the MPD, the city council, and the Nation of Islam, questioning the efficacy of "Operation Clean Sweep."

CRITICISM OF "OPERATION CLEAN SWEEP"

The law enforcement techniques used by the police in its operations were not without critics. The FOP's Gary Hankins lambasted Mayor Barry and Police Chief Maurice Turner for using the high visibility patrols in high crime areas as a media stunt to gain coverage on the war on drugs at the local level:

> The high visibility patrols now being used . . . is a short-range solution to the pervasive drug problem there. If the city is to ever make a significant impact on this problem, collective citizen participation is essential, along with the involvement of both the private and public sectors.[35]

In the Sun-Hope area, the so-called "secret raids" of crack houses were often preceded by a mob of television and newspaper reporters.[36] The highly visible police presence in Sun-Hope was aimed to reassure the residents that police were at work in their neighborhood. There were still not enough officers, however, to maintain a presence around the clock.

To compound the problem, the layout of Sun-Hope continued to present the police with a burden. The neighborhood, large and surrounded by parks, was difficult to patrol by just a few officers:

> There was a lot involved in that. Part of that is just the layout of [Sun-Hope]. It's on twenty two acres, has a park all around it. There are fences and a park you can run easily. It's one access and one exit so you can weave your way through the building if you are fast from police and the cars, and you are probably younger and in better shape. Because of the design of the buildings with breezeways around inside . . . they'd run from one project to another even. So instead of having twenty two acres to do a chase on, they have fourty-some-odd acres to do a chase on, and escape through the park to who knows where. So, physically, it was a problem. I think the police were spread very thin.[37]

Another resident added:

> The reason why the police can't hardly get to them is the place is so wide open it has its own alarm system. As soon as police come within a block, everyone knows.[38]

The sporadic police raids, undercover surveillance, street blockades, and the arrests of scores of drug dealers did not seem to deter potential drug dealers and buyers. For one thing, many of the dope peddlers on the street were underaged teenagers who were very knowledgeable about their status in the criminal justice system.[39] Compared with the profits to be made in the drug business, the risks of incarceration for minors were small—a few weeks, if at all, in a juvenile detention center. The police, therefore, were faced with the problem of dealing with underage teenagers who felt invincible in the face of the law.

As a law enforcement technique, "Operation Clean Sweep" masked structural problems facing communities such as Sun-Hope. The reality of chronic unemployment, lack of education, absentee landlords, and inadequate public services pervasive in the neighborhoods ravaged by drugs were unaddressed. The police arrested many people on drug-related charges.[40] But the streets were not swept clean of trash, drugs, and abandoned property, as was initially proposed by the mayor.

In effect, "Operation Clean Sweep" generated its own dilemma. On the one hand, the district government sought and gathered resources to eliminate neighborhood drug trade areas.[41] On the other hand, the Barry administration had no resources to eliminate the root causes of the drug trade: the lack of education, deterrence of consumers, a lack of marketable skills, entry-level jobs and detox centers. The neighborhoods continued to be plagued with unemployed youth and adults. Thus, for many of young men living in the neighborhood, the street-level drug trade continued to provide a source of income.

In Sun-Hope community, "Operation Clean Sweep" was short-lived and its benefits were few. Commenting on the ineffectiveness of Clean Sweep, Police Chief Maurice Turner Jr. stated:

> I don't see it having any impact on the demand for drugs. . . . Arrests are not the answer. [We have] crowded court calendars in D.C. Superior Court and pushed prisons above their capacities.[42]

Soon thereafter, Chief Turner resigned his position. Declaring their efforts a sham, the police department scrubbed Clean Sweep. "Don't give me more [police] people," the new Police Chief Isaac Fulwood, Jr., frankly informed the public. Those entertaining the belief that arresting drug pushers can drastically reduce crime, the embittered Chief concluded, were "missing the boat."[43]

Exhausting the Law Enforcement Agencies

Arguing that an effective anti-drug control "requires that simultaneous actions be undertaken over a sustained period of time," Gail Peterson issued what amounted to directives to Mayor Barry. The first directive asked the Mayor to:

> create a command control center to coordinate the activities of the many local and federal agencies working on this problem. A partial list of participants would include: the Metropolitan Police, the FBI, the Drug Enforcement Agency, Park Police, the U.S. Attorney's Office and the U.S. Marshal's Office.

The "partial list" of coercive agencies invoked an image of impending occupation. The fact of the matter was that all these agencies had been involved in the anti-drug campaign in one way or the other in the city.[44] In Sun-Hope, the FBI agents and the Metropolitan Police officers had collaborated in various ways to apprehend drug dealers, fugitives, and investigate criminal cases.[45]

The second directive urged multiple actions geared to frustrate nonresident drug dealers and buyers. The directive stated:

> Access to outsiders who come to buy and sell drugs must be cut off. This will deprive the drug dealers of many of their customers. We suggest the following:
>
> •Establish checkpoint/guard house at the intersection of [Crab Avenue and Sunset Boulevard] and further along the "horseshoe" where the pedestrian bridge path from [D.C. Park] intersects Rust Place. These two points should be lit with high-intensity lights.
> •Management will issue Parking Permits to all residents. Non-residents without guest permits would be subject to towing from parking lots.
> •Increase Park Police patrols in [D.C. Park].
> •Obtain restraining order barring known convicted drug dealers and tenants evicted for illegal activities from entering the property. This would make such persons subject to prosecution for illegal entry. This recommendation requires exploration with the U.S. Attorney's Office.[46]

These measures suggested to the Mayor were put into effect with minor success, although the fourth was difficult to implement because of legal complications. In response to the first issue of the directive, the intersections where the drive-by drug buyers and drug hawkers transacted business were illuminated with flood lights. The anticipation was that the bright lights would discourage the drug dealers and buyers from exposing themselves to the full view of police surveillance. In fact many street-level drug dealers preferred to deal close to well-lit areas where they too could monitor prospective clients, identify possible undercover officers, "stick up men" or rival gangs. At best the flood lights were useful in providing visibility to undercover and surveillance officers to monitor the drug trade at night. But this strategy was insufficient to deter the drug dealers and buyers from the area.

The strategy to regulate unwanted individuals with cars in the area involved issuing parking permits to legitimate residents. Although parking permits were issued to all residents, it was not unlawful for the drug dealers and buyers to park on designated parking spots on the street. At best, the parking decals enabled legitimate residents to regain access to parking spaces near their apartment units. The enforcement of the parking rules, by towing away cars without the appropriate decals, discouraged nonresidents from parking in areas meant for the residents. This strategy, however, had minimal effect on the drug trade. The drug dealers and buyers conducted their business on the sidewalks. "Are you look?" drug dealers inquired. "Are you working?" the buyers responded.

Operating on the assumption that maintaining a presence would deter drug dealers and buyers, the police department stationed one of its Mobile Police Units in the central parking lot of Hope Mansions. As Council member Charlene Drew Javis (D-Ward 4) stated succinctly: "The idea is to disrupt the business of buying and selling—to keep the buyer and the pusher from finding each other easily."[47] As one older tenant observed:

> They even brought a mobile van down here—the police department—and sat it right outside here, right in front of where the ice cream truck was sitting. They had a display out here of all the big guns and stuff they had confiscated. You know they had a display out here and all the big wheels from downtown came out here to show off. That was supposed to scare everybody, but that didn't do anything. They were there for a good little while. Everyday, they

stayed off for the night; they'd come back and the glasses on the van would be broken. It was a waste of money. I'd tell it to you like I saw it. Had the police been better organized, they'd had this thing cleaned up in no time.[48]

The presence of the command and control unit, emblazoned with the D.C. police seal, had a minimal deterrent effect. As a mark of disrespect for the police, unknown individual(s) vandalized the mobile unit while officers were off duty.

Calling on the National Guard

In tandem with the social control mechanisms mentioned above, Gail Peterson sought the Mayor's assistance in using the National Guard to intervene in Sun-Hope:

> Our request that the National Guard be summoned at this time is not a criticism of our fine police department or the efforts of your Administration. The [Sun/Hope] community has received every form of assistance the City has to offer including the concentrated effort of Operation Clean Sweep resulting in 1300 arrests in the community in the past year. The current situation is nothing short of an invasion by a ruthless mercenary force. It must be combatted with extraordinary measures.[49]

The request for the presence of the National Guard was strongly supported by Councilman H.R. Crawford, who said:

> We owe those people who live scared some immediate relief. We don't need more summits, more meetings, more discussion. If this is really war, let's declare war.[50]

The request for the National Guard's assistance in the "war" was drowned in political debates. A response from the Government of the District of Columbia Office of Emergency Preparedness (GDCOEP) detailed the political and procedural reasons:

> Unlike the national guard of the other states in the union, the D.C. National Guard is not under the immediate control of the city's Chief Executive, Mayor Marion Barry, Jr. Simply stated, the Mayor does

not have the authority to order the National Guard to duty for any mission or assignment. The D.C. National Guard is activated through a seven-step process involving the Under Secretary of the Army and the Attorney General of the United States. The troops are actually "federalized" when activated, and thus are subject to laws and regulations applicable to military forces. The activation process has been in effect for many years, and as stated above, is completely different from the authority that a governor has to make use of a state National Guard.[51]

The suggestion and the request to deploy the National Guard to wage war on drugs generated contention among factions of city councilmembers.[52] Although the National Guard had been deployed for various missions in the District, a public controversy erupted whenever a proposition was made to deploy the National Guard to deal with drug-related crimes in the city.[53] This request presented the Mayor with related dilemmas: first, how to deploy the National Guard to patrol black neighborhoods without making many blacks feel they were under siege, and second, how to deploy the Guard without exacerbating the MPD's legitimation crisis. Moreover, the deployment of the National Guard inevitably would be interpreted by critics as a mark of excutive ineptness to use the MPD control a local problem. In the end, the Mayor opted not to request the assistance of the National Guard.

SUMMARY

Similar to many neighborhoods, Sun-Hope presented the police with a seemingly intractable problem, namely, an open-air drug trade and its attendant violence. Mayor Marion Barry announced "Operation Clean Sweep" with the goal of ridding neighborhoods of open-air drug markets. In the Sun-Hope neighborhood, the police department employed various law enforcement techniques, raided many apartment units, confiscated drugs and property, and arrested and charged several hundred people with dealing drugs. The police, collaborating with the new owners and concerned tenants, took draconian measures such as street blockades, searches and seizures to control the drug trade.

Results were dismal. The designers of the war on drugs policy failed to understand the root cause of the drug trade—poverty. The drug trade is prevalent in low-income urban areas largely because, in the absence of jobs, the drug business offers the best opportunity to earn money. In the 1980s, as business moved to the suburbs and the local economy contracted, blacks in the inner-city and low-income areas suffered the most. Blue-collar jobs, which were once the backbone of many black communities, relocated. The result was a dwindled taxbase, and the local government was forced to cut back public services and housing for the poor.

Understanding the structural imperatives of the political economy of the inner-city drug trade and the making of segregated impoverished black neighborhoods illuminates the underlying dilemma confronting city governments and ordinary actors. How could the police eradicate the drug trade (which was the source of subsistence for some residents and revenue for some legitimate businesses) in a neighborhood where a disproportionate number of the residents were socioeconomically marginalized? At best, "Operation Clean Sweep" was a stopgap measure. It did not address the underlying socioeconomic isolation attracting drug dealers, prostitutes and some of the neighborhood residents to the illegal business. On the one hand, the MPD demonstrated its effectiveness by making thousands of arrests. On the other hand, the arrests resulted in more problems for the justice system: clogging court calendars, overflowing jails, and costing millions of dollars in police overtime-pay, ironically, adding to the city's expenditures and its inability to provide for its residents.

After the police department's unsuccessful effort to rid the neighborhood of drug dealers and the mayor's refusal to solicit the assistance of the National Guard, Gail Peterson (and other low-income housing owners) turned to the Nation of Islam's security services, namely, the Fruit of Islam (FOI). The next chapter examines the clash between the FOI and the MPD over approaches to reduce the pervasive drug trade in Sun-Hope community.

NOTES

1. The selection of this period is intentional. Although the menace of the drug trade became evident to residents as far back as 1983, it was between 1987 and 1988 that the new owners, management and tenants collaborated to seek legal and extra-legal assistance to rid the neighborhood of the drug dealers.

2. Nancy Lawson, *The Washington Times*, 5 July 1991, B3.

3. Rene Sanchez and Carlos Sanchez, *The Washington Post* 22, April 1988, C1.

4. Police Detective, personal interview, 21 October 1991.

5. Ibid.

6. Ibid.

7. This problem is typical of many impoverished neighborhoods in Washington, D.C. For example, on a typical Thursday in May 1996, 98 police officers actually reported to work although 341 officers were assigned for duty. See Steve Vogel, "Poor Areas Wait Longer for Hard-Pressed D.C. Police," *The Washington Post*, 2 June, 1996, A1, A20.

8. Sari Horowitz and James Rupert, "Chief Denies Antidrug Patrols Cut Police Protection," *The Washington Post*, 27 April 1988.

9. Tenant and LJTP staff member, personal interview, 16 June 1992.

10. Tenant, personal interview, 17 October 1992.

11. This duration was purposively selected because there was a general feeling in the community that things had improved. The percentages columns may add up to over 100 due to rounding. Data source: D.C. Metropolitan Police Department.

12. Police Detective, personal interview, 21 October 1991.

13. Tenant and FOI member, personal interview, 6 April 1992.

14. See John Ward Anderson and Nancy Lewis, "D.C. Police Allegedly Protected Drug Dealers," *The Washington Post*, 6 October 1987, A1; Paul Duggan and Michael York, "FBI Probe of One D.C. Officer Became a Bureau's Dozen." *The Washington Post*, 17 December 1993. For similar police corruptions, see Gerry Yandel and Christi Parsons, "Drugs Turn community into Tragic Crime Zone," Atlanta Journal Constitution, 16 July 1989, C1.

15. See Nancy Lewis, "Suspect Alleges D.C. Officer Stole More Than $1,000 in NE Drug Raid," *The Washington Post*, 30 August 1987, B10. One of the most notorious police corruptions in recent history involved ex-police officer Michael Dowd's account to the Mollen Commission in 1993. See John Marzulli, "Corrupt Cop Tells His Tale," *The Daily News*, 28 September 1993, C5.

16. Tenant, personal interview, 15 May 1991.

17. The stranded drug dealers came to the vendor often to borrow money to make their trips back to their out-of-state homes, with promises to repay him upon their return.

18. Tenant and Hope Community Center manager, personal interview, 13 May 1994.

19. Mayor Marion Barry Jr. "Talking Points For Mayor Marion Barry, Jr. Judicial Training Conference for Judges and Hearing Commissioners of the Superior Court of the District of Columbia." Charlottesville, Virginia, 5 April 1987.

20. Gail Peterson, a letter to Mayor Marion Barry, 6 June 1987.

21. Sari Horowitz, "D.C. Police Arrest 12 In Alleged 'Crack' Ring," *The Washington Post*, 17 June 1987, D4.

22. Ibid.

23. *The Washington Post*, 18 June 1987, D4.

24. Douglas Stevenson, "D.C. Police Arrest 72 in Drug Raids," *The Washington Post*, 30 August 1987, B2.

25. Marion Barry, Jr. Press Release, 15 August 1987.

26. Douglas Stevenson, "Washington Police Arrest 72 in Drug Raids," *The Washington Post*, 30 August 1987, B2.

27. See Carlos Sanchez and Rene Sanchez, " D.C. Officer Shot in NE Drug Mart," *The Washington Post* 2 December 1987, C2; Sari Horwitz. "N.Y. Youth charged in Police Shooting," *The Washington Post*, 3 December 1987, D1.

28. Lewis, Nancy "Out-of-Town Drug Dealers Invade Area," *The Washington Post*, 28 July 1987, A1.

29. Police Detective, personal interview, 21 October 1991.

30. *Focus Group*, May 1987, 9.

31. Property Manager, a letter, 30 June 1987.

32. Ibid.

33. When the open-air drug market dwindled sharply as a result of the twenty four-hour intensive patrol in the neighborhood by members of the Nation of Islam, Joe Kline, the owner of the convenience store reported a 15 to 20 percent decline in sales in tandem with the neighborhood drug raids. He stated, "I never realized how much of our business was linked" to the neighborhood drug trade. See James Rupert, "Muslims 'Dopebusters' To Widen Patrol," *The Washington Post*, 30 April 1988, B1.

34. "Muslims Gain Barry's Support and Find Services in Demand," *The Washington Post*, 22 April 1988, C1.

35. Sari Horowitz and James Rupert, "Chief Denies Antidrug Patrols Cut Police Protection," *The Washington Post*, 27 April 1988.

36. Horowitz, Sari "Clean Sweep Drug Teams Cut in SE Area," *The Washington Post*, 12 March 1988, B1.

37. Shelter Inc. staffer, personal interview, 5 July 1991.

38. *Focus Group*, May 1987, 10.

39. D.C Police found increasing numbers of children engaged in drug dealing during Operation Clean Sweep. See *The Washington Post*, 13 August 1987, A1.

40. According to a "Progress Report on Operation Cleansweep as of August 16, 1987," (a year after it was initiated), 23,153 people were arrested; 2378 people were arrested in the Sixth District area were Sun-Hope is located.

See DC Metropolitan Police Department, Field Operations Bureau Memorandum, 28 August 1987.

41. In a letter to Senator Brock Adams, Chairman of the D.C. Subcommittee on Appropriations, Mayor Marion Barry requested: "an emergency appropriation totalling $36,197,675 that will enable us to be better prepared to fight the war on drugs, utilizing tactics of vigorous enforcement that go beyond traditional law enforcement strategies." 7 April 1989.

42. Nancy Lewis and Victoria Churchville, "Turner Says Clean Sweep Has Failed: No Impact on Drug Market," *The Washington Post* 1988, A1, A24.

43. Washington, D.C. has more police officers per capita—8 officers/1000 citizens—than any other city in the country. Baltimore rates second; 3.9 officers/1000 citizens.

44. Editorial, "The New Mob," *The Washington Post*, 6 March 1988.

45. Tracy Thompson, "Drug Ring Boss Faces Life Term; Tough New U.S. Law Provides No Parole," *The Washington Post*, 18 July 1989, B1.

46. Gail Peterson, a letter, 9 May 1988.

47. The police trailer, a mobile control and command post, has been used in other high drug trading neighborhoods in the city with effective, but short-term, results. See Debbi Wilgoren. "Turning the Corner on Fear; 4th Police District Trailer Delivers a Sense of Security," *The Washington Post*, 27 February 1992, J1; Linder Wheeler, "Reclaiming Cliffton Terrace: NW Neighbors Wage War on Drug Dealers," *The Washington Post*, 3 March 1987, B1.

48. Tenant and Hope Mansions community center manager, personal interview, 13 May 1994.

49. Ibid.

50. Jeffrey Goldberg, "Calling In The Troops," *The Washington Post*, 26 February 1989, D1, D6.

51. A letter to Gail Peterson from the Government of the District of Columbia Office of Emergency Preparedness, 2 May 1988.

52. Jeffrey Goldberg. "Calling In The Troops," *The Washington Post*, 26 February 1989, D1, D6.

53. See Mayor Marion Barry, "Remarks for Capital Guardian," Speech, 29 September 1987.

CHAPTER 6
The Fruit of Islam (FOI)[1]

Security patrols organized by the Nation of Islam (NOI) have brought relief in some of the nation's impoverished and drug-infested African American neighborhoods. Residents and some sympathetic city officials have credited the NOI's patrol team, the Fruit of Islam (FOI), for doing—in a matter of days—what local police and federal law enforcement agencies failed to accomplish over years.[2] Although they patrol unarmed, FOI members have confronted drug dealers, buyers, and users effectively, reducing drug-related violence and homicides. But in some neighborhoods, FOI actions have drawn the group's members into a war of words with the police and city officials.

To understand the passion with which the FOI members pursue their objectives, one must understand the Nation of Islam's (NOI) mission and ideology. One of the central objectives of the NOI is to achieve a separate nation of American blacks:

> We want our people in America whose parents or grandparents were descendants from slaves, to be allowed to establish a separate state or territory of their own—either on this continent or elsewhere. We believe that our former slave masters are obligated to provide such land and that the area must be fertile and minerally rich. We believe that our former slave masters are obligated to maintain and supply our needs in this separate territory for the next 20 to 25 years—until we are able to produce and supply our own needs.[3]

This objective is consistent with the NOI's belief that because of the enslavement of American blacks by Caucasians, any effort to integrate the two peoples will be futile:

> We believe that the offer of integration is hypocritical and is made by
> those who are trying to deceive the Black peoples into believing that
> their 400-year-old open enemies of freedom, justice and equality are,
> all of a sudden, their "friends." Furthermore we believe that such
> deception is intended to prevent Black people from realizing that the
> time in history has arrived for the separation from the whites of this
> nation.[4]

The group's ideology extends to the total liberation of black people
everywhere from their historically oppressive relationship with white
people. NOI leaders assert that although white oppression of blacks
varies during different epochs, its content, born out of colonist-slave
relationship, has been sustained. From FOI's perspective, American
blacks—through white oppression—have become instruments of their
own oppression. Without the intervention by a visionary leader to
awaken blacks out of their stupor, they are bound to self-destruct with
tools and ideologies (guns, nacortics, negative self-images, self-
loathing) supplied by the white establishment.

Nowhere is FOI's assertion of the self-destructiveness of American
blacks more evident than in the various impoverished urban
neighborhoods where low-income American blacks are concentrated. In
Sun-Hope, NOI members saw their community patrol effort as a matter
of

> love and concern for our people. We knew [the residents] had lost the
> knowledge of themselves and they were acting other than themselves.
> We've believed that black people are people of righteousness and
> they've been made unrighteous by the deceiver. And because of
> knowing this, we came here not to hurt our people but actually just to
> move the drugs away and teach our people at the same time. So we
> came to them with a righteous motive, and that was just to help them
> see themselves, and it wasn't so much to jump on them and beat them
> up.[5]

To understand why African Americans were "people of
righteousness," who have been made "unrighteous by the deceiver
[white people]" and, as a consequence, "lost the knowledge of
themselves," one must turn to the conspiracy theory advanced by the
NOI's leadership. The NOI's ideology is premised on a theory about
the American black-white relationship and the proliferation of drugs in

African American communities.[6] A central theme of the conspiracy theory is that the white establishment has been orchestrating the systematic demise of African American people, especially the black man.[7]

Through the U.S. government's complicity both abroad and at home, the theory suggests that lethal weapons, alcohol and assortments of narcotics have proliferated in African American neighborhoods. "The epidemic of drugs and violence in the black community stems from a calculated attempt by whites to foster black self-destruction," Minister Louis Farrakhan, leader of the NOI, told an audience at the D.C. Armory.[8] Under the guise of waging a war on drugs, various coercive agencies are waging a war on American blacks.[9]

Statistics show that African Americans and Hispanics have become the casualties of the "war on drugs"; they are disproportionately arrested, incarcerated and/or sentenced to death in drug-related cases.[10] Given the evidence of persistent racial and economic injustice against African Americans, the conspiracy theorists' view gains ground among the disenfranchised African American population. The conspiracy theory is a manifestation of a deep-seated suspicion fueled by conditions of everyday life for many black Americans.

THE FOI'S MISSION AND ACCOMPLISHMENTS IN SUN-HOPE

The FOI movement perceives itself to be on a mission to save and to minister to their African American "brothers" and "sisters" whose lives are being ravaged by drugs, homicides, unemployment and hopelessness. Dr. Abdul Alim Muhammad, the National Spokesman for the NOI, articulated their mission in impoverished urban ghettos this way:

> We have a mission to defend our people and ourselves against the wickedness and evil of a world that has historically sought our destruction as a people. . . . Drugs have become the favorite weapon to destroy men, women and children—in fact entire communities and nations are being destroyed.[11]

A majority of the residents of the Sun-Hope neighborhood were aware of the reputation of the FOI patrols and had confidence the group would eradicate the open-air drug market. The initial invitation to the

FOI to patrol came from Sunrise's owner and tenant council. The presence of FOI members in just one section of the neighborhood resulted in a marked decline in illegal drug dealing within days. The FOI members cleared the courtyards, stairways, vacant basements, and laundry rooms of loitering adults and youth. Groups of people who gathered to buy, sell and use drugs departed with little resistance at the FOI members' orders.

The presence of the FOI patrol teams brought a sense of calm to the Sunrise Apartments. The situation in Hope Mansions, however, got worse. The drug dealers and derelicts flocked to available spaces and vacant apartments, aggressively peddling their drugs to any person going to or coming from the neighborhood.[12] Within three days, the drug trade reached an almost feverish pitch as the buyers and users sought each other out throughout the night.

In Hope Mansions, the Tenant Council complained bitterly about the consequences of the FOI's actions. Tenants who were concerned about their safety but had lost faith in the police started discussions about how they could solicit the FOI's services:

[Sam] and I, we talked about how do you control this crime. I told Bill you have to bring in *a force that is totally alien* to this particular region so there will be no affinity with the people that you are disciplining. Okay? So from that cue, he went out and encouraged the Moslems to come into this through this woman, [Betty Allen].[13]

Betty Allen, president of Hope Mansions Tenant Council, remarked about the Moslems to a news reporter:

They need to extend their services to us or get the hell out of [Sunrise]. They're creating problems. What do we do? They're pushing the drug addicts into [Hope], shuffling them from one end to another. We would like to sleep like the people in [Sunrise] are sleeping now.[14]

In view of the police department's inability to rid the neighborhood of drug dealers, Shelter Incorporated president, Gail Peterson, looked to the FOI to do for Hope Mansions what they were doing in Sunrise Apartments. According to a Shelter Incorporated field manager:

[FOI members] first actually went to [Sunrise] and were their security force first. At [Hope Mansions] we didn't have a security force. We had an intensive police effort because of all the drugs. We originally arranged to make some contribution to the Mosque if they would perform security duties at [Hope Mansions]. And [NOI] formed, as a result of their activities from these two complexes and some others, a security company. And they now are an official security company in the District—The NOI Security. In that function we do pay a fee for them to provide those services. And they are doing this on a twenty four-hour basis at this point, both for the security of the residents and the security of the construction materials.[15]

In addition to the 24-hour patrol, the FOI security members assisted Sun-Hope management/owners by identifying drug-dealing households for eviction. The FOI members gathered evidence, and reported culprits to both the police and management. One elderly tenant recalled:

I was in [Building] Number 1 when [FOI members] came in here. I know one thing. They cleaned up a lot of [the drug dealers]. Of course a lot of people moved out you know. A lot of them got put out. They catch your son or daughter or somebody with drugs in your place, that was it. [The Management] give you a notice to know you're gonna be evicted.[16]

In instances where the tenants contested their eviction, the management called upon the FOI members to testify in court. A member of the FOI patrol team explained their task:

Having been a hustler myself, I could automatically tell when a person is selling drugs. There is a certain way they dress, a certain time they hang out, the length of time they hang out and the amount of crowd that hang out. All you have to do is to stand back and observe, and you will see drugs being sold. So when drugs were being sold, all we had to do was get a report on the drug, the place that the drugs were being sold, then our command post call a number of brothers to go and remove the area clean. And then we report who we saw selling the drugs to the rental office, who will then in turn evict the people who were selling the drugs off the property. These people can no longer come on the property, so whenever we saw them, we had to escort them off the property.[17]

In the past, police officers had had difficulty facilitating prosecution of drug dealers and violent criminals. Potential witnesses were often too intimidated to testify in court. This situation changed when FOI members testified against the drug dealers. Unlike the tenants, FOI members were not concerned about taking days off from work or losing income for time spent in court:

> They brought the Moslems in here with what I thought was the understanding that these people came here with a network in the prisons. A network in the prisons and they have [an] organization. If you mess up here, you challenge them here—with your name address and telephone number—when you go down the court you can be identified. And if you are brought into a system where you are constantly confronted with this Moslem situation, then you are more likely to think twice about it.[18]

In the eyes of many residents, the FOI was the protector of last resort, and residents saw results from their patrols:

> I felt that it couldn't get any worse. We were at the lowest peak. When the Nation of Islam came aboard first they were at [Sunrise] and the positiveness caught on. . . . [Drug dealers, buyers and addicts] started to dwindle away and saw that things were coming, and there were good things that were gonna knock them out. I felt good about it—the positive change.[19]

Another resident added:

> The only people that was helpful around here was . . . the Moslems. The Moslems, they were out here, raised a little hell. They did what the police were supposed to do but the police wouldn't do. They got things rolling the way it should be, and the owners decided to start to make things better for the tenants.[20]

The FOI patrols undermined the neighborhood drug market. Many of the drug dealers renting or using vacant apartments to store, process, and distribute drugs evacuated on their own volition. Among them were the notorious Jamaican Posse, a group that controlled a substantial share of the "Sun-Hope market." Referring to the Jamaicans, one FOI member stated:

> When they heard the Nation of Islam were cleaning up Sunrise and they were working their way down to [Hope Mansions], they fled. They cleaned their house and left with no fight. They just left just like that.[21]

A neighborhood resident of twenty-five years said:

> What happened was that a couple of them got locked up—the Jamaicans—and little by little they filtered out into other areas. And they did that on their own. But before that, they were so thick in here you couldn't walk down the street without bumping into one of them. And they were running everything.[22]

The dissolution of a three-year-old illegal open-air drug market within a week of the first FOI patrols raised a number of questions. Why was the FOI successful in ridding the neighborhood of open-air drug markets and dealers that had eluded the local police? How did the success of the NOI/FOI shape their relationship with the local police? And what has been the general reaction of public officials and citizens to the NOI/FOI?

The Making of the FOI-"Dope Busters"

When the FOI members set out on their maiden patrol at Sunrise Apartments on April 18, 1988, little did their national leaders know that they were going to be the best weapon in the war against drugs. Little did the Moslems know that their effectiveness would engender renewed national debates about the policy of the war on drugs. That evening, five pairs of well-groomed men carrying walkie-talkies strolled the grounds, stairways, basements, and attics of Sunrise Apartments. The men were clean-shaven, sported close-cropped hair, and wore pressed shirts, suits, red bow ties, and polished shoes. They were polite, addressing every person, as "ma'am" or "sister," "sir" or "brother." In courteous but firm voices, the FOI members coaxed those gathered to depart to their respective apartments. The FOI members escorted the belligerent ones without apartments off of the premises. In two days the clusters of drug dealers and users who had become part of the landscape after nightfall dwindled (See Chart 6.1).

Drug Dealing Arrests

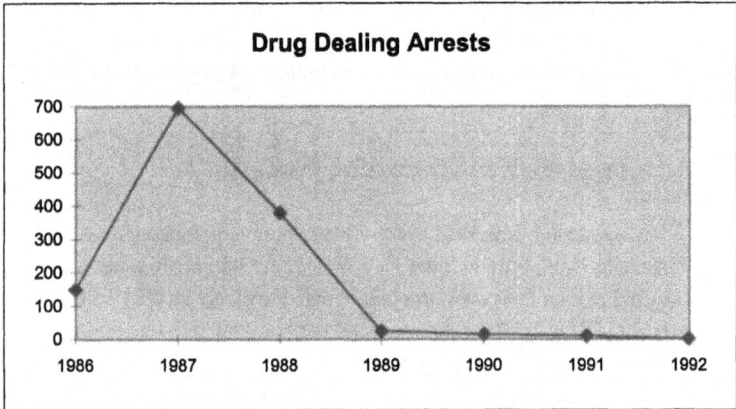

Chart 6.1 Hope Mansions Drug Dealing Arrests

The culture of the drug dealers has been to intimidate, silence, and/or co-opt anyone who threatened their business. Tenant group leaders who openly campaigned against the drug dealers received threatening phone calls. Others had their cars vandalized. The drug dealers were not used to confrontation from seemingly ordinary and yet fearless citizens challenging them to give up their turf.

On the fourth day of the patrol in Sunrise Apartments, an altercation occurred that catapulted the FOI's Sunrise Apartments anti-drug activities onto the national spotlight. On April 21, 1989, shortly before noon, a man wielding a shotgun threatened a group of ten FOI members on patrol. To the amazement of tenants and other drug dealers on the scene, the FOI members wrestled the gun from the man and beat him mercilessly. For the ensuing days, the FOI/NOI received continuous media coverage and analysis. The group acquired the title "Dope Busters":

> The name "Dope Busters" was given to us by the press. Since we was cleaning up dope from the neighborhood, we accepted the name and we went along with it. But our minister he said he didn't like the

name because we are Moslems. That was more like a title and it wouldn't allow people to see us as their brothers. They will think we was some kind of agents coming in to lock them up. So we did not agree with the name.[23]

The FOI's notoriety, however, engendered discussions about the ability of the local police to protect citizens—especially low-income citizens—from the drug-related violence.

Why the FOI Succeeded Where the Police Failed

The District of Columbia Metropolitan Police department, like many others in major cities in the country, was faced with they type of legitimization crisis that arises when state agencies of social control appear inadequate, obsolete, inefficient, and otherwise fail to meet their organizational objectives.[24] When the ordinary citizen views the police as a "joke," "corrupt," and "untrustworthy," he or she may withdraw the authority vested in the agency. This posture expresses itself in increasing unresolved violent crimes and decreasing participation in civic concerns prevalent in many lower-class neighborhoods.

As the tenants were apprehensive about their community's disrepute in the eyes of the police, so were the police officers distrustful and suspicious of anyone living in a neighborhood they had aptly designated "Hell's Horseshoe" and "Little Beirut." The lack of cooperation between the police and the residents emboldened the drug dealers. They had neither fear nor respect for residents or the police. According to an undercover agent who purchased an assortment of narcotics as part of law enforcement techniques:

Sometimes [drug dealers] decide that you are the police and they figure they'll sell you drugs and take your money and get away before the rest of the people [uniformed officers] come and arrest us. . . . When you go in an old ratty shirt and tennis shoes and jeans with your hair all messed up to buy drugs, they know even if you are the police, whatever is going to happen is not going to happen for a good five, ten, fifteen minutes. You're not the threat, it's the people that come behind you.[25]

Dealers and ordinary residents were not the only ones questioning the efficacy of the police; HUD officials were concerned, too. Reviewing the situation in Sun-Hope, a HUD auditor stated:

> [T]he project has been the focal point for uncontrolled crime. There have been many shootings, killings, assaults, and break-ins. *At present, the project does not provide additional security over and above police patrols provided by the city.*[26]

What was unknown to the auditor was the inadequacy and inefficiency of police patrol in the neighborhood.

When the owners and residents' persistent attempts to get law enforcement agencies to rid their neighborhood of drugs had failed, they resorted to the FOI's services. The effectiveness of the FOI rested in the fact that its members presented the drug dealers with a challenge unequaled by the police. From the beginning, the FOI had a clear mission to tackle the neighborhood drug problem until it was out of sight and/or considerably diminished in Sun-Hope. To accomplish this feat, the FOI employed tactics unequalled by the police, while its members earned the respect of the community.

Demonstrating the commitment to maintaining a sizeable and constant presence, after the altercation with the gunman in Sunrise Apartments, reinforcements of FOI members arrived from Chicago and elsewhere:

> I think [it is] the unity of the Nation of Islam that kept the drug dealers away. The brothers [FOI members], when they came, they came 200 at a time to patrol the neighborhoods. And when you look at 200 people, you don't want to fight against that many people because you know there is no way to win. So any time there is any type of competition, [the drug dealers] pack up and leave because they know they cannot make any more money. [The FOI patrol members] will go up to the buyers and tell them there is no more drugs out here to buy and that they should move on.[27]

In addition to their sheer number, the FOI members were so vigilant that the owners of both Sunrise Apartments and Hope Mansions offered them office space from which to operate. A few members also rented apartments there:

> But what made it different is that when we moved out here, we stayed
> on patrol twenty four hours, day and night, until the drugs were
> actually gone. We didn't give [the drug dealers] the chance to come
> back.[28]

One undercover detective who operated in Sun-Hope concurred
that the lack of manpower needed to maintain a sustained and
prolonged patrol was one of the main weaknesses of the police. Unlike
the police, the FOI members rooted themselves in the neighborhood:

> They were there twenty four hours a day, seven days a week. En
> mass, just the way the citizens could have been but weren't, and [the
> FOI] decided they were going to do what the police didn't have the
> time or the manpower to do. Like I said before, you can as a group
> but you can't one-on-one.[29]

One of the most effective methods used by the FOI to control drugs
sales was their constant presence anywhere youths gathered. Among
these areas were near the vending truck and the basketball court:

> Because that is the area that the drug dealers come to hang out.
> So by [the FOI members] standing there, the drug dealers won't stay
> there. They just get in their cars and leave. I have seen a lot of people
> hanging out in crowds. And when people are hanging out in crowds,
> they don't really have anything to do. So we have a rule where there
> is no soliciting, no loitering. So we follow the rule by keeping the
> area clear.[30]

Adding to their effective methods of patrolling the area was FOI
members' "presentation of self" in the African American community.[31]
As one observer noted, the group was "set apart." Unlike the police and
the drug dealers, the tenants did not see them as tainted by the drug
business. In their own distinct subculture of norms, values, and beliefs,
and political ideas, they were moral crusaders. In general, the
movement stresses economic self-sufficiency for African Americans,
independence from the white ruling establishment, sexual morality,
healthy diets, and abstinence from tobacco, alcohol, and drugs.[32] These
defined lifestyle objectives were often lacking in many of the
neighborhoods into which the FOI members were invited. In Sun-Hope,

even residents who did not care for the movement's messages admired the groups's devotion to the community:

> One of the secrets I've been taught is that when you come in and you're different, everybody notices you. They don't understand you so they are not too quick to jump. When people see the police coming, they've seen the police all their lives. But they've never seen black men come in, clean, in suits, ties, and talking about moving out drugs. They were skeptical. They didn't know what to do or what to say. They knew that we had come in, that there was something good about us. They didn't understand what it was at the time. But it seemed that there was a force, God, was with us and they didn't want to attack us. They just moved right on up. The Police came in with guns and everything. All they did was to fool the policemen. After the police was gone, they get back on with the same routine.[33]

Although the group maintained its sense of being different, it nevertheless reinforced its presence in the neighborhood. On Sunday mornings, the FOI members engaged in rigorous calisthenics. These were followed by jogging through and around the apartment complexes with chants of "[Sunrise, Hope]." FOI members brought a mystique to Sun-Hope: there has been a shared belief among residents and drug dealers that the FOI is a powerful organization made up of fierce, disciplined, community-loving, loyal members. Thus, any drug dealer who attacked an FOI member was, in principle, up against the entire national FOI organization (not excluding those in jails and prisons).

Very often, the local police officers operating in drug-ravaged African American neighborhoods did not enjoy the mystique or reverence residents accorded the FOI members. As one neighborhood activist explained, the drug dealers saw in the FOI patrol,

> the threat of being confronted out here with the Moslems. All the Moslems had to do when you go on trial, to court or [prison], or wherever, you had another Moslem who you had to confront. Whether it is religious training, or through intimidation practice, or camaraderie, you couldn't get away from that possibility. This is where I was coming from in terms of saying when you bring in an alien force—totally alien to the folks who are living here and are being victimized, . . . you don't have to deal with hurting anybody's feeling or anything like that. So when you brought the Moslems into

this thing, you had this perpetual confrontation with folks who had a certain belief and philosophy. You heard about the arresting of the guy with the gun, the "Dope Busters" and all the things that go along with it. For example, the head Moslem here is in contact with the head Moslem in the prisons. . . . We are talking organization.[34]

The FOI's mission went beyond the control of narcotic trafficking and sales. Unlike the police, the FOI members made themselves available to residents in need of help:

People did call the Nation of Islam. They will call us with gratitude. Because we would be right there whenever they needed us. Somebody was calling us, and they said they will be coming home late, and they needed somebody to come out and help them with their bags. We will be right there. Just like a brother will do for their sister.[35]

The FOI members volunteered to help youngsters with problems and were willing to converse with anyone who had the time to exchange few words with them. In some instances, they mediated and helped resolve conflicts:

If somebody had domestic problems at their house—man and wife— they will call us instead of calling the police. Most of the time, they will call us for the fact that if they call the police, it will take them about an hour to get there or they would not come at all. So they get tired of relying on the police, and call us and we would be right there. And this built the rapport and the respect for us for being there and helping them resolve the situation or dealing with the problem.[36]

The transformation of the Sun-Hope from a neighborhood reigned by armed drug dealers to a tranquil one was explain by a former president of Hope Mansions Tenant Council as nothing short of a spiritual feat:

I think some of the factors are that the Nation of Islam organization is a very strongly organized unit. They ain't going for nothing. They are focused to do what they are doing. I don't want to get into the other part, but they are not dealing [in drugs]. I think they sincerely care. That makes a difference. I think they are concerned. I think that the police have so many other things that they do, or are attempting to do—they are not focused. . . . But I really believe the Nation of Islam's spiritual love for the people—know what I'm saying—is their driving force and they don't look for any pay. . . . They want that unity, and people to be together.[37]

Although NOI members adhered to strict modes of conduct, that did not prevent them from mingling with alcohol-drinking, cigarette-smoking potential converts. Thus, when they were invited to neighborhood parties, the NOI/FOI members saw an opportunity to proselytize. Their lifestyle testified to their mission. At community or private parties, the NOI/FOI members often contributed their own jars of fruit juice. A few residents did not embrace the FOI members' "clean lifestyle":

> They were jealous of them. See, they are respectable and [some residents] don't like respectable people. Because it reflects on their own loose lifestyle you see. You see they don't drink, I don't think they smoke, and they are interested in social action. These [residents] are not tuned to those things. . . . Of course, a lot of these old people drink a lot of whiskeys and their own reputations aren't so good. None of the Moslems I know drink. When they come to our party they bring a big jug of orange juice.[38]

Another tenant stated that initially:

> Most people didn't want them here. I think maybe because of negative publicity and negative things they've heard about them. But I'm always here to point out—if it works—do it. If it is positive let's go with it. "Yeah, but they stand for this, they stand for that." I said, "All that's well and good and I don't agree with that. But what you can see is that these things have taken place in the process of them being here." And you have to give credit where it's due. *They are very disciplined; they are very organized. And they have been able to do things that the police haven't been able to do. And I think the relationship is better with the Nation of Islam—some of their members are attending our community meetings and are interacting more with the community and kids and all.* So, it's a better relationship over all. But at first there was some apprehension.[39]

The support, respect and awe the FOI members enjoyed in the community contrasted with that accorded to the police officers. The drug dealers, an NOI member argued, have no respect for law enforcement agents, and with justification:

> When they see policemen who are bringing drugs into the community, taking the drugs or taking the money and letting the person go, [the drug dealers] lose respect for the police. So when the policeman comes, they are not afraid of them because the policeman to them is just like them. So when we [NOI] come out, we actually live an example. Not something that they can say that "Moslems sold drugs, or the Moslems smoked drugs." Because we know that will destroy our nation.[40]

Certainly, not all the police officers were corrupted by the drug trade, but the pervasiveness of the drug trade in low-income African American neighborhoods, the massive arrests of predominantly African American males, the seeming inability of the police to rid these neighborhoods of the drug trade, and the absence of drug treatment facilities for those addicted left many ordinary African Americans suspicious of the goals and objectives of the federal government's "War on Drugs" policy and its local implementations.[41]

The Nation of Islam was among the foremost organizations in voicing its suspicions concerning the Reagan-Bush/Bush-Quayle administrations' War on Drugs policy and the army of law enforcers. And whenever they were invited into a neighborhood, the FOI perceived the local police officers as accomplices to the neighborhood drug trade. Likewise, some city officials tended to view the FOI as agitators of the urban poor. By virtue of their confrontational posture toward political authorities, the NOI/FOI left City Hall fractured. Some city officials recognized the movement for its grassroots empowerment of the disenfranchised urban blacks. Others despised the organization for its anti-establishment and anti-Jewish stance. What follows is an analysis of the FOI's and the District of Columbia Metropolitan Police Department's (DCMPD) confrontation over ridding the Sun-Hope of its drug market and violence.

THE CONFLICT: THE NOI AND THE POLICE IN SUN-HOPE

The conflict between some city police departments and NOI members is not a recent phenomenon. Some of the movement's members and the Los Angeles Police had a bloody confrontation in 1962, which resulted in the death of one Moslem and the wounding of six others.[42] More recent clashes with the police in L.A. have resulted in the death of an NOI member and the arrest of a few members.[43]

In Sun-Hope, the relationship between the two organizations was far from amicable. The police arrested and charged one FOI member for assault, and a war of words ensued between the NOI leadership and the police. These events occurred a few days after the NOI initiated its neighborhood patrol. At the core of the antagonism was a contest of legitimization.

On the one hand, the police wanted to maintain a public image of doing all it could to control the drug trafficking and sales and drug-related crime in Sun-Hope. But the drug raids orchestrated for television and newspaper reporters had little effect. At best, such raids disrupted the open-air drug trade for a few hours.

On the other hand, owners and ordinary residents of Sun-Hope had heard of the NOI/FOI's successful anti-drug efforts in Brooklyn, N.Y., where, with the local police department's approval, the organization was able to shut down the drug trade.[44] New York Assistant Police Chief Louis Rilford, Jr., who authorized the FOI's patrol, remarked to a news reporter:

> I'm searching like any other public official for an answer, and the Moslems have made a very clear statement, that this blight can be fought. . . . Simply the way they carry themselves has a major impact. Within the black community, the Moslems have enjoyed respect, even by the bad guys. They have a strong sense of discipline and that is one reason I was able to endorse this. That crucial element of discipline may not be in another group[45].

Another officer concurred:

> The people have a smile on their face now. Without the Moslem guys, this street would be a mob of dealers. You could not walk here two months ago with all the people.[46]

Convinced by these accolades, Sun-Hope owners, with the residents' support, enlisted the services of the FOI.

But unlike the situation in Brooklyn, the relationship between the FOI and the DCMPD was not cordial. From the perspective of the Moslems, the police despised them because they were doing in Sun-Hope that which the police had failed to do. An FOI member recounted:

> The relationship between us and the police, at that time, had been bad. Because the police had been here for years—in and out of the community with everything happening with their guns and bullet-proof vests—and they still didn't move the drugs out. But when we came without guns or pen knives, what we did was move the [drug dealers] out. And this news went back to the police department and the police chief actually made the policemen look so bad because we didn't have guns. And it made them look bad because they were here all their lives trying to remove drugs, and it built a hostility between the police and us. We will almost be like any enemy to the police department when we first came out. But [it is] because of the Grace of Allah that one of the policemen seen the plot against us as the Moslems cleaned up the neighborhood. [The policeman] would give us information telling us when the police is plotting against us and we will move out. We will not have competition with the policemen.[47]

There is no way to substantiate the allegation that the police department was plotting against the FOI, but our data show that the FOI's anti-drug effort directly undermined the Department's credibility. The FOI caused public doubts about police efficacy in dealing with the drug problem. This situation generated intense antagonism between the NOI/FOI and the MPD.

The FOI strategy to rid Sun-Hope of drug dealers generated controversy from segments of the city. The core of the controversy was the FOI members' altercation involving a gunman and TV cameraman. While disarming the gunman, the Moslems inadvertently attacked a television camera crewman filming the incident. In a public statement of apology, one of the ministers of Muhammad's Mosque No. 4 stated:

> Our brothers disarmed [the alleged gunman], as they are taught, and neutralized his ability to do harm. We acted in self-defense of the community. In the midst of this action, a news reporter and a

cameraman were inadvertently roughed up. We were in hot pursuit of
a drug dealer. We apologize for any unintended roughness.[48]

The incident only served to generate tenant admiration and support for
the FOI:

> I don't know who brought the [Nation of Islam] in here. . . but I give
> them credit. The police were here before they came, but [Nation of
> Islam] did more in 12 months than the cops did in three or four
> years.[49]

Increasingly, the NOI became more accessible to residents. Instead
of calling the police, residents requested services by calling the FOI
command and control centers in both Hope Mansions and Sunrise. One
resident stated to a news reporter what the police dreaded the most:

> Tenants are trusting [the black Moslems] more than they were
> trusting the police. When you would call the police, you had to say
> you had heard shots before they would want to come down and
> investigate.[50]

The issue of residents' diminished reliance on the police was one
of the numerous questions posed to Mayor Marion Barry by news
reporters. His response was indicative of the problems the scores of
open-air drug markets, and Sun-Hope in particular, presented to the
city:

> [The residents] probably do [trust the FOI more than do the police]. I
> don't have an answer. Mayors are being put into the position they
> don't want to be put in. I don't bring drugs into America. I don't
> manufacture drugs. I am being burdened with problems I didn't
> create or even America didn't create. . . . [The black Moslem patrols]
> are not a solution. It's a stopgap measure.[51]

The Moslems' "stopgap measure" was the best relief from drug
dealers Sun-Hope residents had experienced in more than 24 months.
So, for many residents the FOI tactics were not of a concern; all that
mattered was that the group helped restore a sense of normalcy in their
neighborhood.

The residents were thankful. In April, 1988, Shelter Incorporated, in collaboration with the Hope Mansions Tenant Association, threw a grand outdoor party that featured the Rosa Parks High School dance troupe and a local band. The fiesta enabled residents to get out, have something to eat, mingle with and appreciate the FOI members for what they had already accomplished in the neighborhood. Among the people who attended the party was Councilmember H.R. Crawford. He praised "the outstanding community services provided by the Nation of Islam [in] assisting us in waging a war on drugs."[52]

In addition to praise from residents, there were voices from various drug-ravaged neighborhoods calling the FOI to extend their services to them. The altercation involving the TV cameraman in April, 1988, from the point of view of many ordinary black people, was excusable given the precarious conditions in which the FOI members had to operate. In a meeting of community leaders in North Carolina, the FOI activities in Washington were exalted:

> The Moslems, with very limited resources and a lot of will and determination, did what the police failed to do with thousands of dollars and much more manpower. I hope what happened in Washington can be a model for the nation. You always have the possibility of abuse, but I haven't noticed that in what the Moslems have done.[53]

The controversial incident drew the FOI into the spotlight, and apartment owners and community leaders in other neighborhoods sought the organization's services to help them rid their neighborhoods of the drug dealers.

For public relations purposes, the police department made overtures to improve its relations the Sun-Hope residents. About a month after the fiesta in the community honoring the FOI, the police department held its "Operation Fight Back" drug rally in Sun-Hope neighborhood, attracting about 600 people. The police served tenants free hot dogs and sodas. There were anti-drug speeches from various community leaders, assistant police chief Isaac M. Fulwood, Jr., and WKYS radio disc jockey Donnie Simpson. The Police Band entertained the residents with Top 40 tunes.[54]

THE WAR OF WORDS: THE NOI AND ITS CRITICS

Nothing threatens the power of the state organization more than when frustrated citizens organize to deal with protracted violent crimes the way they see fit. This is especially the case when the police department fails to acknowledge its limitations and solicit community members' involvement. Thus, the NOI/FOI's celebrated patrol of the Sun-Hope neighborhood became a thorn in the side of the police department. To save face, the police intensified their presence in Sun-Hope apartment complexes:

> [The police] became more effective afterwards. Because the eyes of the city were on what they were doing there, they put more effort in and got better results. Some of it is because of all the attention. Some of it is that the activity dropped off because of all the attention. There were cameras out there, not just from Channel 2, but from other stations. And drug dealers don't like to be seen on TV.[55]

The efforts of the NOI/FOI, however, were not fully embraced by some members of City Hall or the MPD. Fraternal Order of Police spokesperson Gary Hankins complained about the FOI's illegal abuse of power. As part of their anti-drug effort, the group members randomly stopped and questioned pedestrians they suspected to be dealing in drugs. On this matter, Hankins stated:

> Everyone shares the goal that Moslems have of ridding that area of drugs, and police share the frustration of the people living there. But that does not excuse throwing out the Constitution in the name of law and order. If police officers did what the Moslems are doing now, we'd be the subject of civil suits and criminal procedures. We just can't do that. And we shouldn't.[56]

Echoing Hankins' complaints, Police Chief Maurice T. Turner, Jr., added:

> No police department can or will support, endorse or condone any group which advocates law and order yet violates the laws they advocate. A society will crumble when people take the law into their own hands[57]

Another detective added:

> Not to mention, if the police go and whip up on your ass, you
> probably have a lawsuit. But if Joe Blow from down the street comes
> and whips up on your butt . . . what are they going to do? So a lot of
> times they had an advantage that the police didn't have because they
> could do things that we couldn't do without repercussions.[58]

The police were also skeptical about the FOI's accomplishments
and said the FOI's activities hampered the efforts of undercover
officers. Gary Hankins complained:

> When we had the drug markets out here, our undercover officers were
> making buys and we could try to investigate midlevel dealers. . . .
> Now, with the Moslems here, we're not able to get in and make
> undercover buys, which hinders the second- and third-echelon
> dealers.[59]

Some police force members also faulted the FOI for generating
controversy, thereby diverting more attention on Sun-Hope at the
security expense of other communities in the city. According to police
informants, Gary Hankins revealed, the drug dealers

> believe the Moslems are unwittingly helping them. . . . Because [this
> neighborhood] has been a magnet for police resources, there have
> been fewer resources elsewhere in the city. They feel safer.[60]

The reason why the police department concentrated a
disproportionate number of police officers in the Sun-Hope community
was not just to fight the drug trade. After the altercation between the
FOI members and the gunman, there was a rumor that the drug dealers
were planning to wage a gun battle with the FOI. Thus, the
concentration of officers in the community was meant to preempt a
potential conflict. This situation, Hankins charged, was responsible for
only five uniformed officers being available to serve the rest of the city
that Sunday, leading to a backup of twenty-five calls-for-services.

Citing the police officers' antagonism towards the NOI's antidrug
effort, on the day that one of the FOI members was charged with the
assult of the gunman, the NOI spokesman Dr. Abdul Alim Muhammad
told an audience that the police "did little to aid us as we continue to

confront the drug pushers, but ten officers drew weapons on innocent brothers in order to arrest brother Maurice, who was not resisting."[61] Dr. Muhammad stated on a radio talk show that the police were "directly involved" in the drug trade, and that: "if one of the Moslem brothers is shot, the first suspect should not be Jamaican. . . . The first suspect should be the police. . . . We know there are certain elements at the police department that are corrupt."[62]

The police department responded to the charges and discredited Dr. Abdul Alim Muhammad for his allegations:

> The representatives from the Nation of Islam have brought to our attention rumors and allegations they have heard about the possibility of a number of officers being involved in illicit narcotics in the [Sunrise] Mansions area. However, no information beyond the rumors and allegations has been developed that . . . would permit us to initiate an investigation.[63]

One of the harshest criticisms of the FOI's anti-drugs effort in Sun-Hope came from Washington Post columnist Carl Rowan. Although he lamented the impoverished conditions that were breeding crime and powerlessness in Sun-Hope, he did not support the FOI's actions to change the neighborhood situation. He called the FOI members the "New Lynch Mobs," "Drug Vigilantes," and "Dirty Harrys." In addition, Rowan castigated the residents for tolerating the FOI's actions in their neighborhood:

> The worrisome truth is that black people across America who live in neighborhoods lorded over by drug peddlers don't much care about the Constitution or civil rights. They are saying that Moslem patrols can act as accusers, judges and agents of punishment as long as they drive away the dope pushers.[64]

The criticisms of the NOI/FOI did not minimize the support the group received from landlords, churches, and residents living in drug-plagued neighborhoods. In fact, the NOI/FOI became vindicated as the Mayor and his police officials publicly admitted that they were losing the war on drugs.[65]

The irony, however, is that while they were criticizing the FOI, some police officials voiced feelings about the dismal failure of Operation Clean Sweep. Police Captain William White III, a police spokesman stated: "It should be glaringly obvious that law enforcement is not the sole answer to the [drug] problem."[66] To the displeasure of Mayor Marion Barry, D.C. Police Chief Maurice T. Turner Jr. also conceded:

> I don't see [Operation Clean Sweep] having any impact on the demand for drugs. Arrests are not the answer. We must reduce the demand side of the drug business. . . . All we have is more arrests [that have] crowded court calendars in the D.C. Superior Court and pushed prisons above their capacities.[67]

THE POLICE AND THE FOI TRUCE

Although the police resented the FOI's presence in Sun-Hope, some city officials took notice of the community support accorded to the FOI for their effectiveness in driving out the drug dealers. Citing the need to end the war of words, Chief Turner stated:

> There has to be some type of dialogue between that organization [NOI/FOI] and the police. We're not going to do anything to restrict their activities. They have rights as citizens to go into that area. But we don't want them taking the law into their own hands.[68]

What ensued was a secret meeting between the police and the NOI/FOI leaderships in which they jointly reported their differences resolved and agreed to work within the context of the law to maintain order in affected neighborhoods. As one police officer stated, "[w]e've all agreed that no one is going to say anything. . . . We're just going to get the job done."[69] Given that the FOI had no arrest powers, they served best as the "eyes," "ears" and "escorts" of the police department. As one FOI member put it:

> You know some of these officers are afraid coming out here. Some of the places don't have lights, and the numbers on the buildings are so small they can't see them. When we call them, we wait for them out on the street and we walk 'em to the trouble spot. We identify the people causing the trouble, and they make the arrest.[70]

The collaboration between the FOI and the police reinforced FOI's visibility in the neighborhood. According to a tenant:

> [The NOI would] report [crimes] to the [management office], and the office had the police come and check those people out. [The police] locked up seventy-five people in two weeks. I was glad they cleaned them out. Scared to go outdoors, the kids scared to go outdoors, shooting and killing folks? People were crazy.[71]

The consequence of this coordinated effort led to a dramatic reduction in the 24-hour open-air drug trade in the community. With the presence of the FOI, the police no longer had to respond to calls without anyone to meet and give them case reports. The police became more effective as the FOI assisted them in thwarting flagrant lawlessness and arresting criminals.

SUMMARY

The culmination of factors discussed in the preceding chapters evidenced the weaknesses, if not the absence, of informal control agents in the community. This in turn undermined the effectiveness of the police in Sun-Hope community as many of the residents came to define the officers as part of the problem and as untrustworthy. The combination of ineffective policing and community disorganization led to the dominance of the drug dealers in the community even as the police expended resources waging the war on drugs in affected communities.

As a law enforcement solution, Operation Clean Sweep accomplished one thing: the arrests of 23,153 people between August 1986 and August 1987.[72] The drug trade and violence, however, continued in Sun-Hope and other parts of the city.[73] Having exhausted the legal avenues to eradicate the 24-hour open-air drug market, a core group of tenants and landlords turned to the FOI for help. First, the relentless patrol by the FOI led to the demise of the open-air drug market and related violence within a few days. This outcome enabled the FOI/NOI to reinforce its conspiracy theory that state actors covertly allowed drugs and guns to flow into segregated low-income black neighborhoods to facilitate their self-destruction. Second, the turn of events showed that the establishment of a sustained community-based mediating institution and improved community-police relations were necessary steps in reducing crime and disorderly behaviors. Although the collaboration among the police, the FOI, the new landlords and residents led to the reduction in the open-air drug market, the economic conditions which engendered it remained. Unless many members of the families in Sun-Hope were employed to earn income legally, the drug trade was bound to re-emerge once social control mechanisms were relaxed. The hiring of the FOI was only part of the grassroot effort to pursue neighborhood improvement. The next chapter analyzes how tenants had been endeavoring to create a community-based mediating institution, to mobilize resources from government agencies to provide skill and job training, and to acquire the property as a tenant cooperative.

NOTES

1. The Fruit of Islam, from its inception, has been the branch of the Nation of Islam (NOI) responsible for providing bodyguards to ministers and disciplining wayward followers. The FOI members have been referred to as "Mighty Men." See R. H. Melton, *The Washington Post*, 24 April, 1988, A17; Dr. Abdul Alim Muhammad, NOI National Spokesman, referred to them as the "Dope Busters." In Chicago, where many FOI members are trained and deployed, they are referred to as "God's Squad." See Andrea Ford and Russell Chandler, "A Growing Force and Presence," *Los Angeles [California] Times*, 25 January 1990. In the 1980's the FOI started to assist neighborhoods ravaged by the drug trade. These days the FOI is an established, for-hire, security service agency visible in various low-income private and public housing projects in neighborhoods in Washington, Maryland, New York, California, and North Carolina.

2. In Baltimore, Boston, Brooklyn, Miami and other areas, the FOI has been able to rid neighborhoods of drug dealers with relative ease. Because of their effectiveness against drug dealers and criminals, the FOI has been awarded several contracts, to the chagrin of many Jewish organizations. See Steven Holmes. "Farrakhan Groups Land Jobs from Government, Debate Grows," *The New York Times*, 4 March 1994.

3. "What the Muslims Want," *The Final Call*, 8 June 1994, 39.

4. Ibid., 39. The call for African Americans to form a separate nation-state dates back to the 1800s. For instance, Edward Wilmot Blyden outlined a plan intended to pursuade African Americans to emigrate to Liberia. He felt relocation was part of a divine plan to return an educated group back to their homeland. See Edward Blyden, "The Call for Providence to the Descendants of

Africa in America." *Negro Social and Political Thought, 1850-1920: Representative Texts*, Ed. Howard Brotz (New York: Basic Books, 1966), 112-26.

5. Tenant and FOI member, personal interview, 6 April 1992. Emphasis mine.

6. In a New York Times poll of 291 blacks nationwide, 23 percent of the respondents concur that the "government deliberately makes sure that drugs are easily available in poor black neighborhoods in order to harm black people." See Michael Kagay, "Poll Says Most Blacks Don't See Farrakhan's Ideas as Theirs," *The New York Times*, 5 March 1994, 8.

7. Ibid. In the same poll, 32 percent say "most white people want to keep blacks down."

8. Howard Kurtz, "Drug Scourge is Conspiracy by Whites, Some Blacks Say," *The Washington Post*, 29 December 1989, A1.

9. Final Edition, "Farrakhan Relates Vision of Race War Conspiracy," *The Washington Post*, 26 October, 1989, B4.

10. Drug use in the U.S. is proportional to the racial/ethnic breakdown; according to National Institute on Drug Abuse (NIDA), *National Household Survey on Drug Abuse: Main Findings 1990*, 77% of drug users are white, 15% American black and 8% Hispanic. The arrest, prosecution and incarceration rates, however, point to an inherent bias at all levels of the justice system.

Testifying before the Senate Banking Committee (May 14, 1992), Congresswoman Maxine Waters stated: "A Federal Judicial Center study of federal sentences for drug trafficking and firearms offenses found that the average sentence for blacks was 49% higher than for whites in 1990, compared to 28% in 1984." Other articles asserting the racial disparities in drug-related injustices include: Sam Vincent Meddis, "Is the Drug War Racist?," *USA Today*, 23-25 July 1993; "A Law Distinguishing Crack from Other Cocaine is Upset," *The New York Times*, 29 December 1990; Associated Press, "Baltimore Report Lambastes U.S. Drug War," *The Washington Post*, 2 September 1992, D1; Editorials, "The Color of Justice," *The Denver Post*, May 31, 1992, I, 2:1.; and Don Edwards, "Congressional Overkill," *The Washington Post*, 8 March 1994, A18.

On differential sentencing, see Peter Chronis, "Equity Sought in Cocaine Sentences," *The Denver Post*, 3 August 1992. See also, Editorial, *The Denver Post*, 31 May 1992. Dennis Cauchon, "Sentences for Crack Called Racist," *USA Today*, 26 May 1993. For death penalty meted to drug-related offenders see Kenneth J. Cooper, "Racial Disparity Seen in U.S. Death Penalty," *The Washington Post*, 16 March 1994. For a detailed analysis of racial disparity in much of the Justice System, see Robert Staples, *Black*

Masculinity: The Black Male Roles in American Society (San Francisco: Black Scholar Press, 1982).

11. Sari Horwitz and James Rupert, "Calm Returns as Police, Muslims Patrol in NE," *The Washington Post,* 20 April 1988, A1, A16.

12. For fear of being robbed of their commodities at gun point, drug dealers often commanded approaching customers to get their hands out of their pockets.

13. Former neighborhood youth organizer, personal interview, 4 March 1992.

14. Patrice Gaines-Carter and James Rupert, "Muslims Gain Barry's Support and Find in Services in Demand" *The Washington Post,* April 22, 1988, C1, C7.

15. Shelter Incorporated staff member, personal interview, 5 July 1991.

16. Tenant, personal interview, 1 June 1992.

17. Tenant and FOI member, personal interview, 6 April 1992.

18. Former neighborhood youth organizer, personal interview, 4 March 1992.

19. Tenant and LJTP staff member, personal interview, 16 June 1992.

20. Tenant, personal interview, 6 August 1991.

21. Tenant and FOI member, personal interview 6 April 1992.

22. Tenant and Paradise community center manager, personal interview, 13 May 1994.

23. Tenant and FOI member, personal interview, 6 April 1992.

24. Jurgen Habermas, *Legitimation Crisis* (Boston: Beacon, 1975).

25. Police Detective, personal interview, 21 October 1991.

26. William W. Hill, Management Review Report Project No. 000-55002. U.S. Department of Housing and Urban Development, 20 June 1988. Emphasis mine.

27. Tenant and FOI member, personal interview, 6 April 1992.

28. Ibid.

29. Police Detective, personal interview, 21 October 1991.

30. Tenant and FOI member, personal interview, 6 April 1991.

31. Erving Goffman, *The Presentation of Self in Everyday Life* (New York: Anchor Books, 1959).

32. William Simbro, "Nation of Islam Builds Ministry to Serve De Moines' Blacks," *Des Monies Register,* 30 August 1992.

33. Tenant and FOI member, personal interview, 6 April 1992.

34. Former neighborhood youth organizer, personal interview, 4 March 1992.

35. Tenant and FOI member, personal interview, 6 April 1992.

36. Ibid.

37. Tenant and LJTP staff member, personal interview, 16 June 1992.

38. Tenant, personal interview, 25 October 1991.

39. Ibid. Emphasis mine.

40. Tenant and FOI member, personal interview, 6 April 1992.

41. See Desmond Lucien, *Pipe Dream Blues.*

42. Andrea Ford and Russell Chandler, "A Growing Force and Presence," *The Los Angeles [California] Times,* 25 January 1990.

43. Andrea Ford and Louis Sahagun, "5 of 6 Muslims in Clash With Deputies Freed," *The Los Angeles Times,* 26 January 1990. See also, Louis Sahagun, "2,000 Attended Services for Man Killed by Deputy," *The Los Angeles Times,* 28 January 1990.

44. Marc Fisher, "Armed With Faith, Muslims Wage War in Brooklyn," *The Washington Post,* 26 April 1988.

45. Ibid.

46. Ibid.

47. Tenant and FOI member, personal interview, 6 April 1992.

48. *The Washington Post,* 23 April 1988, A25.

49. Tenant, personal interview, 1 June 1992.

50. Patrice Gaines-Carter and James Rupert. "Muslims Gain Barry's Support and Find Services in Demand," *The Washington Post,* 22 April 1988, C1. See also, Steve Vogel, "Poor Areas Wait Longer for Hard-Pressed D.C. Police," *The Washington Post,* 2 June, 1996, A1, A20.

51. Dorothy Gilliam, "Proceed With Caution," *The Washington Post,* 25 April 1988, D3.

52. James Rupert, "Muslim 'Dope Busters' To Widen Patrol," *The Washington Post,* 30 April 1988.

53. *The Washington Post,* 24 April 1988, A17.

54. *The Washington Post,* 15 May 1988.

55. Telesis staff member, personal interview, 1 July 1991.

56. *The Washington Post,* 23 April 1988: A1, A13.

57. Patrice Gaines-Carter and John Mintz, "Muslims Nurture Legacy of Power," *The Washington Post,* 20 April 1988, A16.

58. Police Detective, personal interview, 21 October 1991.

59. *The Washington Post,* 15 May 1988. Of all the police law enforcement techniques, nothing seems more baffling to residents in low-income communities than the technique of letting go the "lower echelons" of drug dealers in hopes of catching the "big" dealers. From the standpoint of ordinary residents, all drug dealers, no matter high or low on the drug distribution chain,

undermine community stability. See, Patrick Symmes, "Good Cop, Bad Cop," *The Washington City Paper*, 19-25 August 1994, 1-26.

60. James Rupert, "NE Police Patrol Dilute Manpower, Officers Say," *The Washington Post*, 26 April 1988, D1.

61. Sari Horwitz and James Rupert, "Calm Returns as Police, Muslims Patrol in NE," *The Washington Post*, 20 April 1988, A1, A16.

62. Ibid.

63. Ibid.

64. Carl Rowan, "The New Lynch Mobs: Drug Vigilantes," *The Washington Post*, 27 April 1988, A21.

65. Rene Patrice Gaines-Carter and James Rupert, "Muslims Gain Barry's Support and Find Services in Demand," *The Washington Post*, 22 April 1988, C1. In 1989, the D.C. Council, approved without debate a resolution praising Minister Louis Farrakhan and his group for ridding Sun-Hope's open-air drug market. The ceremony honoring Farrakhan at the D.C. Armory attracted an overflow crowd of 10,000 people. See, Nathan McCall, "D.C. Votes to Praise Farrakhan's Anti-Drug Work," *The Washington Post*, 25 October 1989, A1.

66. Rene Patrice Gaines-Carter and James Rupert, "Muslims Gain Barry's Support and Find Services in Demand," *The Washington Post*, 22 April 1988, C1.

67. Criticizing the policies of the Mayor and the Police Chief, Gary Hankins, chairman of the Fraternal Order of Police, remarked: "We're watching politics as usual over a mounting stack of dead constituents. This shell game has gone on long enough." See Nancy Lewis and Victoria Churchville, "Turner Says Clean Sweep Has Failed. No Impact Seen on Drug Market," *The Washington Post*, 8 December 1988, A4.

68. Sari Horwitz and Michael Abramowitz, *The Washington Post*, 21 April 1988, D1.

69. Rene Sanchez and Carlos Sanchez, *The Washington Post*, 23 April 1988, A1, A13.

70. FOI patrol leader, Tenant Meeting, June 14, 1991.

71. Tenant, personal interview, 1 June 1992.

72. D.C. Metropolitan Police Department (Field Operations Bureau). "Progress Report on Operation Cleansweep as of August 16, 1987."

73. In the fall of 1988, there were six homicides compared to five in 1986. See Chart 9.1.

CHAPTER 7

Grassroots Restructuring and Tenant Empowerment

In 1985 the Faith Church of Christ (FCC), owner of the Sun-Hope, sold the twin apartment complex as separate entities. A group of investors led by Jason Saunders, a former chairman of the FCC, purchased Sunrise and began to upgrade the complexes. In 1986, Gail Peterson, the president of Shelter Incorporated brokered funding from private and public investors to purchase Hope Mansions.[1] In the midst of the drug trade and the sounds of gunfire, Shelter Incorporated attempted to restore normality to the neighborhood. The management company was replaced, and tenants delinquent in rent and/or found to be operating crack houses were evicted. For nearly a year, Shelter Incorporated stopped leasing Hope Mansions apartments. The vacancy rate was 50 percent by the time renovation started in 1990.

As a mark of separate ownership, a high wooden fence was erected between Sunrise and Hope Mansions. In addition, all of Sunrise was enclosed with a high steel fence, with access limited to four locked gates that could be opened by electronic keys issued to residents. The landscape, which was formerly bare and strewn with trash, was cleaned up and cultivated with grass.

In both apartment complexes, the sudden change in ownership left many residents concerned about the security of their tenancy. Often, when a low-income residential property is acquired by developers and speculators, residents become vulnerable to possible gentrification and rent hikes.[2] As a result, tenants without adequate income are often dislocated or forced to depend on government rent subsidies in order to stay in their apartments. In 1980, in an attempt to protect low-income

tenants from dislocation, the District government legislated the First
Right Purchase Assistance Program (FRPAP):

> The First Right Purchase Assistance Program, administered by the
> Department of Housing and Community Development, is designed to
> help tenants buy their buildings when the owners propose to sell or to
> convert those buildings from rental properties to condominiums or
> cooperatives. Money is available to tenant groups to make an earnest-
> money deposit with their contracts to purchase the building, to make
> down payments, to plan to undertake rehabilitation, and to do
> marketing to promote sales.[3]

The policy provides government assistance to encourage residents of an
apartment complex on sale, where more than 50 percent of the
households earn low to moderate income, to organize as a business
entity to acquire the property. Although the idea of homeownership is
appealing, the process can be problematic, especially for low-income
residents.

The process of "cooperative homeownership" among low-income
residents requires visionary leadership, mobilization of apathetic
residents, and the garnering of public and private resources in order to
acquire the property. Also, the process can be slow, complex, and time-
consuming in instances where many of the residents involved lack
adequate education, organizational skills and technical know-how.
However, the FRPAP motivated Sun-Hope's residents to pursue homeownership.

COOPERATIVE HOUSING ENDEAVORS AT SUNRISE APARTMENTS

Sunrise Apartments was selling for 10.8 million dollars. In order to
organize the residents toward acquiring the property, the tenants group
leaders sought the assistance of the Community Housing Improvement
Initiative (CHII). CHII staff trainers conducted four tenant-workshops
to educate residents about the acquisition process. The effort to
mobilize and educate Sunrise residents, however, was unsuccessful.
According to CHII's low-income housing advocate, Joan Johnson, "this
happens from time to time, particularly in a larger project when you're
talking about large sums of money."[4]

The Sunrise demographic data was telling. Fifty percent of the residents were single heads of households, and 65 percent of the residents received federal housing subsidies to pay a large proportion of their rent. Although the idea of cooperative homeownership appealed to many residents, the majority of them were intimidated by the financial responsibilities associated with it. For others, not having a steady source of income, the idea of "homeownership" was fanciful. The Sunrise tenant leadership was unable to sustain residents' interest in their bid to purchase the property. One resident faulted the leadership for their poor managerial style:

> You see our former president was an alcoholic. She was not a very effective person. But she got the job because nobody else wanted it. . . . We have one now who never returns phone calls. I've been trying to get in touch with him for a while now.[5]

The tenant group abrogated its right-to-purchase, and Jason Saunders and fellow investors acquired the property. On August 9, 1988, Mayor Marion Barry officiated the ribbon-cutting ceremony commencing the rehabilitation of Sunrise.

COOPERATIVE HOUSING ENDEAVORS AT HOPE MANSIONS

The sale of Hope Mansions to Shelter Incorporated took a different turn. The resident group was not given prior knowledge of the sale. Concerned that Shelter Incorporated's acquisition of Hope Mansions would lead to gentrification, and subsequently the eviction of the largely low-income residents, a group of concerned residents started to mobilize their fellow tenants. As a result, the Tenant Council, which had been dormant for years, was revived. A former tenant and one of the principal architects of the tenant cooperative initiative stated:

> I did not get involved with the Resident Council until 1984. Ms. Betty Allen invited me to come out and be part of the resident organization. The Tenant Council that existed had died and we were trying to form it again. . . . The owner was selling to a private company without the tenants' knowledge. We found out that we had the first right to buy so we hired a lawyer to help us know our rights and to put things in perspective. We didn't want to lose the complex. Many of us did not

want to be forced to move when the new owner took over and maybe
decided to convert the buildings into a condo or something like that.
So we hired a lawyer to explain to us about what we need to do.[6]

In addition to retaining a lawyer, the tenants solicited the
involvement of their Councilman, H.R. Crawford. The tenants'
activism led to the formulation of a contractual agreement between the
Tenant Council and Shelter Incorporated detailing an eventual turnover
of the property to the tenants. The agreement was signed at a reception
sponsored by Councilman H.R. Crawford (D-Ward 7) at the District
Building on October 28, 1987. With more than 100 Hope Mansions
residents assembled, Councilman Crawford assured the audience that
the proposed rehabilitation would result in homes "surrounded by a
beautiful landscape, in a neighborhood in which you will enjoy living
and a place where you can rear your children free from the elements of
crime and drugs."[7]

The crucial item in the agreement was the tenant group's deferment
of the purchase of the property until Shelter Incorporated completed
renovation:

> the residents of [Hope Mansions] are willing to forego their present
> right to purchase under the Act and decline the Offer of Sale pursuant
> to the Act presented on January 4, 1987, in consideration of the
> granting of certain other rights and opportunities for future
> homeownership pursuant to this Agreement which provides for an
> Option Agreement to be entered into by the parties if certain
> conditions precedent are satisfied.[8]

The residents' "rights and opportunities for future ownership" included
a series of workshops to be offered by the People's Advocacy (PA) and
funded by Shelter Incorporated.

At the request of the tenants, the PA outlined various workshops
aimed to make the tenant group become effective in forming and
sustaining a viable cooperative. The workshops focused on matters
such as:

> Fiduciary duties and decision-making techniques; Roles of officers
> and committees; How to plan and conduct meetings; Problem-solving
> attitudes and conflict resolution; Building management and

maintenance; Cooperative finances and budgeting; Community planning; and Member communications and cooperative image.[9]

The overall focus of these workshops was to provide the necessary know-how on board development, resource mobilization and homeownership/management to a core group of residents in accordance with the contractual agreement. It states:

> The Parties agree to the plan set forth herein to convert [Hope Mansions] to resident cooperative ownership. The objective of this plan is to provide sufficient time and resources for residents to organize, obtain training and gain experience in ownership and management responsibilities, and to raise the funds required to carry out the active participation by the residents in improvements to and the operation of [Hope Mansions] during the Partnership's ownership.[10]

Commenting on the contractual agreement, Patricia Mason, the former executive director of the People's Advocate, added:

> And in the training agreement . . . we got involved in developing a proposal for training services, with the cooperative itself. They then submitted it to [Gail's] office. Because they didn't have their own funding, [Gail] agreed to cover some of their expenses. Basically, our role went beyond the limited training resources that they had. Our feeling was it was an important project as far as the size and scale. . . . It had to be one of the largest in the country as far as conversions go.[11]

The first stage of implementation in the contractual agreement was geared towards:

> Strengthening of the resident organization; training in cooperative ownership and management; formation of a nonprofit cooperative housing corporation by residents of [Hope Mansions].[12]

As I have stated, when Shelter Incorporated acquired Hope Mansions in 1987, the existing Tenant Council was all but dormant. The fear of the perceived impending gentrification, however, became a rallying point for the Tenant Council. Much of the enthusiasm generated among residents can be attributed to the fact that the new owner and management promised the residents better living conditions. Also, the existence of a signed agreement between the owner and the tenant group made the goal of tenant ownership seem achievable in the near future. According a Shelter Incorporated project manager:

> There were some people who had been there a long time . . . who liked living there, and had a vision that it could be again a very nice place to live. They were very discouraged by the circumstances. On the other hand, they still had a vision of homeowner possibilities. One of the things, a couple of months after I came on board, was the signing of the agreement for a cooperative at the end of 1987. The slate had not had any renovation done to it yet. They saw that this was something that they did want to own and they met with HUD to have that happen.[13]

The tenant group retained the PA to assist them in organizing as a nonprofit cooperative corporation. The PA was tasked with a) conducting needs assessment of the residents, b) applying for project grants, c) training residents in conducting meetings, presenting grievances and becoming effective in achieving their organization goals, d) setting up a job placement and referral programs to assist residents in finding employment opportunities, and e) assisting residents in forming a viable organizational structure—a housing cooperative in the waiting—to acquire the property. All of these objectives combined to form the tenant empowerment project aimed to eradicate the factors which contributed the community's state of decay and decline.

In an effort to establish and prioritized the needs of residents, the PA initiated a survey project. Although the survey was merely a tool to assess the needs of the residents, it became the first major effort to recruit the active involvement of tenants in the process—as interviewers in their own neighborhood:

> The first thing that I did was to work with the residents and also with some trainers in the implementation of the survey. That survey, what we did was to hire residents to serve as surveyors. So they initially went out with a sheet of paper stating that a survey was going to be held for each building out here and got the individual to sign something saying they will attend. Then the day before they went

back out [to further remind the residents of the commitment they had made], and the day the residents went to take the survey, we actually gave an oral survey. We gathered all the residents in one room and administered an oral survey and at the end of the survey, each resident was given $5.00 for participating.[14]

The survey results became essential in plans for the rehabilitation of the buildings and the restructuring of community. For example, over the years, several of the households had outgrown the number of bedrooms in their apartments. In the survey report, the PA indicated that 36 percent of the households mentioned an increase in size. Of the households responding to the questionnaire, 37 percent of families occupying one-bedroom and 21 percent of families occupying two-bedroom apartments requested additional bedrooms as a result of overcrowding.

In addition, many senior and retired citizens indicated a preference for apartment buildings separate from households with children. The survey results also indicated that "51 percent of the Hope residents wanted to own, instead of just renting." Of these residents, however, 32 percent were unsure of homeownership and 40 percent knew little or nothing about co-op living.[15] The tenant survey also generated a list of services (i.e., day care, laundromat) and vocational training (i.e., apprenticeship, GED) needed by tenants.

REFORMING HOPE MANSIONS TENANT COUNCIL

Critical in the tenants' acquisition of Hope Mansions was the formation of a stable mediating institution through which tenants could achieve their goal. One of the top priorities of the PA in Hope Mansions was the restructuring of the Tenant Council into a cooperative entity with a board of directors charged with decision-making. According to a former PA field worker:

The first thing we did was to meet with the residents. [Patricia] actually talked to residents and it was about what they've been doing in the past, their organizational structure: Were they incorporated? Was there leadership?, and so on. Based on her assessment of where they were at that point, she wrote a proposal in which there were several different dynamics outlined which the [People's Advocacy] would do.[16]

The proposal outlined a series of workshops on the formation of a board and a management team, as well as the incorporation of a housing cooperative.

The Tenant Council as it existed before restructuring was a "closed" organization made up of a core group of friends. This circle of friendship had made them insensitive to reaching out to other tenants who attended meetings regularly and paid their membership dues:

> Another issue is the leadership because certain people have been in leadership for a long period of time. I think that knowing how to lead, knowing when to delegate and knowing how to get others involved in the process is another challenge which they had. When I was there, the "old guard," as I called it, had decided upon one route on getting people to the meeting.[17]

Because the core members had made no effort to attract the tenants, the majority did not know about the Tenant Council. Lacking organizational and leadership skills, the Tenant Council had been unable to mobilize and to raise the consciousness of the residents regarding community concerns.

Traditionally, the organization had had a problem drawing and retaining new members. Whenever some of the core group members had introduced others residents to the Tenant Council independently, they tended not to stay. The reason, as the PA staff determined, was that the "old guard" had no way of enabling willing individuals to become part of the organization:

> Residents have some problems with the ability to organize too. The fact was that there was such a large site and only a small group of them who were in control of the resident organization. Part of what we tried to do was to help them understand that they had to get more people involved. And they had to be representative of the whole by getting greater participation. We advocated that they expand the board of directors, which they did, reluctantly. But that ended being of help. Instead of five people running everything, they got about a dozen on the Board and Building Captains. That was a small step but they began to get more participation.[18]

As part of the restructuring, a new and expanded cooperative board of directors was formed. As a business entity, the Board retained the services of an attorney to formulate its organizational by-laws. The attorney was charged with the task of incorporating the organization as Hope Mansions Cooperative. Board members were selected through a democratic process—by ballot. Prospective candidates seeking membership on the Cooperative Board collected signatures to secure nominations for a scheduled election publicized by fliers delivered to each household and by door-to-door solicitation. The community-wide election was crucial for two reasons. First, it ensured that all the households were informed about the budding tenant cooperative initiative. Second, the electoral process compelled those seeking nomination to go door-to-door to meet and tell their fellow residents about the pending changes in their communities.

Making Things Work in Hope Mansions

The case of Hope Mansions reveals that it is easy enough to outline a community's objectives and goals, but it is far more difficult to achieve them. The most difficult stage of the conversion was the "[p]articipation by Hope Mansions residents in management decision-making, followed by a sharing of management responsibilities by members of the cooperative housing corporation."[19] This segment of the contractual agreement was problematic because it required not only the tenants' expertise, but also the willingness of the management company to work with them.

Consistent with the empowerment process, a number of residents were to be selected to participate actively in the various phases of the rehabilitation. By so doing, it was anticipated that tenants would have acquired the technical skills necessary to manage their own cooperative housing eventually. A former PA field manager explained the process:

> I was the Project Coordinator for the resident empowerment process. Basically what it entailed was creating a structure within the resident association in which the residents would be responsible for issues and concerns which involved them, management, and then the owners. And so, it would be a sort of a tripod in which the things that affected the residents—they would have to vote and control it and be able to report back to the management. So then they will have a working relationship with the management and the owners also. Because the goal with HOPE was for them to own the property, the whole hypothesis was that if the residents understood the process, then it

would make it an easier transition when they became the owners of the property. So as a project manager, I was to implement that.[20]

After the signing of the contractual agreement between the tenants' group and Shelter Incorporated, the tenant group leadership and its members received at least three training sessions dealing with various dimensions of cooperative business management. The last of such training occurred in the spring, 1994.

In light of all the workshops, the tenants' organization regressed over time. Commenting on the last workshop organized for the tenants in compliance with HUD's HOPE II (Home Ownership for People Everywhere) grant, one of the PA program managers stated:

> Many of the tenants attended the workshops not because they were interested in actively participating in the Cooperative. From what I hear, many of them came because it was some kind of vacation for them. They brought their husbands or boyfriends because each member had a room to themselves. After the training, I started working with tenants to get their homeownership program going, but you know, many of them did not come to the tenants' meetings, and those who came seemed not to understand what is going on. Some of them just don't know how to participate.[21]

Some the Cooperative members, however, saw their situation differently. Tenants complained about their lack of opportunities to apply the lessons learned from the workshops to real situations:

> You see, they've been taking us to go to retreats in Virginia for a weekend to train us on how to become homeowners, and the way things should be done at our board meetings. We got all these handouts about co-ops and finances. But you know, how can we manage when we have no way of practicing what they've been teaching us? . . . So after a while you done forget because you don't use them.[22]

Furthermore, many of the residents simply did not grasp the concepts of real estate management. In light of the fact that a disproportionate number of them had less than 12th grade education, many of the tenants had a hard time understanding what was being presented to them at the workshops. An elderly tenant expressed the plight of many of the workshop participants, stating:

> You know the weekend retreat they've been taking us to? We go out to a camp in Virginia, leave Friday evening and come home Saturday night. They give these workshops on a bunch of things that are way over your head. Much of the time you don't know what they've been teaching you.[23]

Another problem facing the tenants was the lack of opportunity to participate in major decision-making concerning the development of "their property." More often than not, it was Gail Peterson who communicated to tenants what they should expect in terms of community improvement, rather than the residents defining and stating their own expectations. Asked about Shelter's contractual relation with the tenant cooperative, a former field manager stated unabashedly:

> [Gail] has not run an open, sharing, interactive corporation with the residents. It did not happen. There are lots of small decisions that add up, and there are lots of decision that had to do with the design, the use of space, design of the space, new businesses. [Gail] has never set up a mechanism for an on-going communication and participation. Communication, in fact, is the easy part. But participation—She's never done that. She doesn't really have any true interest in doing that. She never invited them into these meetings.[24]

Independent of this field manager's observations, one of the Cooperative Board members concurred that:

> [Gail] did the renovation and did not ask anyone as to anything they wanted to go out here. As far as the Co-Op office, the space that she's given us, she didn't ask us if this space is big enough? Does this meet your standard needs, that you need to put an office into? Any of the constructions going on out here was what she wanted. Point blank.[25]

Landlord-Tenant Negotiations

Although the tenant group members did not actively participate in major decision-making concerning the rehabilitation project, they had some of the demands, as outlined in the contractual agreement, met. By 1992, the Cooperative Board had been successful in soliciting various support services from the owner. These included a converted one-bedroom apartment serving as the Cooperative Office. Also, the tenant group and the owner/management dealt with the drug problems by retaining the security services of the NOI, as discussed in a previous chapter.

In addition, the tenant group pursued plans to encourage community involvement, to find subcontracts for residents with construction-related skills and jobs for the youth, to participate in selecting future tenants and to realized the formation of a cooperative. First, at the request and recommendation of the tenant group, Shelter Incorporated hired a local clergyman, Rev. Donald, to serve as the Community Liaison. Rev. Donald, counseled families, conducted Bible studies on Tuesday evenings and held church services on Sunday afternoons. He also canvassed households, encouraging their active participation in the cooperative endeavor. Acting as a mediator, Rev. Donald settled interpersonal conflicts in the neighborhood.

Second, the HMC confronted Shelter Incorporated on its hiring and subcontracting practices in the community. The tenants drew Shelter Incorporated's attention to its failure to subcontract minority-owned firms. Peterson obliged. The residents, however, noticed that:

> [Shelter Incorporated] had subcontracted to two minority-owned companies. But do you know that none of the people hired by these companies didn't live out here? . . . When I first moved out here, I was working with one of the construction companies but the majority of the work was done elsewhere. When I left them I started working for the government. Then me and another resident decided to put a company together because I knew that when I was working in here, a lot of the work was supposed to be done by the residents to get more involved in where they lived. But it was not happening. . . . So we pushed her and said: "Hold up. When you wrote up your proposal to HUD saying you will train everybody and you were portrayed in the newspapers that you're helping black-owned companies build up and you're helping the residents out here, and none of these is being done."[26]

Although there were many unemployed men living in the community, very few of them were hired in the rehabilitation of the community. At a tenant meeting, one tenant complained that:

> They've got all these forked-tongue [Hispanic] people working out here but our men have no jobs. What's Gail doing not hiring any of the folks living out here?[27]

These complaints resulted in awarding contracts to Hope Builders Incorporated (HBI), a community-based organization formed by two residents. This resulted in job opportunities for some unemployed tenants as laborers. Others took up apprenticeships in carpentry and bricklaying. HBI rehabilitated the Community Center (which houses also the daycare center, learning center and the community laundromat). In addition, Shelter Incorporated awarded HBI a contract cleaning out debris from the renovated buildings. Between 1991 and 1994, HBI provided temporary jobs to a total of 40 young adults and teenagers in the community. This, no doubt, improved the morale and pride of the young men in the community.

Despite its effort to get Shelter Incorporated to sign a contractual agreement to relinquish future ownership and control of Hope Mansions, the tenant organization was unsuccessful in its third goal of influencing Shelter Incorporated to allow a few capable tenants to participate minimally in the operations of the property. As part of its effort to establish an effective tenant cooperative housing, the Board members sought to be included in screening prospective tenants. The leadership surmised that the inclusion of a few members to screen in-coming residents would achieve two results. First, it would enable the residents to ensure that prospective households moving into the neighborhood did not have criminal histories and inclinations. Second, it would provide an opportunity to draw in-coming tenants into the budding cooperative.

The idea of tenant participation in interviewing and selecting prospective tenants was threatening to the management company. Even tenants' partial participation in the process would, in effect, enable the tenant group to recruit applicants favoring cooperative housing. Subsequently, this might diminish the management company's power and the eventual termination of their contract.

This issue generated antagonism between management and the Cooperative Board. The Cooperative Board members frequently commented on the resistance they experienced when attempting to participate in the decision-making process. Not allowing the tenants to play a role in screening prospective tenants weakened the incipient Cooperative in two ways: the Cooperative was unable to screen for tenants who valued civic participation, and second, it was unable to attract like-minded tenants committed to the idea of cooperative homeownership. In sum, the Board members saw Shelter/management's resistance to their participation in significant decision-making as a way of thwarting their effort to own the property in the near future. Expressing her antagonism towards the property manager, one Cooperative Board member stated: "The first person we're gonna fire is Jim Casey when we become homeowners."[28]

Final stage of the contractual agreement was the "homeownership" goal. This is to be accomplished by 1996. According to the agreement, Shelter was expected to transfer ownership and control of [Hope Mansions] to the cooperative housing corporation formed by its residents.[29] Completion of this final stage did not materialize. The tenant organization, as I will discuss later, was plagued with internal bickering and animosity between factions. At this juncture I will assess the changes in the neighborhood, Hope Mansions Cooperative's accomplishments and difficulties in raising and sustaining tenant consciousness in the community.

"[Hope Mansions] Regained"

"[Hope Mansions] Regained" was the title of a newspaper editorial detailing the transformation in the community after Shelter Incorporated had purchased the apartment complexes. The physical transformation included the sandblasting of the buildings, rendering them virtually new. The lush vegetation of grass, shrubs, interspersed with trees, pleased longtime tenants and invited prospective tenants. The mailboxes previously located in each building were now strategically located at the walkway intersections in the courtyards. This was a deliberate and additional architectural design employed to entice residents out of their apartments and into social interaction.

Other features which guided residents to acknowledge each other were the garden benches situated along a network of wide concrete walkways throughout the apartment buildings. Especially appreciative of these benches were the senior citizens who strolled within the neighborhood visiting friends. The benches served as rest stops between the large courtyards. Given that the apartments units were without porches, the benches also became common areas where tenants met to socialize with each other.

There were a total of seven playgrounds scattered in various courtyards and a newly constructed basketball court which was well-lit for evening games. Near the basketball court was a decorative water fountain flanked by three dolphins which spewed water from their spouts when the tap was turned on. The children in the community played in the water to cool down during the hot summer days. To keep the facility operative, a ground maintenance crew cleaned the premises daily and mowed the lawn as required.

The rehabilitation of Hope Mansions generated a sense of security many long-time residents had not experienced for almost a decade. The newly functioning security intercoms tied into the main electronic security doors enabled each household to screen persons seeking entry into each apartment building. Parents evaluated the level of neighborhood safety by the degree of worry they entertained about letting their children play outside without having to watch over them. Fearful parents who once had stood guard while their children played outside now did not find it necessary to do so. The renovations, the cleanliness of the community and several planned activities for the neighborhood children and senior citizens all contributed to a shared sense of well-being many residents had not known over the past decade.

But as in any low-income community, a communal sense of safety (and decent living conditions) was dependent on an improved economic well-being. In other words, the community was in danger of declining in the near future unless the economic conditions of majority of Sun-Hope tenants improved considerably.

THE STATE OF THE HOPE MANSIONS COOPERATIVE (HMC)

The Hope Mansions Cooperative (HMC) was a product of the activism of a core group of tenants and the acquiescence of the Shelter Incorporated. The organization had an office space, office equipment such as a photocopier, a fax machine, a functioning computer, a laser printer, and a telephone. The HMC was made up of several committees including: Building Captains, Fundraising, Grounds, Security, Entertainment, Communications, and Personnel Committees. The two paid office staff members were residents of Hope Mansions. The tenants applied for the jobs and were selected from 189 applicants. The Communications Committee published a monthly newsletter, "The Hope Sun," which kept residents abreast of community concerns.

The development of the HMC, however, cannot be discussed in isolation: since its inception, the Cooperative had evolved under the guidance of the PA. Operating on the behest of the Cooperative, the PA wrote proposals and was awarded grant moneys to implement life- and community-enhancing projects. Among the projects were the (Department of Health and Human Services) DHHS-funded Livelihood Jobs Project (1991-92), the Washington Gas funded Energy Conservation Training Project (1991-1994), and the Housing and Urban Development (HUD) funded Homeownership for People Everywhere (HOPE II) Project (1993-94).[30] These grant implementation projects constituted the community empowerment strategy to help needy and willing tenants become economically self-sufficient.

HOPE II and Schism among The Cooperative Board Members

In 1986 when tenants celebrated their agreement with Shelter Incorporated regarding their eventual ownership of the Hope Mansions, only a few Tenant Council members at the time had a true sense of how they were going to own Hope Mansions as a collective. This idea of "homeownership" became more realistic in November 1992. Housing and Urban Development Secretary Jack Kemp came to Hope Mansions in person to inform the tenants that their HOPE II grant application had been approved. The $500,000 grant would enable the Cooperative to develop a formalized administrative structure, to conduct a feasibility study of homeownership, and to educate and empower tenants to take control over their neighborhood.

The grant award generated excitement followed by a bitter internal conflict. There erupted an internal power struggle between the "old guard," older and less educated tenants who had formed the original core group of the tenant organization since 1985, and the "new guard" a group of young college-educated tenants whose tenancy ranged from two to three years. The young tenants disrespected the old guard for being unrefined and unprofessional in their ways. From the viewpoint of the old guard, the young people were opportunists who had joined the organization for financial motives and self-aggrandizement.

In 1992, the "new guard" orchestrated a "coup d'état." With the help of the organization's lawyer, they amended the organization's by-laws requiring that board members be residents of Hope Mansions. This provision led to the forced resignation of Betty Allen, a former resident but an ardent community organizer and president of the Cooperative.[31] In essence, although the HOPE II grant engendered hopes of ownership, it also generated struggles for leadership and for recognition.

Essential to the grant implementation was the restructuring of the Cooperative to ensure that the organization was democratic and to attract effective residents. By the spring of 1994, the PA organized a two-day workshop for the Cooperative Board members and selected residents. The workshop included topics such as Board Development, Financial Management, Cooperative Housing Management and Conflict Mediation and Resolution.

Nearly two months after the workshop, there was a battle within the Cooperative Board over hiring practices and leadership. The grant implementation required the hiring of two paid staff: an administrative assistant and a Home Ownership Coordinator (HOC). One resident was hired, out of 189 applicants, by the Cooperative Board for the administrative assistant position. The HOC position, however, was not advertised.

Through some internal maneuvering, one of the tenants was appointed to position of HOC by the Personnel Committee without the knowledge and ratification by the Board of Directors. A letter signed by the Cooperative president and the Personnel Committee chairman sent to the PA's Project Manager stated:

Please be advised that the [Hope Mansions] Cooperative, Inc., Board of Directors has selected Ms. Childs as our new Administrative Assistant and Ms. Puttnum as the Home Ownership Coordinator. The aforementioned selections were approved by unanimous vote by the Directors of the organization in our Board of Directors meeting held on December 8, 1993. We are looking forward to Ms. Childs and Ms. Puttnum beginning work as soon as possible. Ms. Childs and Ms. Puttnum will report to you[r] office on December 27, 1993, at 1:00 pm for orientation. Please make the arrangement required to bring our new employees on board[32]

The filling of the HOC position came as surprise to all but two Board members: the Personnel chairman who wrote the letter and his girlfriend—a board member—who got the job. Contrary to the content of the letter, the only position "approved by unanimous vote" was that of Ms. Childs as Administrative Assistant.

Instead of bringing their concern to the Board meeting, some individual Board members wrote letters to HUD's Field Office complaining about the Cooperative's internal rivalry. Others wrote letters complaining about their disenchantment with the PA. The first letter sent to HUD officials stated:

> My name is Constance Knott and I am a member of the [Hope Mansions] Cooperative, Inc. Board of Directors. I was also the Assistant Secretary of the Board until the recent election of January 22, 1994.
>
> I spoke to you on January 28, 1994 regarding my concerns about the way things are being handled with the HOPE II Grant on behalf of the cooperative.
>
> One of my concerns is the way in which Ms. Puttnum acquired her position as Home Ownership Coordinator. . . . When the letter of recommendation was presented to [the president], however the position for Ms. Puttnum had been upgraded to Home Ownership Coordinator. . . . Ms. Joyce [the president] voiced her disapproval to Ms. Puttnum concerning the upgrading of the position; however, Ms. Joyce signed the letter because she felt that it was extremely necessary for the Administrative Assistant position to be filled, and both job positions were on the same letter. . . .
>
> My question is this—can Ms. Puttnum be hired by the Board of Directors and still maintain her position as an officer on the Board? I feel that Ms. Puttnum hired herself, and is her own supervisor. I definitely need clarification on this issue.[33]

The Cooperative president, Ms. Joyce, who "had resigned from the board of directors, but [had] not sent an official letter of resignation," sent a similar letter to HUD Field Office complaining about "the way Ms. Puttnum acquired her position as Home Ownership Coordinator."[34]

The controversy about the hiring of the HOC generated animosity among Board members. Some of the members complained that Ms. Puttnum not only failed to do her duties, but had become unbearable as a colleague. Claiming that the president and the other Board members were slow and ineffective, Ms Puttnum consistently over-stepped her administrative boundaries by taking initiatives on behalf of the organization without going through the proper channels of approval.

Subsequently, within a week the president and four Board members (constituting a majority of the old guard) submitted their resignations. One Board member's resignation letter stated:

> In re-prioritizing my life, I realize that it is time for me to concentrate more on my family and my other interests. Therefore, this letter is to officially inform the Hope Mansions Cooperative, Inc. Board of Directors of my resignation that will be effective as of April 12, 1994.[35]

The president of the organization, who served only 3 months of her one-year term, added:

> I am relinquishing my position as president and Board Member of the Hope Mansions Cooperative, Inc. effective immediately. There are other interests that I am attempting to attain. Great success with the HOPE II Grant and Homeownership in [Hope]. Keep the eyes on the prize [sic].[36]

The other board members did not issue resignation letters but made their intentions known at the board meetings. Four months after the stealthy hiring of Ms. Puttnum, a majority of the Board members resigned, questioning her qualifications and leadership skills as a Home Ownership Coordinator.

Fall Out with the PA

The departure of all the "old guard" set the incipient Cooperative into a decline. With the presidency and the various board positions vacant, Ms. Puttnum propped herself up as the acting president while searching for new board members. The rash of resignations incapacitated the remaining Board members: they were unable to hold official meetings without a quorum, let a lone make decisions.

In her brief term as acting president, Ms. Puttnum took the necessary steps in an effort to undermine the PA as the principal grant manager. In a letter to a HUD case manager, Ms. Puttnum complained about what she considered to be exorbitant charges PA had made against the grant money for workshops provided to the Cooperative members. She stated:

> In reviewing some of those invoices we find several questionable charges. For example, the invoice submitted on September 4, 1993 charges $18,300.76 for "organizing the Resident Management Council." The Organizational activities included the dissolution of a former organization, incorporation of a new entity, preparation and filing Article of Dissolution, Articles of Incorporation, By-laws, Resolutions, Minutes of Organizational Meeting, Waiver of Notice, Oaths of Office, conducting the Organizational Meeting, and other meetings, all of which were done by our Attorney, [Mr. Christmas], who accompanied me to our meeting on May 12. We have no idea what organizing [PA] did to justify the sum billed.[37]

The conclusion of the letter summed up the sentiment of the "new guards'" or Ms. Puttnum's desire to rid itself of the PA:

> We have long been dissatisfied with [PA], but were not quite sure what to do. The Board is in total agreement with terminating that relationship and has authorized me to entertain a proposal from Marshall Heights Community Development Corporation, Inc. to replace PA.[38]

At the time Ms. Puttnum made this complaint to HUD, the Hope Mansions Cooperative had spent nearly $80,000 and was about ten months into the grant implementation. Unfortunately when asked about the Board's accomplishments, individual board members were unable to identify any positive gains made by the organization towards fulfilling their goal of cooperative homeownership. The organization had become a hotbed of conflict. The internal schism among the Cooperative Board members did not stop there. The former and current Board members registered their dissatisfaction with the PA's handling of the Cooperative's business, as well. Some of the resigning members wrote scathing letters to the HUD officials concerning the PA's incompetence in ensuring the hiring of qualified and experienced personnel for the organization.

The irony was that earlier, the Cooperative Board had refused any assistance from the PA's staff in hiring qualified applicants for the positions. The only role the PA project managers played in the affair was to comply with the directives contained in a letter from the Cooperative's president and the personnel committee chairperson. Their letter stated:

> by a unanimous vote by the Directors of the organization in our Board of Directors meeting held on December 8, 1993, "[the appointed staff] will report to you[r] office on December 27, 1993, at 1:00 pm of orientation . . . make the arrangement required to bring our new employees on board."[39]

This evidence, however, did not prevent some of the Board members, not excluding the president who had signed the letter, to write to HUD blaming PA for the illegal hiring of Ms. Puttnum. In a letter to HUD explaining PA's position, the project manager stated:

> All individuals hired under the HOPE 2 Grant were hired with the final decision being made by [HMC]. [HMC] established a Personnel Committee who screened all responses to the advertised positions, interviewed all applicants, and forwarded to [PA], in writing . . . the names of the individuals selected to be hired for the approved staff positions.[40]

Although individual Board members berated the PA for providing exorbitant training the Cooperative members did not need, the condition of the organization contradicted their claims. At the time the acting president wrote the scathing letter to HUD, there was no functioning Board of Directors. Consequently, there was no evidence that "the Board was in total agreement with terminating" their relationship with the PA. As a PA Project Manager stated to HUD officials:

> I am not sure what "Board" she is referring to, nor have I been provided with confirmed documentation who are the members of the HMC Board of Directors. I would suggest to you that the referenced letters is a clear example of the Board of Directors' inability to function properly and that additional training will be needed for the new members of the Board of Directors.

The complaints from individual tenants, however, led HUD to suspend temporarily the grant implementation and expense reimbursement to the PA while HUD officials investigated the matter. They did not find any wrongdoing on the part of PA. At the recommendation of HUD officials, an oversight group—made up of two Cooperative Board members, two PA project managers, and a housing consultant—was formed. Their investigation of the operations of the Cooperative led to the dismissal of the acting president and the Personnel chairperson. They were found to have misappropriated funds and acted in ways inconsistent with the requirements of the grant implementation guidelines.

The Tenant Cooperative without Tenants' Cooperation

Sometime in 1991, the Cooperative Board initiated its then unnamed newsletter to communicate with tenants. The second issue had a plea from the president that stated: "Tenants, it is time for us to band together for a common goal; a better life for our families in [Hope]."[41] The irony is that since the president's call "to band together," the Cooperative had been in a state of disarray. Between 1992 and 1994 the HMC had four presidents, but none of them completed their terms in office. The other characteristic of these community leaders was that they frequently moved out of the community when they became frustrated at not being able to accomplish their objectives. Those who stayed in the community withdrew their membership from the nascent Cooperative, avoided participating in any community endeavors, denigrated the efforts of their rivals, and discouraged other tenants from joining the organization. Expressing his frustration about the effects of the internal strife in the organization, one of the few men and one of the most active members of the organization stated:

> We need somebody that is going to buckle them. Somebody that is going to stand up and say "look, open our eyes," and make us see what is going on around here. Because first of all, most of the people around here, the only one that can do our bid is Betty Allen [the deposed president]. The Board out here now, they're all full of shit. They got too much plan, they're all money hungry, they got certain individuals on the Board all they think of is money and getting promotions on other little things except for the [whole]. They're using the Board for what they want to do. Power struggle that's all there is. As far as getting things done, you might see a little group

here doing a little bit, a little group there doing a little bit, . . . but the
tenants are not cooperating because they don't give a darn.[42]

The power struggle within the HMC was also linked to both the
members' distrust of each other and of the PA staff. On one hand, the
HMC was dependent on the PA staff to provide all the essential
technical support as outlined in the grant proposal. On the other hand,
once the grant money was awarded, some of the group members felt
that they should have been in position to administer the grant. This
combination of dependency and distrust led to bitter confrontations
disrupting the HMC's progress towards its homeownership goal. As a
former project manager stated:

[Hope Mansions] had a dependency problem. They just have a
negative, negative attitude. They like to feed into the negative aspects
of stuff versus just deciding: "Well okay, this is a bad situation but
what is the higher purpose? What else can we do to get to other
things?" And, that was the thing that Patricia [former PA Executive
Director] always reinforced saying: "Okay, this is where we are at but
what can we do to go to another higher level" or something like that.
The people I met, the old guard, they were kind of negative, and I
guess they just have lived in that situation and gone through some
traumatic situations.[43]

The animosity between the different factions of the Board of
Directors invariably affected the way uncommitted tenants viewed the
HMC as a community mediating institution. The persistent schism
among board members accounted for the organization's inability to
attract and retain members. Residents who became familiar with the
organization often pointed to the strife between individuals and thus did
not want to join the organization. Others had misgivings about the goal
of cooperative homeownership. Many of the residents confronted the
HMC by asking what it was going to provide them if they were to join
and pay their membership dues.

"Delivering the Goods"

Advocacy groups and leaders of low-income tenant organizations must
often confront intense challenges bridging the gap between good
intentions (talk about what ought to be), and delivering the goods

(achieving concrete results). The legitimacy of any tenant organization is dependent on the leaders' ability to prove to their constituents that they are capable of working at their behest. As one Board member explained:

> The main purpose of the Board is to get the tenants' view on the current issues in Hope Mansions, such as the renovation, moving dates, security deposits, lease, etc. Your views are very important to the Board, and all tenants have a right to voice their views. Your views are also important because they can affect decisions made on such issues as rent increases, maintenance, and activities and services you feel are needed to enhance our community.[44]

In Hope Mansions, the Cooperative Board had been successful in signing a contract with the owner for eventual tenant ownership and control of the property. Through the influence of the Cooperative, Shelter subcontracted the construction and cleaning jobs to a tenant-owned company. But despite these achievements, the HMC Board of Directors faced a legitimation crisis: many tenants did not see the organization's impact in their households. The organization failed in two crucial ways to sustain tenants' support regarding concerns about rent increments and its inability to pressure the Shelter Incorporated to install a laundry facility for the 650 households. The residents had lived without a laundry facility for ten years.

After the renovation was completed in 1991, Shelter Incorporated proposed and was granted two rent increments by HUD. In response to the first proposed rent increment, a group of tenants, under the auspices of the Cooperative, collected signatures to protest the rent increment. The Cooperative Board members, however, after deliberation, decided not to present the petition against the rent hike to HUD for consideration formally.

The second rent increment proposed by Shelter, however, was met by a protest initiated by one of the Board members. She complained that her husband had been laid off and that she was supporting a family of five on her meager income. After securing the support of the Cooperative Board, she orchestrated a signature drive to avert the rent increment. Having collected the signatures of nearly 90 percent of the households to avert the rent increment, Miss Taylor presented the list to the Cooperative to forward it to HUD and Shelter Incorporated.

Reporting to the tenants the status of the campaign against the rent increment, the presidents stated:

> Thanks to all of you for participating in our Stop The Rent Increase Petition. Our petition had the signature of a majority of [Hope] residents and was accompanied by a very well-thought-out and -written rebuttal of management's reasons for seeking the increase. It was submitted to the Dept. of Housing and Urban Development (HUD) on November 14, 1991.[45]

Shelter Incorporated countered the tenants' rent protest. Convinced, HUD officials granted Shelter Incorporated the permission to proceed with the rent increment. The Cooperative Board conceded defeat with grace:

> Although HUD granted management the right to increase rents, our concerns were considered. We can feel very proud of our effort in coming together in our common cause.
> All is not lost on this issue, because management's reasons for the increase included more security, more maintenance workers, groundskeepers and other staff, an up and running laundry center, community and youth activities, and a prettier and improved [Hope].
> From this increase we should come to expect and hold management to providing a safer home and community for our families, jobs for our unemployed and a quicker and more pleasant response to our maintenance needs. Also, *we should soon see a safe, clean and accessible laundromat*, and regularly scheduled community activities for our young people, our seniors—all of us.[46]

The tenants' request for a community laundromat predated the arrival of Shelter Incorporated. Many of the new tenants moved into Hope Mansions with an understanding that a laundromat would be available "soon." Two years after the above consolation to the tenants, another president of the Cooperative stated:

> Like as far as the management and their saying that a laundromat is coming, that is a key thing to the residents out here. . . . It's been five years yet . . . the [laundromat] hasn't gotten here; [Shelter] hired a new employee. She [Peterson] came out and made an announcement at one of our community meetings, saying the laundromat was going

to be started in a month or so. That was over two months ago and nothing has been done. . . . Instead of saying to the residents, "it still isn't here yet. We talked to you about getting a laundromat, management says it's coming and now they are giving no reasons to why." No explanation. Instead a bunch of "it's coming, it's coming."[47]

At a general tenant meeting, the acting president responded to tenants' complaints about the lack of a laundromat by blaming the owner. Unsatisfied by the performance of the Cooperative Board, a tenant castigated the president by stating:

You've been here since 1985 and you've been complaining about a laundromat, and you've been talking about it all the time and you ain't got one. So what's it you've been talking for? You ain't got nothing done? All they've been doing is talking but getting nothing done. They're wasting my time.[48]

Another stated:

We meet and we talk about the same thing over and over again. They've been talking about the same things we talked about two years ago and nothing has changed. We never seem to get beyond the talk to get anything done around here. But they keep telling folks to join the cooperative to buy this place.[49]

After the meeting, one tenant expressed disappointment with the president for the self-deprecating manner in which she addressed the tenants on the laundromat matter. She stated:

I don't like the way they explain things. Did you hear the president saying that "the owner don't think us niggers need to do our laundry?" What kinda talk is this? This is no way to talk to folks at a meeting. They are so negative around here. That is all you hear. Negative.[50]

The Cooperative Board was confronted with a dilemma. On the one hand, the Board wanted tenants to recognize the Cooperative as representing the community, a body to which tenants could present unresolved complaints. On the other hand, many of the tenants found that the Board members were just as powerless as they were when it came to making the owner and management respond to their needs. The bottom line, a PA staffer conceded, was:

> I think we don't have a strong lobby of residents. We have some 650 units and 400 and something are occupied. If this is a community of conscious consumers, what will it take for 400 households to say we are not paying rent until this, this, this, and this is done? You can point to a number of things.[51]

The "number of things" included rent strikes and tenant protests, but these actions were unattainable given that many of the tenants did not pay fair market rent. Tenants shared collective consciousness about issues which affected them, i.e. rent increments, the laundromat and crime, but that was the extent of their solidarity. When it came to acting collectively as conscious consumers to alter their circumstances, a majority of the tenants had the tendency to shirk away, citing personal concerns: fear of eviction, loss of their Section 8 rent subsidy or doubt that their actions would change the situation for the better.

SUMMARY

In Hope Mansions, the nascent tenant Cooperative experienced intense conflict among new and old members over the control of the finances and leadership. Tenants not only distrusted each other; they distrusted the very advocacy organization which had guided them to make great strides as a functioning body. The core problem of Sun-Hope neighborhood, however, was the lack of community-wide loyalty. Although demographically Sun-Hope had become a predominantly low-income and racially homogeneous area, the residents shared varying levels of education, economic security, community consciousness and activism. Activist tenants who attempted to mobilize others to keep "their community in order" often discovered only a few neighbors shared their sentiments and level of concern. Typical of many impoverished neighborhoods, tenants with little stake in Sun-Hope were not community-conscious.[52]

Frustrated, some community leaders withdrew from the organization, and those with the financial means moved out. Some of the consequences included the following. 1) Community mediating institutions were weakened by the discontinuities in leadership resulting from high turnover. 2) The lack of community-wide loyalty made it impossible for the enthusiastic few to achieve their cooperative homeownership goal. 3) The neighborhood lost human resources needed to stabilize the it: the departure of community activists, leaders and gainfully employed persons upon whom others depended for guidance and support. These factors implicated both interpersonal and organizational difficulties facing community advocacy groups in addressing problems in low-income neighborhoods.

Housing desegregation, as noted earlier, was viewed as a means to promote racial integration. This resolution, however, has led to an intense racial and class isolation of low-income blacks in many urban neighborhoods like Sun-Hope neighborhood. Although Sun-Hope was not racially integrated initially, it was transformed into a predominantly lower-class black neighborhood when various *de jure* desegregation housing policies encouraged the exodus of well-to-do blacks from predominantly mixed-class black neighborhoods.

The ramifications of segregation, as the next chapter suggests, have had a tremendous impact on the lives of isolated poor blacks. Its effects include developers and unionized contractors not hiring jobless residents whose buildings they were refurbishing. In response, efforts were made to help unemployed and willing tenants find employment through a community-based job training and placement program: the Livelihood Jobs Training Program (LJTP).

NOTES

1. Shelter Inc. generated a total of $20.2 million for the rehabilitation. The financial sources were as follows: Fannie Mae (Direct Loan) $1.7 million; Owner Equity $2 million; City (CDBG) $3 million; HUD (Flexible Subsidy) $4.5 million; and Fannie Mae (MBS) 9 million.

2. John Gilderbloom and Richard P. Appelbaum, *Rethinking Rental Housing* (Philadelphia: Temple University Press, 1988). See also, Ralf Goetz, *Understanding Neighborhood Change* (New York: Ballinger, 1979).

3. See *Indices: A Statistical Index to District of Columbia Services* (Washington, D.C. 1990), 212.

4. *The Washington Post*, 25 July 1985.

5. Tenant, personal interview, 25 October 1991.

6. Former Tenant and president of the Hope Mansions Tenant Council, personal interview, 6 June 1992.

7. Douglas Stevenson, *The Washington Post*, 29 October 1987.

8. Shelter Inc.-Hope Mansions Tenant Council Contractual Agreement, 28 October 1987.
9. Tenant Empowerment Agreement, 1989.
10. Ibid.
11. Patricia Mason, personal interview, 3 March 1994.
12. Tenant Agreement, 1989.
13. Personal interview, 5 July 1991.
14. Former PA staff member, personal interview, 11 March 1992.
15. PA Survey Report 1987. The percentages are faulty. It appears that either the results were interpreted incorrectly or the respondents checked more than one response for the same question. That being the case, 50% of the residents who wanted homeownership also may have responded they did not know anything about cooperative homeownership.
16. Former PA staff member, personal interview, 11 March 1994.
17. Ibid.
18. Former PA president, personal interview, 2 March 1993.
19. Hope Mansions Contractual Agreement, 1989.
20. Former PA staff member, 11 March 1992.
21. PA project Manager, personal interview, 23 January 1994.
22. Tenant, personal interview, 20 September 1991.
23. Field notes, 12 September 1993.
24. Former Shelter Inc. staff member, telephone interview, 15 February 1992.
25. Tenant, personal interview, 16 June 1993.
26. Tenant and Hope Mansions Cooperative president, personal interview, 16 June 1993.
27. Field notes, 20 May 1992. Some of the leaders were racially antagonistic towards Gail Peterson who is white, but this was the first time I noticed a tenant scapegoating Hispanics working in the community for taking their jobs. Similar antagonistic relations are found between poor blacks and Korean merchants in predominantly low-income African American neighborhoods where blacks perceive being exploited by the merchants. See Michael Specter, "Day by Day, Racial Schism Grows on Church Avenue," *The Washington Post*, 20 September 1990, A3; Calvin Sims, "Black Shoppers Call Korean Merchants Hostile and Unfair," *The New York Times*, 17 May 1990, B1.
28. Field notes, June 9, 1992.
29. Hope Mansions Contractual Agreement, 1989:3.
30. The HOPE program was a set of initiatives and goals about housing for low-income people unveiled by President Bush on November 10, 1989. The

program was structured to empower public- and Section 8-assisted housing groups in three principal ways: "Empowering people with the opportunity to manage and own their own homes and apartments; Empowering people to enter the economic mainstream by removing barriers to jobs, entrepreneurship, and economic growth; Empowering people with better access to affordable housing and homeownership opportunities, especially for first-time home buyers." See *HOPE: Homeownership and Opportunity for People Everywhere*, U.S. Department of Housing and Urban Development publication HUD-PDR-1246(1), March 1990.

31. Betty Allen and her sister were raised in the community. Betty moved out of Hope Mansions in 1986 but continued to be active in the community. Her sister still lives there. The reason why Betty remained the president for four years was that she was trusted and respected by many of the residents. It was her intention to move back to Hope Mansions once the tenants took ownership of the property.

32. A Letter dated December 7, 1993. The names in this quotation are not the original ones.

33. A tenant's letter to Mr. Lance Hylton, Housing and Urban Development Field Office, dated 14 February 1994. The names in this quotation are not the original ones.

34. A letter to Mr. Lance Hylton, The HUD Field Office, dated 15 March 1994.

35. Resignation letter to the president, 13 April 1994.

36. Resignation letter from the PMC president, 13 April 1994.

37. A letter sent to Mr. Marshall Messimer, HUD Residents Initiative Office, 18 May 1994. This letter questioned every dimension of the PA's involvement in the grant implementation.

38. Ibid.

39. Letters sent to the People's Advocacy Project Manager, signed by the Cooperative president and personnel chairperson, 27 December 1994.

40. A letter from People's Advocacy to Mr. Messimer, HUD Resident Initiative Coordinator, 22 June 1994.

41. Newsletter. "Tenant Awareness." (Undated, circa summer, 1991).

42. Tenant, personal interview, 23 July 1993.

43. Former PA staff member, personal interview, 11 March 1992.

44. Newsletter. "Tenant Awareness." (Undated).

45. Newsletter 9 (December 1991).

46. Ibid.

47. Tenant and acting president, personal interview, 20 August 1993.

48. Field notes, 19 February 1994.

49. Field notes, 7 May 1994.
50. Field notes. At their general meetings, some tenants have the tendency to explain the owner's response to their problems in terms of race relations: because, "we are "niggers," or "because we ain't white folks," the owner takes her time to pay attention to their complaints. 7 May 1994.
51. LJTP manager, personal interview, 3 March 1992.
52. In a petition drive against rent increment, one woman refused to add her signature for reasons that management might terminate her rent subsidy. She paid $25.00 per month for her two-bedroom apartment.

CHAPTER 8

Empowerment through the Livelihood Job Training Program (LJTP)

The physical environment of Sun-Hope had been rehabilitated, but the socioeconomic situation of many of its residents had not changed. The development and stability of the Sun-Hope community depended also on the improvement in the socioeconomic conditions of the tenants. The situation of a majority of the tenants, however, was complicated by their own cultural capital: lack of education and marketable skills and familial constraints as single parents.

Many impoverished tenants responded with suspicion to corrective services directed at them. Tenants dependent on public welfare were particularly apprehensive when asked to provide extensive background information, such as occupation, sources of income, household size, and marital status.

Another problem project managers and community organizers confronted in low income neighborhoods was tenants' sense of insecurity. Program managers expected that needy residents in a low-income neighborhood would be responsive to programs designed to assist them to improve their socioeconomic conditions. The prospective participants, however, were apprehensive about sacrificing a few weeks in a skills training program which would not change their situation for the better. Moreover, prospective participants were aware of the limited incentives work has to offer, especially when one is the lowest tier of the segmented labor force. For the welfare dependent, the critical question about the types of jobs and wages offered expresses, on the one hand, their desire to work and forgo their public aid, but on the other hand, their knowledge that they would not be able to support their families on their meager wages. The Livelihood Job Training Program (LJTP), as will be discussed later, with it best intentions, revealed the inherent frustrations experienced by the employment seekers and placement managers assisting them to enter the mainstream labor market.

In 1991, the Department of Health and Human Services (DHHS) awarded Hope Mansions Cooperative, the People's Advocacy (PA), and Shelter Incorporated consortium a $500,000 grant. This grant had a dual purpose: half of the money was ear-marked for the rehabilitation of the community center, and the other half was to be used for setting up job training, referral and placement services to unskilled and unemployed residents. The grand expectation was that by the project's end, alienated and jobless adults and youth would be reintegrated into their own community, and subsequently into the mainstream labor market.

All will agree that decent, safe and affordable housing is a necessity. But it is problematic to maintain decent and safe living conditions when a significant number of the adult residents and youth lack marketable skills, employment, competitive wages/salaries and adequate education. The Hope Mansions' rehabilitation was designated to focus on the residents. This was important, as one of the site managers explained:

> because it begins to look at the rehabilitation of the people, not just buildings. I think we've seen a lot in the past where, particularly, public or federally subsidized housing has been rehabed structurally and then five years later is back to where it used to be because usually there is no attention given to the rehab of people, and rehab of people's thought about living.[1]

Given their impoverished background and neighborhood isolation, a majority of the young adults in the Sun-Hope community lacked the negotiating skills to make their way into mainstream society. Many able-bodied men and women gave up any hope of gaining employment after repeated rejections. In a 1989 assessment, a PA researcher stated about residents:

They needed jobs. That was a big issue. A lot of them were unemployed. They needed assistance with children. I guess the most important thing was they needed hope to know that they could overcome whatever was out there. Again, I use the word, powerlessness. They seemed powerless for being in that situation. And, they seemed mad.[2]

When Shelter acquired Hope Mansions in 1988, the PA staff members who worked with the community members often used words such as "powerlessness," "hopelessness," "negativity," and "apathy" in referring to the disposition of many tenants. These characteristics were symptomatic of a people living with the specters of unemployment, low wages, and fear of eviction. The task was to resocialize a community of residents distrustful of each other and outsiders. As a PA project manager explained:

Rehab of people implies that the conditions they are living in is a reflection of some thought that they are having about themselves and their ability to do things and to change or not change their condition. So it implies that we are building on people's skills, people's knowledge, people's exposure to other things that are important to growth. . . . People need to be nurtured. It is like you construct a building and it has to be painted, you have to change the carpet, fix the plumbing. I don't mean to reduce us to bricks and mortar, but we need even more so maintenance.[3]

In a community meeting in the fall of 1991, 25 tenants (99 percent women) were introduced to the framework for implementing the DHHS grant. Using a diagram, the program coordinator explained the various components of LJTP, which included credit counseling, budgeting, job training, job placement, job referral and personality assessment. For those not needing these services, a consciousness-raising class was organized, where participants read and discussed a text about life and living. Although many tenants welcomed the project, some doubted that "good-paying" jobs would replace their public assistance. One skeptical tenant queried: "What kinda jobs they're gonna give us? We don't need no $5.00 an hour jobs here. We need good paying jobs."[4]

Given the uncertainties of the labor market, and partly as a consequence of their lack of marketable skills, many of the single mothers were unprepared to accept precarious entry-level jobs that paid them less than their public assistance stipends. The shared reality among many of the women who declined or subsequently dropped out of the program was that the gap between their public assistance stipend and potential wages was a source of discouragement:

> Sometimes you can't get the high paying job that you want . . . and the jobs are so way out and you have to worry about a babysitter. And you can't leave your child with any and anybody because they might not be there when you get back. When I say good paying job, I mean something paying over $16,000 and $17,000.[5]

The concerns about finding a babysitter and about the cost and access to public transportation to jobs in the suburbs deterred many residents from enrolling in the program. This explains why the first 15 women who participated in the initial round of the LJTP were unmarried and without children: they did not qualify for public assistance and, thus, had no choice but to look for employment.

MARKETING THE LJTP

> The Livelihood program includes the assignment of individual trainees to small peer groups after initial determination of eligibility employment screening.[6]

With a fanfare of music, food and promotional gifts, the program managers inaugurated the DHHS-funded LJTP to the Sun-Hope community. Residents in search of jobs for themselves or their relatives turned out to get information, and news about the LJTP also spread quickly by word of mouth beyond the community. People from outside the community—Moon Crescent and convicts in the DC half-way houses—came to enroll in the program.[7]

Virtually any tenant-focused program implemented in the Sun-Hope community drew tenants' attention when cash or gift incentives were advertised.[8] The promotion of the LJTP in Sun-Hope was no exception:

> The way the Livelihood each program was promoted was that [participants in the program] had $500.00 coming their way. Couple of the clients found out that wasn't exactly true. Other people came through here with their own agendas and could not see themselves

working within the setup. You see, we wanted an awful lot from the clients. We wanted them to commit to three pages of things on the application. "Yes, I will do that," "Yes I will do my budget," "Yes I will . . . report to my financial counselors."[9]

The program asked for each participant's commitment to refrain from crime and from using, selling, or associating with anyone involved with illegal narcotics.

The $500 incentive was real and useful to participants who wanted to acquire skills in masonry, machine tooling, or carpentry but who lacked the money to cover the cost of necessary tools, transportation, gloves and uniforms. LJTP promised to establish a bank account for each participant. As one of the LJTP manager stated:

These accounts are for use by participants for purposes related to attaining employment and/or training, i.e. union fees, transportation, tuition, child care, uniforms, physical exams. Other uses for these funds include emergencies. An intended outcome is to develop a good banking experience among participants.[10]

The participant could only withdraw funds to purchase items within the framework of the program, and with the authorization of a case manager. The program was designed with the expectation that as the participants completed their job training programs and became gainfully employed, they would repay the money borrowed from the account. The funds would then be used to support other participants enrolled in the program. Based on the results of their background assessments, some participants were encouraged to modify behavioral patterns that undermined their social and economic progress, and/or to acquire life skills essential to negotiating their way through mainstream society.

Although the LJTP was conceived as a job training and placement program, the managers knew that the program goals would not be achieved without individual and group counseling in life-skills. The core component of the LJTP, one staff member explained, was

a life assessment program. The way you live your life. Some people need to change the direction they are on, some people need a little bit of assistance, other people just need to be aware that there is something else [other life choices]. We don't try to make a decision for them of where they should go. The best example—and I point back to the finance—is if you smoke a carton of cigarettes a day, yeah it could be bad for your health, but I'm not going to say you can't do that. As long as you budget it in your budget for a carton of cigarettes a day, that's fine with me. I would discourage you from trying to smoke cigarettes. We will try to address that in one of the other facets of the program on health. But we don't try to make a moral or ethical decision on what you want to do. We try to advise you, and then you go from there.[11]

Every facet of the program was aimed at empowering participants to take control of their lives, take responsibility and remedy past actions thwarting their life improvements, and hopefully to be fully self-sufficient through gainful employment.

CREDIT AND FINANCIAL COUNSELING

An LJTP report to HUD revealed that over 56 percent (the total of "Fair" and "Poor" categories) of the program participants not only had credit problems, but had no regular sources of income to pay off their debts (Table 8.1). Because these individuals were unable to make the minimum monthly debt payments, the financial institutions had blocked their credit lines, and the individuals were being sought by debt collectors.[12]

TABLE 8.1
Participants' Credit Status

Categories	Number of Participants	Percentage
Good credit	5	5
No Credit experience	37	39
Fair Credit	36	38
Poor Credit	18	18
Total	96	100

One of the ironies of this data is that although some of the participants did not have bank accounts, they had credit lines with various financial institutions. One of the program managers stated in a quarterly report to DHHS:

Most of the participants never had a checking or savings account at a bank, savings and loan, or any established financial institution. Of the 96 participants, 39 had banking experience while 57 participants had no banking experience. Those without banking experience generally cashed checks at a liquor store, grocery store or a check cashing facility.[13]

For the group of the program's young women participants who received public assistance, having a bank account would have enabled them to conduct transactions at a lower cost than they incurred at check cashing outlets. Many of them, however, refused to open bank accounts for fear that social workers might learn about their other sources of income in addition to their public assistance.[14]

Of the participants with banking experience, eight had infractions such as bounced checks and uncovered overdrafts from previous accounts. In an effort to reconcile these participants with their former banks, the program managers negotiated with the banks to resolve those infractions:

[T]he financial counseling portion of the program . . . offers them a chance to keep their credit good if it is already good. If it was bad credit, [the goal was] to repair their credit and to get them on the track of thinking about more than just today and about getting further than just survival.[15]

The credit/financial counseling component of the LJTP attempted to assist participants to repair their credit, to budget their expenditures, to abide by their budget, and to practice living frugally. Although program managers were careful not to judge their spending habits, some of the participants found the process demanding. As one program manager explained:

With the finance, it was work. It was not passive, it was active. You prepared your budget and you worked on your credit. We put together how for you to do it, but unless they do it themselves they'll never learn how. So, it was work. It took a conscious effort on their part to complete the things that we proposed to them.[16]

Among the participants' responsibilities was tracking their daily expenditure:

With the financial training, we had a little card—the daily expense card. Now [with] the daily expense card what you're suppose to do is write [the amount] down whenever you spend any money. No matter what you spend it for, you're suppose to write down. Most people will tell you: "I know where I spent all my money." Ninety percent of the people we talk to will tell you that. But if you ask them: "tell me where you spent every dime," they are not able to. Now when these people sat down with this card and went through where they bought a candy bar, they bought cigarettes, they bought soda, they saw where their money was going. That ain't the way of changing their behavior, but it allows them to see where [their money] went. So if they make a conscious decision to change, they have the information. This program is not going to change anybody overnight, but if it can get someone into the long-run thinking about changing then that would be more of a success.[17]

To reinforce this "long-run thinking," the program managers invited financial experts to lead discussions and to answer participants' questions on subjects such as health insurance, life insurance, credit card applications, credit for apartment application, checking accounts, savings accounts, investment strategy, auto purchase/lease and financing of major purchases. All of these workshops combined to provide participants with a comprehensive financial education essential for participating in the mainstream social life.

NO QUICK SOLUTIONS

Because the credit/financial counseling required major behavioral modifications on the part of the participants, some of them (25 by the end of the program) dropped out of the program at various points. Those who stayed with the program benefitted from job referrals and placements. The majority of the participants who entered skills training or started their own small businesses utilized the $500 in their individual bank accounts. Unbeknown to the program managers, some of the participants, however, abused, misused, or stole the funds.

Although the funds in the individual bank accounts established for the participants could be drawn on with the approval and co-signature of program managers, the process was not foolproof. At a particular Riggs Bank, the staff were fully informed that LJTP accounts were to be co-signed by any of the three program managers. But after discovering that the restriction was unknown to other Riggs branches, seven participants withdrew all the funds through branches that were not informed about the program.[18] These participants were dismissed from the program, and the program managers were unsuccessful in recovering the money, as shown in Table 8.2.

TABLE 8.2
Outstanding Loans (November 1991)

	Amount	Number of Accounts	Percentage Outstanding
Total Current	250.00	2	20
Total Delinquent	6,540.14	20	64
Total Unauthorized	3,500.00	7	34
Total	10,290.14	29	100

The other participants who worked within the framework of the program and used the money as authorized, however, were not too eager to repay their debts, even though some of them were working and earning incomes. Based on participants' income or wages, the program managers designed a payment plan by which each participant was to repay the loan. At the closing of accounts in January, 1993, sixty participants had received a total of $30,000. Of this, $8,849.35 has been repaid: the program lost $21,150.65.

PUTTING PEOPLE TO WORK

Although the LJTP was, by design, intrusive, some of the participants were willing to subject themselves to its rigorous demands. The reasons are three-fold: first, LJTP was implemented in close proximity to their community; second, many of the participants, especially the men, felt more comfortable dealing with case managers who were not strangers to the community members; and third, the Livelihood Support Fund (revolving loan) was attractive to help participants wanting to overcome financial barriers.

The characteristics of a majority of the tenants who sought assistance through LJTP indicated the level of impoverishment in the community and the political disenfranchisement of many of the people. According to one program manager:

Most of them are in need of high school diplomas; most of them are not high school graduates. I think there is a literacy problem among a good number of them. We've been working with some of them on basic skills, reading, writing, but serious educational deficiency is there looking at the people that come through us. That is not to say that they are the majority of the people who are out here.[19]

Under severe recessionary economic conditions, even those with adequate education and skills do experience lay-offs and unemployment.[20] Economic recession is especially worse for those with deficient education and marketable skills. To help overcome this handicap, 33 (45 percent) of the participants requesting job training were evaluated and placed in a GED/Literacy program to acquire reading and/or writing skills as shown on Table 8.3.

TABLE 8.3
Participant Placement in the LJTP

Type of Training	No. of Participants	Percentage
Barber	1	1
Construction Skills	16	22
College Degrees	4	5
Computer Maintenance	3	4
Computer Skills	6	8
GED/Literacy	33	45
Hazardous Waste	2	3
High School Diploma	1	1
Secretarial Skills	5	7
Nursing/First Aid	3	4
Total	74	100

Because of inadequate education, a disproportionate number of the LJTP participants seeking employment found that they were only qualified for menial jobs that paid minimum wage (without benefits), and were likely to be the first laid off. Consequently, many of the LJTP participants not only experienced chronic joblessness, but whenever they had jobs, they are usually underpaid. Some people are undereducated, unskilled. They are left out by the government, left out by the politicians. There are a lot of the people who could do a whole lot more than they are doing. But because of their circumstances, they have a mind set that they've gotten into. They think they are not capable of doing anything, or don't know what they are able to do for themselves.[21]

This lack of aspiration is rooted in their education, lack of institutional resources and a vital social network into the public and private sectors.[22] As one LJTP staff member observed:

A lot of broken spirits come through that door. They are unemployed and they don't want to hear nothing else but they want a job. When they leave out of here we try to let them leave out of here with more than a job because it's going to take more than that to get them through.[23]

What the program manager referred to giving participants "more than a job" entailed:

Getting people ready for jobs, teaching people what they are suppose to do when they go to a job. We have some people that have never had a job; they have no idea what to do. No idea why it is important to be on time. No idea why it is important to show up everyday. Those are the things that we go through and teach people [to] . . . get them training to get a better job, and those types of activities.[24]

The types of activities also included: assisting participants in preparing resumes, training them in self-presentation and interviewing techniques, coaching them in proper workplace demeanor, vouching for participants who were late getting back to the half-way house, and tutoring some participants in reading skills to enable them to take tests. In total, the program participants were undergoing resocialization.

The type of training LJTP offered points to the dire conditions in which many of the young men and women lived:

[T]hey all come with the desire to work and to make some money which they place strong emphasis on, and in my opinion, that was just . . . a band-aid effect. The thing of it is that they don't have any income at all, and my job is to get them focused on career goals and I would do that along with trying to get them some kind of income to ease their immediate frustrations. But the thing that I do is to get them back to school, get them a job and get them back on some career plan or something like that.[25]

Given the desperate situation of some the participants, a few of the program managers found themselves providing assistance outside the boundaries of the program.[26] This included doing things such as: giving out-of-pocket money to participants to catch the bus to attend job interviews, driving some participants to the social security office to replace lost social security cards, and buying food for hungry and desperate men.

JOBS TRAINING AND EDUCATION HURDLES

The focus of the LJTP was to place individuals with at least a high school diploma in training programs to acquire or upgrade their marketable skills. There were some participants, however, who had no skills to upgrade or lacked the basic educational requirements for entry-level jobs. According to one of the program managers:

We have a lot of illiteracy. I'd say 20 percent are illiterate. They cannot read or write. And another 40 percent are functionally illiterate. If they try to read something, they won't get the expressed meaning out of it. And many of them are not high school graduates.[27]

This situation presented a dilemma for the program managers; without a high school diploma and a marketable skill, it was impossible to place an individual in job, and yet, frequently the individuals who came to the LJTP office expected a quick solution to their jobless situation. The program managers devised ways to assist this segment of participants whose backgrounds were inconsistent with LJTP's framework:

We recognize that first and foremost, people need income. They need to make money and that is why they come to us and they need a job. We don't do a formal assessment of basic skills, ability to read, and write and all that. *We do assessment of people's sort of natural ability. We suggest to everybody that you do have some capacity to do work, to do things, some ability.* Sometimes some natural things.

So we begin to look at their natural ability or inclination to do some type of work, and try to direct their search for jobs. Our assistance with their search for jobs is in the direction they are naturally inclined to go. . . . We start to direct them into job search in areas that will require the use of their hands . . . because what we've learned is that . . . you do better in something you have natural inclination to do. You will show up on time, you will show up period. And you are likely to last longer. And if it is something that totally goes against your natural grain, you're not likely to be there very long.[28]

Many of the participants had to choose between enrolling in jobs training programs—which meant deferred wages—and getting an entry level job to earn wages, even if for the short term. The dilemma some of the participants confronted was that even after attending a job training program for four to six weeks, they often found themselves in the same position as before the training: unable to secure steady employment.

The majority of the participants were placed in temporary and/or seasonal jobs such as construction laborers, janitors, stock clerks and movers. Moreover, many of these jobs lacked fringe benefits such as sick leave and health insurance and offered the participants little more than meager wages and some work experience.[29]

TABLE 8.4
Wages of LJTP Participants (1991-93)

Wage Ranges	No. of Participants	Percentages
$4.50–5.50	55	58
6.00–7.00	32	34
7.50–8.50	1	1
9.00–10.00	7	7
Total	95	100

With 92 percent of the LJTP participants (in Table 8.4) placed in entry-level employment earning between $4.50 and $7.00, the program managers continued to encourage participants to look beyond their immediate achievements and to aspire for careers of some kind:

So our thinking is not short term—just to get somebody a job,
because it is going to be just that—short term job. Even though entry
level jobs are not very high paying jobs, people are starting to
recognize what skills they do have and what it takes to get where they
want to be. We also deal with folks on the long term sense. What is it
really that you want to do? We had one guy say he wants to be a
lawyer. He had a couple of years of undergrad. He wants to be a
lawyer. Well, all we did was to look at where he is now, where he
wants to go, and map it out so he can see on paper clearly what it is
that he has to do to get where he wants to go.[30]

Further, as one program manager stated:

Now this program is not going to be around a long time forever and
ever to show people the push and pull. But what we want to try to do
is to show some people a map. Some people have not had that kind of
purpose, focus, life plan given to them, and their designs and their
goals. So we think nothing is too far-fetched. We are dealing with
people twenty years old, strong, healthy. You feel you want to own
your own company, and you're here and you want to get here. There
is a way to get there. We map that out. We also do that in terms of
time, how long it is going to take to get there, what kinds of moneys
is going to be needed, sources. Not just time needed, but in terms of
energy you need to devote to certain things. We just spend time doing
that. So [we are] looking at the long term plan, short term needs, and
the natural inclination to do things.[31]

Unfortunately, participants who found employments and began to
earn wages became complacent and stopped meeting with their jobs
counselors. Consequently, some of the participants thwarted their own
employment advancement and/or missed out on new job opportunities
as they become available through the LJTP office:

Education is one of the big things. Education on several phases.
Education for the level of job that they are applying for. Most of these
people are high school or less-than-high-school educated. Manual
labor positions are about the only things open to them. Jobs where . . .
they would have to have a lot of inner drive to succeed. Somebody
could go on as a plumber's helper at $5 an hour, learn to be a
plumber, join the union [and] become a plumber making $25 an hour.

But you have to have a lot of drive to do that. A lot of these guys are bringing home $175 a week. This is the life. "I've never made that much in my life." And for them to look beyond that . . . "I'm making $7 an hour." But they fail to realize they are on a bubble, too. Construction project [is over] quick, and they are back to zero.[32]

As much as the program managers did all the could to assist the neighborhood residents find and keep jobs, their efforts were doomed to the extent that wage and temporary labor were seasonal and few, and competition for them was stiff.

COMMUNITY-INDIVIDUAL EMPOWERMENT THROUGH THE LJTP

Livelihood Program is a large effort to empower residents—or at least that is how I've understood it—and the idea being to move people toward self-help and self-sufficiency.[33]

The PA staff viewed the LJTP as the heart of the community empowerment—the process of providing needy people with the tools necessary to enable them to move from the margins into the mainstream political, economic and social life of the society.

We have motivational speakers come in. It's a whole array of things. We have assessment. That's new for some people who have never been exposed to it. And we are a fairly new program; we've been around three months. We took in about 102 applications and we have 47 participants active. We also have group discussions where we talk about political issues, different topics that the members, or participants, are interested in. And they have assignments on a weekly basis that they bring back. It's very interesting. It's one of the few programs to just take off on-site of the complex.[34]

The group discussions, or "rap sessions" as some called them, enabled many of the participants to articulate some of the predicaments facing their community, their personal lives and their plans of action to deal with these predicaments.

One of the collective accomplishments of the group was getting the District of Columbia Department of Recreation to revitalize the abandoned playground in the community located near J.F.K.

Elementary School. The significance of this task for the group was that, by making the playground a concern that deserved community attention, they were then faced with finding out which city administrations were responsible for maintaining the playground. They searched for the addresses and telephone numbers of the District government agencies responsible, wrote letters to the division heads, and sent copies of the letters to their councilmember and their neighborhood's Advisory Neighborhood Commissioner.[35] The D.C. Department of Recreation and the Department of Public Works responded to the group's request and restored the playground for the neighborhood children. This process was both a learning and an empowering endeavor for the participants; they learned that ordinary people like themselves could effect change if they organized.

The idea of community empowerment was also consistent with the concept of cooperative homeownership. Tenants empowered by the LJTP, program designers surmised, would consequently become more productive citizens, and consider the merits of cooperative homeownership. In fact, it is more realistic to educate people about homeownership when they have regular jobs and earn incomes. A long-time tenant and LJTP case manager, who later became the president of the Cooperative, stated:

> Empowerment is getting people, hopefully, to work toward the same goal. To be committed, hopefully, make [Hope Mansions] a better place to live. We don't have any place else to live. So, this is our home until we move up and leave it. Getting that common goal in sight is what we are about.[36]

While community empowerment and individual self-help are rewarding to participants, the process is demanding. The irony, however, is that the people most likely to be attracted are the ones who have considerable employment history, the confidence to face the imminent challenges in the labor market and who are looking to upgrade their skills, or to switch to better paying jobs. This group of residents tends to approach the tenant-oriented programs with the commitment required of them. The program, however, was not targeted for this group.

While the LJTP's aim was to help tenants find employment, many of the tenants enrolled in the program expected the process to be simpler than it was. Many of the participants, however, found themselves being advised by the program managers to make drastic or moderate modifications in their individual behavioral patterns. The fact that program managers made no promises that participants were assured employment deterred some participants from investing their energies in the training program.

(OVERCOMING) EXTERNAL BARRIERS TO HELPING THOSE IN NEED

As I have mentioned in chapter 7, in collaboration with the tenants cooperative, the LJTP managers had the best intentions to assist many of the disenfranchised residents in the Sun-Hope community. But the managers had to overcome several problems, such as the institutionalized labor unions that controlled access to certain jobs, subcontractors failing to hire neighborhood residents as laborers, and ensuring that tenant-own construction-related businesses got bids to perform jobs in the community. In a status report to DHHS, the PA director lamented that six months after the LJTP was initiated:

> On-site hires of residents in construction, management and human services jobs have not been realized to the extent proposed for several reasons. . . . To date, only 25 of the proposed 102 placements were made on-site in construction and one in management. These jobs were for unskilled laborers and came available during the project period of the high turnover in this type of work. The low skills levels of resident participants, with the exception of one carpenter, contributed to the program's inability to place them in any higher-skilled jobs that may have come available.[37]

The unionization of the construction project, in particular, presented a double bind to some of the LJTP participants. On the one hand, unionized jobs are controlled by the labor unions which control the hiring of prospective applicants. On the other hand, to maintain an army of unionized workers, the union stewards ensured that all prospective employees were dues-paying members of a local union or would become one upon employment. This meant that individuals unable to afford the initial membership dues of $350.00 could not gain employment unless they signed a letter-of-intent to have a portion of their wages paid directly to the unions towards their dues. Union jobs, however, offered higher wages, benefits and apprenticeship opportunities. Drawing on their Livelihood Start-up Loans, a few of the participants were able to pay their union dues in order to take entry-level jobs as laborers.

Having secured the jobs for some LJTP participants, program managers had to deal with another hurdle. The LJTP workers, now union workers, had their hopes dashed upon discovering that the skill-upgrading and apprenticeship training opportunities available to them through the Laborers' Union were limited in scope. They offered general, rather than job-specific, training. This was problematic to both LJTP participants and managers, because without job-specific training the participants would have no specialized skills to keep their services in demand:

> Skill upgrading and apprenticeship training opportunities have been made available to all on-site workers through their respective union affiliations, however most program workers have not taken full advantage of this union benefit. Since nearly all the Livelihood Program participants on site are laborers, their affiliation is with the Laborer's Local #74. This union offers on-going training in general construction to its members. For trade specific (i.e. carpentry, electrical, plumbing) apprenticeship training, a worker must be affiliated with that respective union. Attempts were made by program staff to place some of these workers in entry-level jobs whose titles (i.e. plumber's helper, carpenter's helper) would allow them to join trade specific unions and thus have access to apprenticeship opportunities in those trades. However, only two contractors on sight [sic] had been responsive to hiring participants and they hired only laborers, with the exception of one skilled carpenter hired.[38]

In general, the on-site contractors were reluctant to hire residents seeking employment. This situation illustrates only one of the many external barriers to securing gainful employment for program participants.

The effort to get LJTP participants employed by Shelter Incorporated and various subcontractors renovating the community was not without additional difficulties. Initially the various companies which were subcontracted to renovate the community were not contractually bound to hire any of the community's people. This led to a confrontation between the LJTP managers and the Shelter field staff. In a memorandum to the PA executive director, one of the LJTP managers suggested the need for "increased oversight and the implementation of measures by PA to correct these shortcomings." She suggested, among others, these ideas for the placement of program participants:

> Any new contract for work [should] . . . include a provision requiring employers to hire [Hope] residents and neighbors through the Livelihood Program. Such a provision should be written by [Shelter] in cooperation with [PA] and included immediately. Contractors with pre-existing contracts must be strongly encouraged to hire [Hope] residents through the Livelihood Program.[39]

The frustrations experienced by the LJTP managers to place tenants in jobs in their own neighborhood was also shared by participants and other residents. From many residents' perspective, the refusal of the construction companies to hire the community's jobless highlighted enduring racial discrimination. Racial discrimination, however, was not the main reason for the construction companies' failure to hire tenants seeking jobs.

The "reason for the slow hires," stated the author of LJTP status report, "was the unionization of the construction project. Union requirements eliminated the hiring of non-union workers":[40]

> [S]ince financing for the rehabilitation of the entire project came largely from the AFL-CIO [American Federation of Labor - Congress of Industrial Organization] Investment Trust, negotiations were lengthy to remove union requirements from this part [the construction of the Community Center] of the construction, which is partly funded by HHS under this grant. The purpose for creating a non-union environment in the construction of this space is to relax hiring and other restrictions in order to attract small minority contractors, like [Hope] Builders, Inc. and [Hope] Cleaning, new resident-owned companies being assisted and nurtured under this partnership.[41]

Herein lies the dilemma. The AFL-CIO's central mission is to assist working people in getting reasonable wages from their unionized jobs while protecting them from capitalist exploitation. It is within the spirit of assisting working people that the AFL-CIO responded to Shelter's call for financial investment in the rehabilitation of Hope Mansions. Consequently, the construction companies and workers rehabilitating

Hope Mansions were unionized by the AFL-CIO to ensure that non-unionized companies and workers did not get subcontracts or jobs in the area. This interlocking organizational interest inadvertently locked out the unemployed residents of Sun-Hope and neighboring communities. This situation generated antagonism between the Hope Mansions Cooperative board members and Shelter president, Gail Peterson.

In an attempt to resolve this dilemma to facilitate the placement of program participants in on-site employment, one of the LJTP managers asked that not only must any new contract for work include a provision requiring employees to hire Hope residents, but Shelter Incorporated should

> provide [PA] with all contractors' weekly payroll listing all workers' name, address, position, length of employment, union affiliation and salary on a weekly basis.
>
> Solicitation for bids for work [should] . . . be made in the environments that will illicit responses by minority and Washington, D.C.-based contractors. These solicitation must be made available to [PA] prior to publicizing. Also, [PA] will reserve the right to announce or make public these solicitations.
>
> [Shelter should] provide [PA] with the hiring needs of [JC Management], the on-site property management company. All solicitations for employment or sub-contractual work with property management must be provided to [PA] prior to publication. [Shelter] must encourage the hiring of residents in property management positions.[42]

The LJTP managers' persistence to make Shelter Incorporated live up to its obligation paid off: the subcontractors, including three tenant-owned and operated ones, provided job opportunities to the community's underemployed and unemployed. In a 1993 report to the DHHS Office of Community Services, the author summarized LJTP's achievements as follows:

> 96 persons have been enrolled in the project (94% of the proposed 102)
>
> 74 have been placed in jobs (19 of which have had 2 placements and 2 have had 3 placements for a total of 97 job opportunities provided).

60 participated in, were offered or referred to, job skills training programs. On-site construction workers were offered construction skills training through their unions.[43]

THE IMPACT OF THE LJTP

A success is having someone come in here and totally change their ways. That would be the ideal. But if we can just get them to think about what they are doing, then we are doing alright.[44]

Although the LJTP was in existence for less than 18 months, it became one of the major institutions in the community. In fact, many households knew more about the LJTP and the names of staff members than they knew about the Hope Mansions Cooperative. Known to community members simply as "Livelihood," the program staff members not only assisted tenants with finding job opportunities, but aided some residents in managing their private lives. Among the letters of appreciation sent to the staff by participants, the most eloquent one summarized the program's impact on the community:

There are many nuances of Livelihood that impress me, but first and foremost I appreciate the programs proximity to those it was designed to serve. This accessibility, in conjunction with the staff's patience, tenacity and genuine concern has proven to be the impetus for success. I (like most young Black males in my community) seem forever entrenched in the insidious and destructive subculture that plagues every urban city in these United States. As a consequence I have wasted far too many years of my life in prison. With the help of Livelihood I have begun to redefine my values and to revamp my ideas and ideals. The Livelihood Program facilitates growth and has surely been a cornerstone in my life. I see an acute change for the better in my overall demeanor, the way I perceive myself and in relation to my outlook on life.[45]

That this man was able to express the impact of the LJTP on his life had to do with the fact he took remedial reading and writing courses while in prison. With his perseverance and willingness to commit to the program's objectives, the LJTP managers facilitated his transition into the labor market.

Another participant stated:

> The Livelihood program has been very helpful to me because of the
> group session held on apprenticeship training, getting a job, budget
> and finance, behavior and attitude. Also the staff workers were very
> pleasant, good listeners and always eager to help anyone.[46]

Despite the accolades about the LJTP, the program managers could
not help everyone who came to consult them about career initiatives.
These individuals filled out application forms but were unwilling to
subject themselves to the program routines to put them on a path out of
underemployment and joblessness:

> We were here to address certain problems such as self-esteem and
> types like that. There were some people we couldn't reach. Maybe
> they've been pushed too far, the prison system has a bit to do with
> many of our clients. Not knowing since they've been out [of the
> prison system], I know it's done some damage to them. That's a
> damage we cannot fully assess and determine and create the
> appropriate program to help them.[47]

Other participants who came to the program managers and
enthusiastically filled out their application forms felt that too much was
being demanded of them:

> In line with their livelihood—the financial counseling, your peers, the
> people you want to be around with, things you want to change within
> your life to make a better life for yourself. All of those things are
> [required] in the application. So some people out of fear of change,
> said: "No this is not for me" . . . Some of the people came here with
> an agenda to get the $500 and skip out. But they filled out the forms
> and never come back. It was a too slow of a process. Livelihood is a
> process, so this part of the process they did not want to fulfill. They
> were not ready to fulfill.[48]

Although some of the participants "were ready to fulfill"
requirements necessary to lead to employment, they were, however,
faced with structural obstructions. Stigmatized by their criminal
records, some of the program participants experienced persistent

rejections for employment. As one program manager explained in regards to an ex-convict filling out a job application:

> [T]he system doesn't really allow them to come back to society without all those marks on. . . . "Have you ever been incarcerated"? "Yeah." "For what?" "Well I don't know if we want to hire you". . . . So all they sell is drugs, drugs. They may get a pinch of no more than a nickel on them, but all they get to sell is drugs most of them. You see, drug is the big scare word.[49]

For many of these young men, the path to the mainstream labor market was marked by obstructions; their criminal records thwarted their chances of getting a job:

> Most of the men have had some run-in with the law. They have been in jail, on probation, on parole, in half-way houses. Without skills. Ninety percent of the people are without skills. Most of the people, if trained properly, could perform well. If given the skills they can perform.[50]

This explains why many of the young men in the community continued to be trapped in conditions of underemployment and unemployment and invariably operated an "underground system" of illegal activities. As one of the program managers lamented,

> First of all, he is back [from prison or jail] being taken care of by somebody. It could be being taken care of by the state [parole officer], by the parents, girlfriend, you know, so he is moving from one state [of dependency] to the other. He is denied the access to the areas [employment, jobs training] where he can start to stand on his own. So to protect his own self-worth, he becomes the baddest of who ever he could be.[51]

Not all the residents who consulted the LJTP staff members for jobs were ex-convicts. Other participants understood their impoverishment in terms of fate. According one of the project managers:

> There are the people who have decided that they have been dealt a hand, that that's the only hand they can play, and that this is their

lives. They've been dealt a hand that says, "I'm to be poor, I'm to be struggling for income, struggling for standards. This is all I am worthy of in life, and I can't change it."[52]

This self-deprecating attitude is fostered under conditions of prolonged periods of economic impoverishment and political disenfranchisement. The prolonged conditions of community decline, underemployment, and frequent failures in finding jobs had eroded some residents' aspirations. As one tenant explained the situation: "Sometimes you just be down so long until you end up lacking confidence in yourself."[53] The lack of confidence further eroded the individual's aspirations:

> There seems to be a lack of hope or a lack of education here. There is a lack of self. I don't want to say morals . . . but standards. There are no standards here to be met. People don't look at any standards to be met. I find it interesting that an awful lot of the men still live with their mothers. They depend on their mothers for support.[54]

In situations where they *were* placed in jobs, these individuals frequently quit in a matter of days because they defined any reprimand as an affront to their dignity:

> Another point on the education, is the education of how to perform in a job. How to be in a work environment. Many people do not know how to be in a work environment. You can't just stop and smoke a cigarette when you want to. The Man is paying you to work; he wants to see you work. Breaktime, you can break at lunch. So we have guys who come in here and say they quit their jobs because the boss talked down to them for being five minutes late to work, or they felt disrespected.[55]

As essential as low paying jobs are to making an entry into the mainstream economy, they can also be a source of discouragement. For disadvantaged people working at minimum-wage jobs in which they are considered insignificant, unappreciated, and dispensable, the workplace becomes an arena of frustration and degradation.

SUMMARY

This chapter focused on the process of community empowerment through a jobs training and placement program. This was the single most important effort to address the economic handicaps of individuals and families living in Sun-Hope neighborhood. Central to empowering the members of the community was the effort to get willing residents trained and placed in jobs. The LJTP managers and many of the participants were beset by dilemmas. The primary target group—AFDC recipients who signed up—were discouraged by the cost of foregoing their welfare benefits (Medicaid, food stamps and rent subsidy) for a low-wage job without benefits. For these women, the fear of being free of public aid was real when they considered their potential expenditures in rent, utilities, health insurance and transportation, to name a few. The kinds of jobs available to persons without adequate education and marketable skills offered little in occupational mobility. There is a widely shared view among conservative theorists and policy-makers that urban ghetto blacks experience persistent poverty because they are lazy—or have made lazy by being the welfare dole for so long—and lack the protestant work ethic. Not only do the poor shun manual labor, but perceive such jobs as degrading. Although there were some residents who were known to program managers to be lazy, the majority of the participants were determined to find jobs which would enable them to become self-sufficient.

The majority of the participants who came to the LJTP, who either registered and dropped out later on or followed through and found jobs, were least concerned with the type of jobs offered them. The foremost concern of all the participants were the meager wages. Unskilled and poorly educated, they were relegated to jobs at the lower tier of the segmented labor market where employment was seasonal and infrequent, where workers were not only disrepected but disposable, and wages were not only low but near subsistence level. Meaningful and gainful employment remains the most important means by which people organize their lives, but without sufficient disposable wages, it is nothing short of exploitation to persuade the poor that work is a socially worthwhile endeavor.

The duration of the job was also another concern. There persistent problem facing the LJTP participants was finding and keeping a job after the job training. Although the LJTP placement managers assisted some in finding jobs, the majority of them were seasonal or temporary.

For women on welfare, this situation was discouraging. Other participants, however, were hamstrung in getting jobs because they were stigmatized by their criminal histories. Although many LJTP participants were enthusiastic about finding blue collar employments, they were constrained or obstructed by institutional "gatekeepers" from getting the kinds of jobs which would have led them out of marginalization, as these testimonies have shown. Critical to understanding the problem of chronic or sporadic unemployment, but missing in the discourse on welfare dependency and the culture of poverty, are the disincentives and the indignities that labor market presents to the poor and marginalized.

NOTES

1. Alice Sand, LJTP manager, personal interview, 9 March 1992.
2. Former staff member, personal interview, 11 March 1992.
3. Alice Sand, LJTP manager, personal interview, 9 March 1992.
4. Field notes, 14 November 1991.
5. *Focus Group*, May 1987, 14. For a detailed case of the difficulties determined poor women face in getting and holding jobs, see Barbara Vobejda, "No Exit: In an Isolated Urban Ghettos, a Better Life Seems a World Away," *The Washington Post National Weekly Edition*, 15-21 March 1993, 6-7.
6. PA Quarterly Report No. 1, (for period 10/1/90 through 12/30/09) to the Department of Health and Human Services (DHHS) Grant No. 90-1-HB-DC-002.
7. The unemployment rate in the District was 6.6 percent (20,000 residents) in 1990. But the unemployment rate in Ward 7 was 8.8% (3,100), the second highest in the city. See *Indices: A Statistical Index to District of Columbia Services*, August, 1991.
8. For almost three years, I was tasked with implementing Washington Gas-funded Energy Conservation Training and Weatherization Program. These services were aimed to educate residents about energy-dollar savings techniques and provide a household energy audit followed by weatherization of their apartment units. All of these services were being provided free of charge. This, however, did not attract the residents to the program until I decided to give out ten dollars cash incentive, a T-Shirt and serve food to household participants attending the training session. The training sessions were held on the premises at the Community Center on Saturday mornings. Although two tenants were hired to go door-to-door signing up tenants for training sessions, the household participation rate was 70 percent. Another problem was that,

once tenants participated in the training sessions and received the ten dollars, many of them refused to continue the program: they were not interested in having their apartment units audited and weatherized although many of them complained of not being able to pay for their utility bills.

9.   Tenant and LJTP staff, personal interview, 16 June 1992.

10.   PA internal memo, "Participant Accounts - Cycle I Closeout," 12 November 1991.

11.   James Park, LJTP manager, personal interview, 13 February 1992.

12.   Debt collectors usually have a hard time finding these debtors because many of them do not have a fixed addresses. But unless these people paid their debts voluntarily, some of them would not be able to request gas, electric and telephone services.

13.   PA Quarterly Report No. 6, (for period 1/1/92 through 3/31/92) on DHHS Grant No. 90-1-HB-DC-002. In many low-income neighborhoods around the city, the absence of banks has resulted in the emergence of check-cashing business places where the poor redeem their checks for hard cash. The redemption fee for cashing one's paycheck or public assistance checks (eg. AFDC) ranges from between 1 and 3 percent of the cash value of the check. See Ruth M. Bond, "Poor People's Money," *The Washington City Paper*, February 1994, 21-27.

14.   Throughout the course of my field research, I had the opportunity of directing Washington Gas Company's energy conservation training program in Hope Mansions. Having been promised ten dollars cash incentive, many of the tenant-participants (who were on Section 8 rent subsidies) wanted to know if I would be reporting their names to management—because it might have meant an increment in their rent. A few of the women I hired to distribute literature about the program asked if they could be paid in cash for their services, and some of them pleaded with me not to report their earnings to the Internal Revenue Services or management.

15.   James Park, LJTP manager, personal interview, 13 February 1992.

16.   Tenant and the LJTP staff, personal interview, 16 June 1992.

17.   James Park, LJTP manager, personal interview, 13 February 1992.

18.   In one instance, two program managers caught up with a dismissed participant in an attempt to get him to repay his loan. He threatened to kill both men should they come to his temporary church-basement residence again.

19.   Alice Sand, LJTP manager, personal interview, 9 March 1992.

20.   For an analysis of the impact of the recent economic recession on the middle class, see Claire Safran. "The New Faces of Poverty," *Redbook* (August 1992): 84-87.

21.   James Park, LJTP manager, personal interview, 13 February 1992.

22. Notable among authors who argue that low-income communities do maintain a viable social network is Carol Stack's *All Our Kin: Strategies for Survival in a Black Community.* (New York: Harper & Row, 1974). As essential as these networks are in low-income communities, they are limited in scope. Without a network into the mainstream economy, many low-income people in the ghetto would not be able to find jobs.

23. Tenant and LJTP staff, personal interview, 16 June 1992.

24. James Park, LJTP manager, personal interview, 13 February 1992.

25. Jack Jackson, LJTP job placement officer, personal interview, 20 October 1995.

26. One of the program managers drew unnecessary attention from a law enforcement agency in Maryland after allowing one participant to use his home address to get a drivers' license. The participant, program managers discovered later, was a fugitive being sought after by the Federal Bureau of Investigation (FBI).

27. James Park, LJTP manager, personal interview, 13 February 1992.

28. Alice Sand, LJTP manager, personal interview, 19 March 1992.

29. Since the termination of the LJTP in October 1992, the PA has not made any effort to find out how many of the participants are still employed or unemployed.

30. Alice Sand, Program Manager, personal interview, 19 March 1992.

31. Ibid.

32. James Park, LJTP manager, personal interview, 13 February 1992.

33. Tenant and LJTP staff member, personal interview, 19 March 1992.

34. Ibid.

35. "In accordance with the *District of Columbia Self-Government and Government Reorganization Act of 1973*, there are 37 advisory neighborhood commission (ANC) areas, established by the council and subdivided into 323 single-member districts. The function of the ANCs is to advise the District government on matters of public policy and to review and make recommendations concerning zoning changes, variances, public improvements, licenses and permits of significance to neighborhood planning and development" (*Indices*, August, 1991. Washington, D.C.)

36. Tenant and LJTP staff member, personal interview, 19 March 1992.

37. Joseph Sanford, PA Executive Director, The LJTP Status Report to Eunice Thomas, Director, Office of Community Services, Department of Health and Human Services, Washington, D.C. January 19, 1992.

38. Ibid.

39. Alice Sand, LJTP Manager, "HHS Project Status and Recommendations," to Joseph Sanford, May 1992.

40. Ibid., 2.

41. Status report to Eunice Thomas, Director, Office of Community Services, Department of Health and Human Services (DHSS) about Livelihood Program. DHHS Grant No. 90-1-HB-DC-002.

42. Alice Sanford, LJTP Manager, "HHS Project Status and Recommendations," to Joseph Sanford, May 1992.

43. Status report to Eunice Thomas, Director, Office of Community Services, DHHS. DHHS Grant No. 90-1-HB-DC-002.

44. James Park, LJTP manager, personal interview, 13 February 1992.

45. A participant's letter to LJTP managers, 20 July 1992.

46. Tenant, letter, 28 March 1993.

47. James Park, LJTP manager, personal interview, 13 February 1992.

48. Tenant and LJTP manager, personal interview, 16 June 1992.

49. James Park, LJTP manager, personal interview, 13 February, 1992.

50. Ibid.

51. Ibid.

52. Alice Sand, LJTP manager, personal interview, 9 March 1992.

53. *Focus Group*, May 1987, 15.

54. Jack Jackson, LJTP placement manager, personal interview, 20 October 1992.

55. James Park, LJTP manager, personal interview, 13 February 1992.

CHAPTER 9

Conclusion

FINDINGS

In this final chapter, I review the study's major observations and highlight some of the conclusions about the various forces shaping the emergence and the perpetuation of the urban black ghetto and its prospects for improvement. In the introduction, I stated that the focus of the study was to comprehend the dynamic micro-macro relations played out in the lives of urban ghetto residents and their struggle to maintain a neighborhood-community. By studying the urban neighborhood ghetto, we gain a better understanding of the sources of the problems facing the residents and the strategies they, using extant resources, adopt to deal with the problems. This approach is important because it is at the community level where we gain insights into the effects of economic trends and local and national policies on the lives of individuals and into the prospects of improving people's lives.

Sociologically, the explanations for the poverty of the urban black ghetto are wide-ranging. The three dominant perspectives include: institutional racism, the culture of poverty and political economy. First, in the 1940s, scholars including Gunnar Myrdal and host of liberal authors proposed that prejudice and institutional racism were the roots of social class inequality.[1] Second, in the post-1960s, conservative scholars misappropriated Oscar Lewis' conception of the culture of poverty, generating a body of work premised on the passivity and lack of a protestant work ethic circumscribing ghetto blacks' relationship to an environment of indigence, crime and various aberrant behaviors.[2] Third, contemporary scholars have reexamined the context of urban

poverty and have found that there is not one single foundation upon
which it rests: instead, a broader, complicated socioeconomic and
political environment perpetuates poverty despite efforts (myriad
programs operated by public and nonprofit agencies) to confront it. A
closer examination of this century's earlier theories will reveal this
complexity.[3]

As revealed by Gunnar Myrdal's 1945 book, since the 1940s, there
has been a longstanding view that the urban black ghetto situation is a
product of structural and institutional practices guided by ideological
beliefs of racism. His work focused on the dilemma between the
ideology of social equality and the reality of pervasive racism, where
"group prejudice against particular persons or types of people
dominated [the individual's] outlook."[4] More specifically, the
contradiction between institutional racism (racial discrimination and
segregation) and the ideology of social equality (equal opportunity) not
only shaped black-white relations; it impinged on the different
opportunities available to middle- and lower-class blacks as well.
However, there is ample evidence of marked improvement in the lives
of African Americans since Myrdal wrote *The American Dilemma*.
Noticeable are the growing population of the black middle-class, their
structural assimilation through colleges and universities, their
occupational mobility, and their access to residential areas previously
closed to them.

In contrast, the cultural and structural assimilation of some
generations of lower-class blacks into mainstream American society is
occurring at a snail's pace. What data shows in this book is that the
contemporary urban black ghetto situation is attributable not to blatant
racism and discrimination *per se* or to psychological and cultural
pathologies specific to poor blacks, but significantly, to factors endemic
to the market society, as an examination of the culture of poverty
within a socioeconomic context will reveal.[5] The historical evidence for
this view lies in the situation of blacks during and after World War II.
The War engendered an industrial boom, and because of the need for all
kinds of labor for decent wages, cultures of poverty and economically
marginalized black neighborhoods in northern cities were not
geographically isolated from the mainstream political economy.
Segregated but mixed-income urban black communities were stable
largely because a disproportionate number of the people were employed
with steady income. Even with minimum wages, household heads were
able to maintain their families. The culture of poverty proponents,

unwilling to take into account the significance of economic shifts, their varying effects on diverse socioeconomic groups, and the disincentives the labor market now presents to the poor, have overlooked the fact that it was only when employment started disappearing and the middle class started exiting the cities, that the seeds of the supposed culture of poverty germinated in the ghettos. Thus the culture of poverty, specific to urban American, is a product of the dominant market culture. Driven by profit motives, the market culture (which engendered the urban ghetto through redlining, blockbusting, and steering and fostered marginalization through structural, seasonal and geographic unemployment of the unskilled) ensured *de facto* housing segregation and the widening income gap between the rich and poor.

Thus, the history of the ghetto since World War II shows that the culture of poverty provides an inadequate or incomplete explanation of urban decay. In fact, the proponents' theory that poor blacks lack a work ethic and fail to confront problems actively simply are untrue or at least simplistic. Specifically, these assertions have been challenged by the Sun-Hope's community-conscious residents' pursuit of a cooperative, by the hiring of the Fruit of Islam (FOI) to rid the neighborhood of crime and by the residents' desire for education and steady work. In other words, poverty is not endemic because of the characteristics of the individuals; it is a product of the environmental factors, including declining employment opportunities, *de facto* racial and class segregation and undereducation. Poverty is the *effect* of these forces on the disadvantaged, but it is the composite reaction to poverty—lawlessness, drug dealing, violence, out-of-wedlock pregnancies, broken families, apathy, hopelessness, and nihilism—that the conservatives fallaciously employ to explain *causes* of the culture of poverty.

In addition to the disappearance of low-skilled employment, the pre-Civil Rights (Act of 1964) years of *de jure* racial segregation gave rise to, and sustained, the urban ghetto. These days, the ghetto is sustained by *de facto* segregation which is driven by the structure and process of our market society, specifically, by the profit-driven real estate market, the disappearance of private and public labor markets previously accessible to low-skilled workers, and the shrinking poverty-level wages for the surplus labor competing for unstable, seasonal and part-time jobs.[6] Although all are influenced by the market society, its adverse multiplier effects impinge on the ghetto poor most severely, as through the housing gap, the shrinking low-skilled job market, the destabilization and concentration of the poor, and the drug dealers who are attracted to neighborhoods of poor people, until finally, poverty undermines the community's will to form or maintain mediating institutions.

In contrast to the theory of the culture of poverty, an analysis of the market culture offers insight into residents' attempts to change their environment and explanations of why those efforts may fail. Like many urban communities, Sun-Hope residents attempted to improve their neighborhood infrastructure and organization, to challenge the drug trade, to form a cooperative, and to secure job training and employment. Their efforts, to which I will return, have been thwarted not by laziness or passivity, but by the market culture in which individuals lacking education, skills, political and economic networks are marginalized and devalued. In particular, undereducation and a scarcity of jobs offering substantive pay create an environment in which poverty remains chronic among the market society's lowest stratum, a group already troubled by its increasing socioeconomic and geographic distance from middle-class America and its driving institutions.

The ghetto persists in many urban areas largely as a result of the "housing gap" (the proportion of low-income household renters being greater than the number of affordable and available low-rental units). Thus, upwardly mobile households fleeing mixed-income and exclusively black neighborhoods are more likely to be replaced by poorer families.[7] Between 1980 and 1990, all the various Washington, D.C. Wards having the largest concentration of blacks recorded the largest decline in the population of modest income-earning households. The single largest exodus occurred in Ward 7, where Sun-Hope is located: an estimated 13,000 people left the area within a decade.[8] The housing gap, by default, steers poor urban families into the few, densely-populated subsidized and public housing areas, where they become racially isolated and economically marginalized. In view of this, Massey and Denton noted that unlike any other ethnic group, "only blacks must attempt their escape [from poverty] within highly segregated, racially segmented housing market."[9]

Escaping poverty, however, requires that one find employment locally, move to where employments open up, or find jobs in areas accessible by affordable transportation. For the urban poor, these options are not readily available. As Andrew Hacker noted, "[a] real obstacle to workforce equity stems from the difficulties blacks have in finding housing in areas where jobs open up."[10] Residing in public and subsidized housing distances away from areas of employment opportunities, undereducated and unskilled blacks find their prospects for upward mobility a daunting task.[11] Unlike many cities, Washington, D.C. has had no industry, its segmented service businesses have dwindled and its construction-related jobs have been limited.[12] And where available, these jobs are often unionized and access to nonmembers is denied. Moreover, even with some job training and job placement for the poor, entry-level employment wages are most often insufficient to support a household. In view of this, a welfare-dependent family in which the household head opts to become wage-reliant stands to lose essential benefits and will face severe hardships sooner or later. The aggregation of these experiences not only perpetuates indigence and hopelessness in the ghetto, but severely thwarts the efforts at forming and strengthening local institutions and civil society. Thus, the social history of Sun-Hope neighborhood over the past forty years is implicated in the advance of market society and its consequences for the urban poor black situation.

THE DILEMMA OF RACE, CLASS AND NEIGHBORHOOD ISOLATION IN A MARKET SOCIETY

Constructed out of *de jure* segregation, the urban ghetto did not wither away upon the advent of *de jure* desegregation. Increasingly and intensively, the market society, organized by various influential interest groups, has become the sorting mechanism by which households escape or remain in the ghetto. Because it is the degree of participation in the market society that makes family asset accumulation and investment possible (or impossible), the market culture invariably shapes the life-chances of families. In 1990 the demographic data revealed the disparity between rich and poor in the District of Columbia to be the largest in comparison to all fifty states. "The average income of the bottom fifth of families in the District was $5,293 a year, while the top fifth made $149,508."[13]

The destabilization trend dating back to the 1970s caused by the middle-class exodus rendered Sun-Hope neighborhood a ghetto—a neighborhood of predominantly one ethnic group with the majority living below the poverty line, experiencing seemingly intractable social problems. Nation-wide, this type of concentration and segregation of impoverished African Americans in housing projects has a tremendous effect on how landlords maintain their property and treat tenants. As the income-reliant tenants move out and increasing number of poor tenants default on their rents, landlords, in turn, disinvest, letting the property decline and decay. In Sun-Hope, the Faith Christ Church's disinvestment in the property engendered an environment of general disorder, lawlessness and criminal enterprises.

As the neighborhood's history reveals, in a market culture, not only are the unskilled and inadequately educated most vulnerable to economic uncertainties, but they have the fewest institutional alternatives by which to pursue culturally legitimate avenues of success. Essentially, the concentration of impoverished tenants in the Sun-Hope neighborhood led to its vulnerability to the drug trade and associated intraclass antagonism. In the early 1980s, the conditions of decay and decline in the Sun-Hope neighborhood attracted gangs of drug dealers. The ghetto, with its predominantly jobless youth and young adults, poor and broken families, provided a labor force desperate for the opportunity to make money and suited the out-of-state drug dealers' need. Faced with extant resources and constrained by inadequate education, lacking marketable skills and experiencing chronic joblessness, some adults—and in some cases whole families— were lured into the drug trade by drug syndicates. For instance, a 1986 survey of Hope Mansions showed that 80 percent of the 152 households reported incomes between $6,000 and $12,000 per year, and 45 percent reported their main source of income as Aid to Families with Dependent Children (AFDC). No able-bodied adults held employment in 35 percent of the households.

The drug dealers, armed with money and other symbols of success, enticed vulnerable youth and welfare-dependent single parents. These parents sublet rooms in their apartments from which drug dealers conducted their illicit trade. The drug trade, in turn, engendered violence and homicide, as drug dealers battled for turf within the neighborhood. The violent and disparaging behaviors of some tenants and out-of-state incomers linked to the drug trade begot fear, distrust and incivility among ordinary residents. Having coopted some of the residents, the drug dealers succeeded in creating an environment where ordinary residents were apprehensive about discussing openly-known dealers for fear of retaliation. It was difficult for poor and intimidated residents to organize openly to oust drug dealers from their neighborhood, not only because they felt powerless and distrustful of each other, but because the lenient law enforcement, especially against the youth, enabled the dealers to operate with impunity.

Neighborhood Organization

In the context of decreasing resources and increasing marginalization, we also find an inverse relationship between an effective community organization and the rise of widespread disorderly conduct. The middle-class exodus had drained the community of leadership and political influence. In the Sun-Hope neighborhood, a majority of the remaining residents expressed concerns about the problems in their neighborhood but at the same time were disengaged from the tenant organization. Although many residents reported knowing something about the dormant tenant group, they saw no need to participate because "it ain't gonna change anything" or because they expressed personal dislike for the "women" in charge.[14] The core group of twenty tenants, predominantly women, met regularly; however, the occasions on which many residents responded to a call to attend the incipient and inchoate Tenant Council meetings included only those times when there was a promise of food or some reward. For many, living in impoverishment has the effect of eroding their belief and trust in governmental agencies, and subsequently on their outlook on their own collective capability to alter the choices affecting their lives. As a result, the few concerned but demoralized residents were unable to maintain a functioning mediating institution to deal with the drug-related problems effectively. The high turnover of inefficient management companies and the lack of a broad-based mediating institution in Sun-Hope, then, facilitated the infiltration of drug dealers into the community. The drug dealers secured access to vacant units by bribing maintenance workers, while the few concerned tenants remained fearful of confronting neighbors dealing in drugs. Without a community-wide consensus, Sun-Hope became a seemingly permissive and tolerant neighborhood where the drug dealers and criminals operated with impunity.

Police-Community Relations

The destabilization and the general socioeconomic decline of the Sun-Hope neighborhood, starting in the late 1970s, shaped the acrimonious police-community relations in later years. Specifically, the decline of the tenant councils of the 1970s correlated not only to the exodus of the middle-class, but also to the decline in both informal and formal social control at Sun-Hope. Depleted of willing and able residents with organizational and leadership skills, it became difficult for ordinary residents to mobilize the resources necessary to deal with neighborhood problems. In a market society, "neighborhoods not only reflect the status of their residents, but confer status upon them."[15] As an impoverished and dilapidated neighborhood, where drug dealers operated a 24-hour open-air drug market defined by violence and homicides, the Sun-Hope neighborhood and residents were stigmatized. Police officers referred to the area as "Little Beirut," implicating the combination of intense drug- and gun-related violence in the neighborhood; however, its Sixth District police princinct was more severely understaffed than any other in the city.[16] This was one reason why police response to call-for-services in the community was the second worst in the city. In general, the poorer the neighborhood residents, the less frequent is the police patrol, the less likely it is that the police will seek out violations, and the poorer is the police response time to call-for-service.

The weak leadership, lack of political clout, community-wide disorganization and tenant-consensus on how do to deal with Sun-Hope's open air-drug market and related violence made it difficult for the police to do their job, and for the residents to have legitimate grounds on which to hold the police accountable. News reports about tenants' unwillingness (due to fear of retaliation, distrust of the police and/or racial politics) to help the police conduct investigations, even in homicide cases, gave the public the impression that residents did not care.[17] The police, likewise, came to share the public's sentiment that Sun-Hope was a haven for disreputable people and a source of their woes, hence the label "Little Beirut." Policing at Sun-Hope was characterized as reactive, at best.

The plight of the Sun-Hope community came to the fore when the new owners took the necessary steps to politicize the neighborhood drug trade. One of the outcomes of new managements' decision led to the clash between the Fruit of Islam (FOI) patrol group and the District of Columbia Metropolitan Police Department (MPD). The relationship between the FOI and the MPD was not a mere conflict between a civil society and a state society over a neighborhood problem: it epitomized the racial and class antagonism rooted in the *de facto* segregation of impoverished and underserved neighborhood residents in the city. In economically depressed black neighborhoods, where a disproportionate number of the residents are trapped in poverty and where residents perceive government agencies have given up on them, residents view the police with ambivalence. While ordinary residents expect the police to rid their neighborhood of the lawless who threaten their sense of security, police tolerance of social disorder or their extended absence from neighborhoods of persistent lawlessness leaves residents with the attitude that they are undeserving of police service. From the viewpoint of many Sun-Hope residents, the drug trade prevailed relentlessly because police presence was often brief, and hardly led to any noticeable decline in the lawlessness. Instead of preventive, policing in Sun-Hope was reactive, where officers dealt with "serious" cases such as homicides or conducted drug busts. So sweeping, too, were the sporadic drug raids, especially when the War on Drugs Policy went into effect, that ordinary residents felt victimized by the paramilitarized police.

The antagonistic community-police relations made effective police and detective work difficult. The police, tenants reasoned, did not arrive in timely fashion when called. And when they did, they were disdainful toward the tenants. In Sun-Hope, the much-publicized or perceived corruption of some officers made residents distrustful of the agency. The antagonism was also the source of the nagging problems confronting the police in clearing heinous crime cases in communities such as Sun-Hope: the police faced the silence of frightened witnesses and neighbors who refused to assist them because they lacked faith in the police to protect them. The antagonism also stemmed from the fact that although the suburban white middle-class drug culture contributes to the drug violence in these communities nation-wide, blacks are disproportionately arrested, charged, sentenced and harshly incarcerated in drug-related cases, while whites, if arrested, receive comparatively lenient treatment. In the Sun-Hope neighborhood, the open-air drug trade dominated because it provided an avenue for some of the area's youth to make easy money. It was within the context of this seemingly entrenched lawlessness and the benign neglect of Sun-Hope by the police that some residents, not excluding the new owners, became frustrated and sought for the service of the Fruit of Islam.

The ineffectiveness of the MPD (or their resignation) in controlling the "Sun-Hope trade" led the landlords and the tenant groups to recruit the FOI patrol team. The FOI's ideology that the police contribute to the flow of drugs into the ghetto through nonenforcement, along with the former's tactic of confronting suspected drug dealers in the community, generated controversy. The police and critics questioned the FOI's mandate to confront neighborhood drug dealers, and the FOI members questioned the MPD's credibility and effectiveness in controlling the open-air drug trade and related violence in the neighborhood. Concerned about its image, the police department took the necessary step to foster dialogue with the FOI, the landlords, the residents' group, and to provide more resources to the community.

The outcomes of the police-tenant deliberations were: 1) the MPD re-evaluated the deployment of officers in low-income neighborhoods and implemented new policing strategies to foster a meaningful relationship between designated footpatrol officers and neighborhood residents; and 2) the MPD implemented a landlord-police program which encouraged police officers to move into apartments in the Sun-Hope neighborhood for a reduced rent. This led to six officers and their families moving into Hope Mansions. Some of the officers assisted with an after-school youth program. Others, aided by volunteer tenants, managed a "Koban," a community mini-police station in a converted apartment. The combination of these measures contributed to the decline of crime and deviant behaviors in the neighborhood. Although the outcome of the "police-as-tenant" program has yet to be evaluated, since its institution in 1995, there has not been a single homicide involving a tenant reported in Sun-Hope community. One major lesson here is that when the community, the landlords, the Coucilmember of Ward 7, the FOI and the police held meetings and arrived at a consensus on what do about the community's problems, reducing the rates of crimes and homicide and eradicating open-air drug markets became easier and sustainable, disproving any monolithic label of passivity and revealing instead the necessity of confronting through community-wide endeavors complex issues of isolation and the resulting demoralization within a market society.

Empowerment and Cooperative Homeownership

Findings related to the preceding examination of the drug trade within the context of the neighborhood's marginalization reveal the often-overlooked conditions which defeat "quick fix" programs aimed at improving the lives of the poor. In contemporary urban America, the single obstruction thwarting the upward mobility of the poor is their lack of education and the means by which to at least alter their life chances. The empowerment and cooperative homeownership undertakings were some of the means to help residents strive toward upward mobility. Among these programs implemented at Hope Mansions were the U.S. Housing and Urban Development's HOPE II (homeownership) and the Department of Health and Human Services' (DHHS) jobs training and placement programs, both aiming to address the sources, not merely the effects, of poverty, but still failing to confront the foundational issues of self-doubt, inexperience and distrust of authority.

The HOPE II program, under Bush Administration, was geared to empower low-income people in public and subsidized housing. By empowerment, the Bush government sought to give poor people the autonomy to own and/or manage their housing projects and to be independent of the underfunded and inefficient Public Housing Authorities. In the Sun-Hope community the implementation of the empowerment program revealed many of the dilemmas tenants faced: inadequate education and the lack of organizational experience. When residents were presented with the opportunity, backed by a HUD grant, to organize and eventually manage their own housing cooperative, many found the idea to be confounding, due to their inadequate education. Tenant leaders were faced with the difficulty of educating both themselves and the others about the cooperative venture. Years of poverty had taken an emotional toll as well. Many of the tenants saw the cooperative "ownership" idea as simply unattainable by virtue of their lives on the poverty line.

Through the People's Advocacy (PA), the nascent Hope Mansions Cooperative (HMC) got the attention of many of the passive residents when the organization obtained a $500,000 grant from HUD. The HMC regressed, however, as a result of a intense struggle between the younger and older members for leadership and over recognition for the emerging significance of the organization. Other members battled over the few paid positions which opened up. As a result, a number of experienced board members resigned, leaving the PMC without the legal mandate to operate. The remaining group, mostly the younger ones, selected new board members and sought to remove and wrestle fudiciary control of the HUD grant from the PA. The PA director obliged. HUD, however, then canceled the grant. This led to the demise of Hope Mansions Cooperative. The contractual agreement between Shelter Incorporated (SI) and the tenant group to eventually own the Hope Mansions Apartments collapsed as a result of internal conflicts and lack of expertise.

While the idea of tenant cooperative homeownership would have resolved the contradiction between rent control (tenants' interest) and profit (landlords' interest), it was, however, not easily pursued even with the support of a generous HUD grant. Sun-Hope residents were faced with two dilemmas. First, the tenant leadership lacked the adequate schooling to enable them to communicate with critical agencies. Residents could not articulate their concerns on paper without the assistance of an experienced advocacy group. Second, the case of Hope Mansions reveals that without a core group of educated and experienced members to provide the necessary technical support, an attempt to embark on a massive project such as cooperative housing is doomed to fail.

One solution is the utilization of an advocacy organization with the know-how to help tenants organize. The tenant-PA relations at Hope Mansions, however, illuminate the underlying antagonism and distrust impoverished neighborhood tenants sometimes feel regarding "experts." Tenants persistently viewed the PA as a "poverty pimp"—an entity deriving income at their expense. In fact, ironically, the PA tenant-empowerment workshops had given a few of the tenants a false sense of confidence that they could manage their own affairs. The collapse of the HMC, however, proved otherwise.

Economic Empowerment: A Jobs-Training Catch-22

Another program utilizing DHHS grant money designed to help the impoverished at Sun-Hope neighborhood was the Livelihood Jobs Training Program. This program was implemented for two essential reasons: to assist residents in freeing themselves from chronic joblessness, and subsequently, to stabilize the neighborhood by raising the median income. But, like other programs, the jobs training and placement program presented dilemmas to participants, and they to the program.

The targeted population of the LJTP was welfare residents. As was stated in the grant proposal, the program objective was to reduce the number of welfare dependents in the neighborhood by 40 percent. The LJTP failed to realized this objective. The welfare-reliant residents did not respond to the program because they were faced with a dilemma. On the one hand, there was consensus among the prospective target group that there was pride one feels being wage-reliant and self-sufficient. On the other hand, those dependent on government subsidies realized the brute reality of not being able to support themselves and their families if they were to take an average $6.00/hour job, and risk losing their subsidies. This is a market society which is as ruthless towards those without marketable skills as it is toward those without access to mediating institutions. In this economic trend where a highly skilled labor force is in demand, the problem facing the majority of the ghetto poor is structural unemployment. Even though they share the American value of work ethic and want to work, many urban poor find themselves unable to gain the necessary training or education required for the job available. Others complain of having had the training only to find that the jobs are inaccessible.

The LJTP, however, offered no iron-clad guarantees to prospective participants. As a result, the only residents drawn to the program were those already employed and seeking to be placed in better paying jobs. The single characteristic of the women who dropped out of the program was their lack of cultural capital, specifically adequate elementary and college education. For some of the program participants, because they were functionally illiterate, the LJTP managers recommended that they first get their GED before being placed in entry-level jobs. In a rapidly changing technological and market-driven society, the lack of adequate education, which serves as the foundation for acquiring marketable skills, remains the major obstruction facing the poor from active participating in adequately rewarding and long-term employment. Even as they seek out job training and employment opportunities, it is undeniable that many face severe odds in their chance to escape poverty. For instance, by the close of the LJTP, there were 97 participants ranging in ages between 18 and 59 years, and averaging 32 years of age.

Of the 39 women participants:

    2 had no formal education,
    1 had completed up to grade 9,
    5 had completed up to grade 10,
    8 had completed up to grade 11,
  18 had completed up to grade 12,
    4 had completed up to grade 13,
    1 had 2 years of postsecondary education.

Of the 58 men participants:

4 had no formal education,
1 had completed up to grade 7,
5 had completed up to grade 8,
6 had completed up to grade 9,
13 had completed up to grade 10,
10 had completed up to grade 11,
17 had completed up to grade 12,
2 had up to 2 years postsecondary education.

What these sub-educational attainment statistics, in conjunction with the average age of 32, reveal, is that these individuals face a bleak future in their effort to overcome poverty. Not only are they likely to remain at the margins of the mainstream society, but the possibility of inching their way into it gets more difficult as the legitimate means by which to bring themselves up by their own bootstraps gets increasingly restricted. They have become obsolete in that they live in a technologically advanced and competitive market society but lack the saleable skills necessary to participate. In their state of socioeconomic obsolence, they are unable to make any significant contribution to their own lives and their community.

In a focus group session for adults, when asked "what two or three things would you change about your life, if you could change anything?", the predominant responses implicated the particiapants' inferior education and frustrated life-chances as a result of it:

> I would have made sure I stayed in school and got all the education I need to get me a good job so I could maintain the goals that I wanted to get to. I would finish high school. . . . I would not have started having babies before I got married.[18]

Another stated:

> I am a product of this school system. I don't even see how I got as far as the 12th grade without having to write too much. And what makes me so angry is that I could be dynamite if I could really write well. Now I'm getting better because I try to write and read and help myself. But I am so mad with the system because some people can get out. I know two people that are functionally illiterates and they graduated from high school in D.C.[19]

Another confessed:

> I am the product of one of the schools too. I don't mind saying it but I'm one of you who cannot read that well. When I was in school, in elementary school, they put me in basic class. Basic class consists of you do what you want . . . . You draw. You see what I'm saying? . . . I don't know how I passed but I went to college. I'm reading better. I'm a little slow now but I've been in school. I even went to college. I passed. I got D's and C's, ok?. . . . I am learning how to do high school math. I'm in vocational rehabilitation now. . . . I'm working at it.[20]

So debilitating was their education, that many of the LJTP applicants needed assistance in filling out the in-take forms. In short, because these individuals lacked adequate education and the employment credentials, they engaged in short-term strategic conducts to meet their immediate needs, and in the long term reproduced their poverty.

Another obstacle facing the LJTP was that many of the program participants were veterans of the "war on drugs." LJTP staff members persistently encountered resistance from potential employers when attempting to place residents who were ex-convicts. Some program participants had resorted to, and were arrested for, drug-related crimes because they lacked adequate education and marketable skills. Now that they were attempting to change their ways, however, having a criminal record thwarted their chances of gaining employment. This kind of frustration accounts, in part, for the recidivism some of the young men in the neighborhood.

SUN-HOPE IN A MARKET SOCIETY: PAST AND FUTURE

As this study has shown, changes in this troubled urban community have been made. Steps toward community empowerment faltered, but the crime rate was reduced, the property was rejuvenated, tenant-police relations were revived and income-reliant families were drawn into the community. Specifically, these inter-connected changes in the Sun-Hope neighborhood are reflected in the general decline in crime rates.[21] This is attributed to the combined effect of change in ownership and management, the refurbishing of the apartment complexes, the improved community-police relations and the FOI members' presence in the area. The marked improvements resulted in attracting income-

Chart 9.1: Violent Crimes

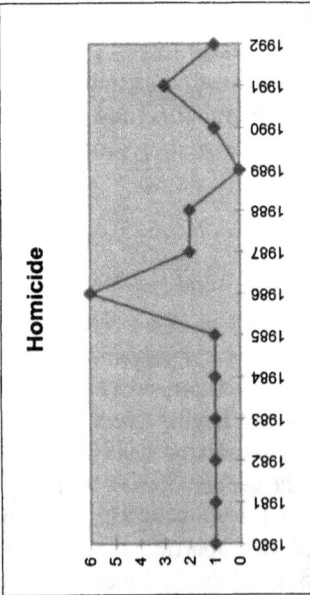

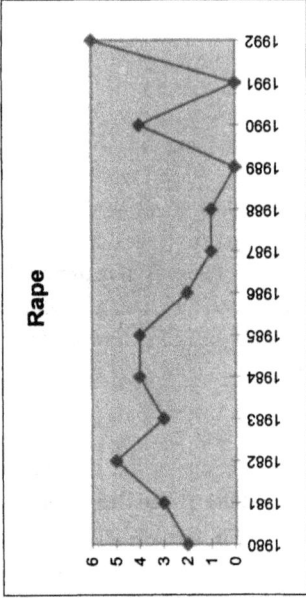

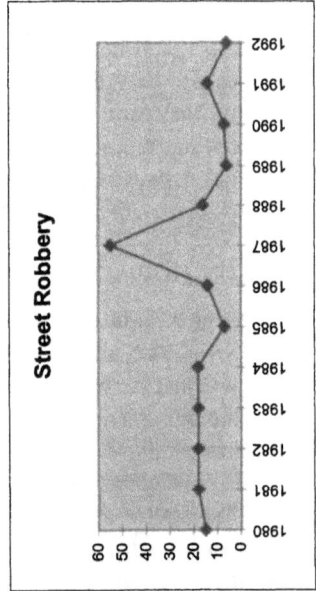

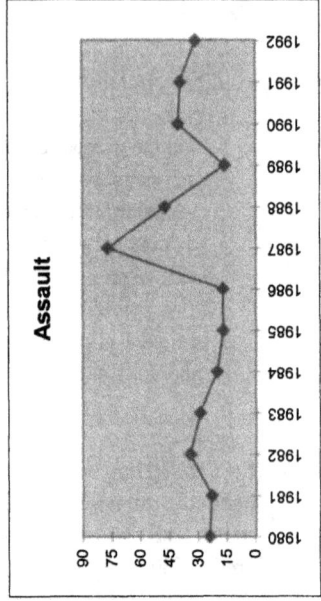

Chart 9.2: Property Crimes

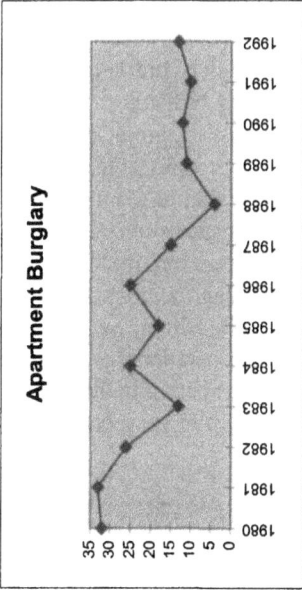

Apartment Burglary

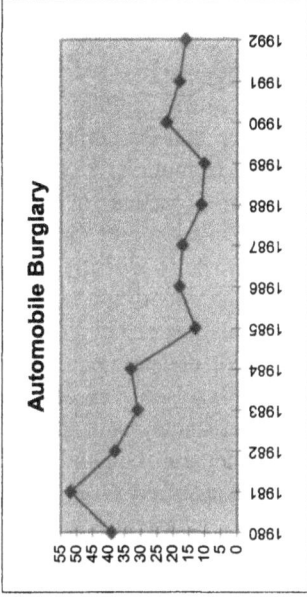

Automobile Burglary

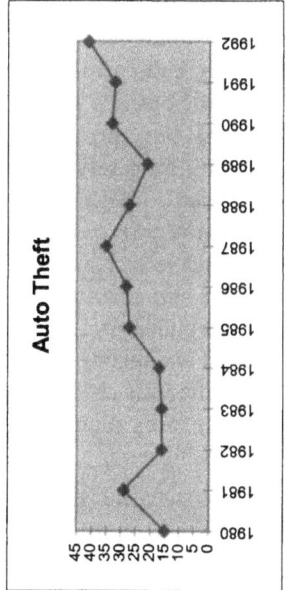

Auto Theft

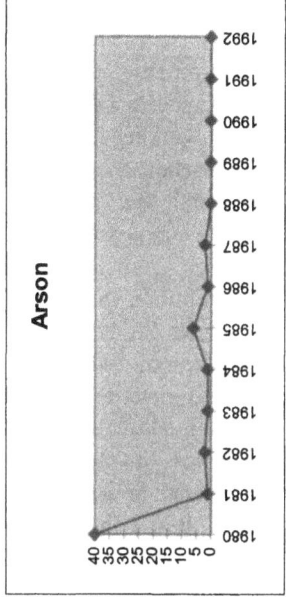

Arson

reliant families back into the community. By 1991 the total number of households had jumped to 568, from 276 in 1986. As an indicator of the working families being attracted into the community, the average household income rose to $14,653 from under $5,000. Such statistics reveal the underlying structural issues of undereducation, underemployment and social class isolation endemic to the urban lower class in an industrialized society. Subsequently, if the improved conditions in the Sun-Hope neighborhood are to be sustained, the deleterious effects of *de facto* isolation of the lower class must be addressed. While the establishment of community-based mediating institutions through which active residents can draw resources and essential government services is essential, even these efforts do not address the structural issues of undereducation and underemployment endemic to the lower class in a market society.

While the Sun-Hope residents themselves have challenged the label of passivity assigned to them by culture of poverty proponents, more complex socioeconomic issues must be addressed before the transformation of the urban ghetto can be realized. A relationship between a sustained mediating institutions (civil society) and individuals in problem-plagued communities must be pursued and fostered, and this relationship must be based on the residents' sense that the professionals involved share a commitment to the community. To this end, critical literacy by which individuals can raise their consciousness and empower themselves must be pursued. Absentee landlords operating subsidized housing projects using federal grants must be carefully scrutinized to prevent abuse and neglect of the tenants. Adults and youth must be able to secure gainful employment nearby or accessible by public transportation, Only when these most basic needs have been met can a future free from material degeneration and chronic violence be secured, can the community's young pursue more than dreams of finishing high school, escaping teen pregnancy and minimizing the prospects of incaceration: once these needs are met, individuals can have a chance at competing in the market society. This case study illuminates the struggles and prospects of transforming the urban ghetto.

NOTES

1. See St. Clair Drake and Horrance R. Clayton, *Black Metropolis: Study of Negro Life in a Northern City* (New York: Harper & Row, 1945); Michael Harrington, *The Other America* (New York: Macmillan, 1962.)

2. Oscar Lewis' culture of poverty thesis is often used out of context, especially by conservative intellectuals and policy-makers because they see the poor as perpetuating their own impoverishment through their failure to conform to the norm of the mainstream culture. In his *La Vida: A Puerto Rican Family in the Culture of Poverty* (London: Secker and Wargburg, 1967: xxi), Lewis, however, argued that "the culture of poverty is both an adaptation and reaction of the poor to their marginal position in a class stratified, highly individuated society. It represents an effort to cope with feelings of helplessness and despair which develop from the realisation of the improbability of achieving success in terms of the values and goals of the larger society." See, Edward Banfield, *The Unheavenly City* (Boston: Little Brown, 1970); Lawrence Mead, *The New Politics of Poverty: The Nonworking Poor in America* (New York: Basic Books, 1992.)

3. William Julius Wilson, *The Truly Disadvantaged: The Inner City, the Underclass, and Public Policy* (Chicago: University of Chicago Press, 1987.); Jacqueline Jones, *The Dispossessed: America's Underclasses from the Civil War to the Present* (New York: Basic Books, 1998.); Jill Quadagno, *The Color of Welfare: How Racism Undermined the War on Poverty* (New York: Oxford University Press, 1994); Andrew Hacker, *Two Nations: Black and White, Separate, Hostile, and Unequal* (New York: Scribner's, 1992.); Mark Robert Rank, *Living on the Edge: The Realities of Welfare in America* (New York: Columbia University Press, 1994).

4. Gunnar Myrdal, *The American Dilemma* (New York: Harper and Brothers Publishers, 1944).

5. See Elliott Currie, "Crime in the Market Society," *Dissent,* (Spring 1991): 255.

6. Examining the census data of the 1980s, Mishel and Frankel discovered that "Real hourly wages dropped by 9.3 percent between 1980 and 1989. . . . In 1987, 31.5 percent of the work force was earning poverty level wages, up from 25.7 percent in 1979. This shift toward low-wage employment occurred in every demographic group. . . . However, the biggest losers were the 75 percent of the work force without college degrees, particularly men (especially black men) and young workers." See Lawrence Mishel and David M. Frankel "Hard Times for Working America: Facts You Ought to Know." *Dissent,* (Spring 1991): 282-286.

7. In 1930, the population of Washington, D.C. steadily rose from 488,000, peaking to 900,000 in 1943. The last 40 years has witnessed a steady decline to its present of 540,000. See D'Vera Cohn, "D.C. Population Still Declining In Latest Count: 11,000 Lost in a Year; Md., Va. Gain Again," *The Washington Post,* 31 December 1996, A1.

8. David Finkel, "Point of No Return: Why the Middle Class is Leaving Washington Behind," *The Washington Post Magazine,* 9 October 1994. By all accounts, even some of the poor people have moved to neighboring wealthier counties in Maryland and Virginia where services to the poor are comparatively better.

9. Douglass S. Massey and Nancy Denton, *American Apartheid: Segregation and the Making of the Underclass* (Cambridge: Harvard University Press, 1993), 9.

10. Andrew Hacker, *Two Nations: Black and White, Separate, Hostile, Unequal* (New York: Scribners, 1992), 115.

11. See David Simon and Edward Burns, *The Corner: A Year in the Life of an Inner-City Neighborhood* (New York: Broadway Books, 1997). The authors provide a vivid account of the life-chances the poor trapped in Baltimore's inner-city.

12. A subject of controversy needing research has to do with the allegation that the Washington, D.C. hospitality industry, namely hotels and restaurants, overlook blacks for low-end jobs. Some leaders in the AFL-CIO have alleged that because African Americans are most responsive to unionization, since the 1970s the hospitality industry has intentionally sought after Latin American immigrant workers who generally resist unionization. In the 1990s, the allegation goes, the Hispanics have became conscious of their exploitative situation and are responding to unionization. In response, the hospitality industry is now shifting its attention to immigrant workers from Asian countries.

13. Blaine Harden, "New York's Richest Get Richer, Poorest Poorer," *The Washington Post,* 19 December 1997, A3.

14. In many low-income black neighborhoods, women not only dominate the mediating institutions; they are often the leaders. Their brash style of leadership in dealing with recalcitrant neighbors engenders admiration, contempt and envy by community members. Three women leaders noted for their fight against blight, drug dealers, and violence in their community are Bertha Gilkey in St. Louis, Kimi Gray in Washington, D.C., and Che Madyun in Boston. For more details, see Jason DeParle, "Cultivating Their Own Gardens," *New York Time Magazine,* 5 January 1992; David Osborne, "The Can't Stop Us Now," *Washington Post Magazine,* 30 July 1989, 12; Peter

Medoff and Holly Sklar, *Street of Hope: The Fall and Rise of an Urban Neighborhood* (Boston: South End Press, 1994).

15. Rodney Stark, "Deviant Places: A Theory of the Ecology of Crime" *Criminology* 25. 4(1987): 900.

16. In 1989, the Hope Mansions Cooperative Board wrote a letter to the Sixth District Deputy Chief Jimmie Wilson "to express our alarm and shock at the comparatively low level of resources being allocated to our police district to continue its fight against drugs, and to aid us in keeping them out as we seek with others to truly rehabilitate our environment." Displeased by the poor police response to call-for-services, the letter added that a group of "tenants are engaged in a nightly patrol of the perimeter of the property (15 buildings in all), but their efforts must have police reinforcement and backup, if they are to succeed."

17. William Raspberry, "Silent Betrayal," *The Washington Post,* 6 October, 1993, A19.

18. *Focus Group,* May 1987, 13.

19. Ibid., 32.

20. Ibid., 32.

21. This is a MPD crime data by city-block.

References

Anderson, Elijah. 1990. *Streetwise: Race, Class and Change in an Urban Community.* Chicago: University of Chicago Press.

Auletta, Ken. 1983. *The Underclass.* New York: Vintage Books.

Becker, Gary S. 1964. *Human Capital.* New York: Columbia University Press.

Blackwell, Jame E. 1991. *The Black Community: Diversity and Unity.* New York: HarperCollins Publishers Inc.

Connolly, Harold X. 1976. "Black Movement into Suburbs: Suburbs Doubling Their Black Populations during the 1960s." *Urban Affairs Quarterly* 9: 91-111

Currie, Elliot. 1991. "The Market Society." *Dissent* (Spring): 255-58.

Drake, St. Clair and Horrance R. Clayton. 1945. *Black Metropolis: Study of Negro Life in a Northern City.* New York: Harper & Row.

Elliot, Liebow. 1967. *Talley's Corner: A Study of Negro Streetcorner Men.* Boston: Little Brown.

Farley, Reynold. 1970. "The Changing Distribution of Negroes within Metropolitan Areas: The Emergence of Black Suburbs." *American Journal of Sociology* 75: 512-29.

Green, Constance. 1976. *Secret City: History of Race Relations in the Nation's Capital.* New Jersey: Princeton University Press.

Giddens, Anthony. 1986. *Central Problems in Social Theory, Action, Structure and Contradictions in Social Analysis.* Berkeley: University of California Press.

Gilderbloom, John and Richard P. Appelbaum. 1988. *Rethinking Rental Housing.* Philadelphia: Temple University Press.

Goetz, Ralf. 1979. *Understanding Neighborhood Change.* New York: Ballinger.

Hacker, Andrew. 1992. *Two Nations Black and White, Separate, Hostile, Unequal.* New York: Scribners.

Hirschi, Travis. 1969. *Causes of Delinquency.* Berkeley: University of California Press.

Harrington, Michael. 1962. *The Other America.* New York: Macmillan.

HOPE: Homeownership and Opportunity for People Everywhere. U.S. Department of Housing and Urban Development publication HUD-PDR-1246 (1), March 1990.

Indices: A Statistical Index to District of Columbia Services. (August 1991).

Jone, Jacqueline. 1992. *The Dispossessed: America's Underclass from the Civil War to the Present.* New York: BasicBooks.

Jones, LeAlan et al. 1997. *Our America: Life and Death on the South Side of Chicago.* New York: Scribner.

Kotlowitz, Alex. 1991. *There Are No Children Here: The Story of Two Boys Growing Up in the Other America.* New York: Doubleday.

Lehman, Nicholas. 1991. *The Promised Land: The Great Black Migration and How It Changed America.* New York: Knopf.

Lewis, Oscar. 1966. "The Culture of Poverty." *Scientific American* 215: 19-25.

Lewis, Oscar. *La Vida: A Puerto Rican Family in the Culture of Poverty.* London: Secker and Wargburg, 1976.

Lusane, Clarence.1991. *Pipe Dream Blues: Racism and the War on Drugs.* Boston: South End Press.

Massey, Douglass S. and Nancy A. Denton. 1993. *American Apartheid: Segregation and the Making of the Underclass.* Cambridge: Harvard University Press.

Massey, Douglass. 1990. "American Apartheid: Segregation and the Making of the Underclass." *American Journal of Sociology* 96: 329-57

Medoff, Peter and Holly Sklar. 1994. *Street of Hope: The Fall and Rise of an Urban Neighborhood.* Boston: South End Press.

Meister, Richard J. 1972. *The Black Ghetto: Promise Land or Colony?* Lexington: D.C. Heath and Company.

Merton, Robert. 1968. *Social Structure and Social Theory.* New York: The Free Press.

Moynihan, Patrick D. 1965. *The Negro Family: The Case for National Action.* Washington, D.C.: U.S. Department of Labor.

Osborne, David. 1989. "They Can't Stop Us Now." *The Washington Post Magazine,* 30 July.

Quadagno, Jill. 1994. *The Color of Welfare: How Racism Undermined the War on Poverty.* New York: Oxford Univeristy Press.

Rank, Mark Robert. 1994. *Living on the Edge: The Realities of Welfare in America.* New York: Columbia University Press.

Ratner, Mitchell S. 1993. *Crack Pipe as Pimp: An Ethnographic Investigation of Sex-for-Crack Exchanges.* Lexingon Books: New York.

Russel, Kathy et al. 1992. *The Color Complex: The Politics of Skin Color Among African Americans.* New York: Harcourt Brace Jovanovich Publishers.

Sackrey, Charles. 1973. *The Political Economy of Urban Poverty.* New York: W.W. Norton & Company.

Safran, Claire. 1992. "The New Faces of Poverty." *Redbook* (August):84-87.

Simon, David R. 1995. *Social Problems & The Sociological Imagination: A Paradigm for Analysis.* New York: McGraw-Hill Inc.

Simon, David and Edward Burns. 1997. *The Corner: A Year in the Life of an Inner-City Neighborhood.* New York: Broadway Books.

Skogan, Wesley G. 1990. *Disorder and Decline: Crime and the Spiral of Decay in American Neighborhoods.* Berkeley: University of California Press.

Stack, Carol. 1974. *All Our Kin: Strategies for Survival in a Black Community.* New York: Harper & Row.

Stark, Rodney. 1987. "Deviant Places: A Theory of the Ecology of Crime." *Criminology* 25: 893-909.

Susman, Marvin B. 1957. "The Role of Neighborhood Associations in Private Housing for Racial Minorities." *The Journal of Social Issues* 13: 31-37.

William, Terry. 1989. *The Cocaine Kids: The Inside Story of a Teenage Drug Ring.* Reading, MA: Addison-Wesley.

Williams, Gregory Howard. 1996. *Life on the Color Line.* New York: PLUME/Penguin.

Wilson, James Q. and G. Kelling. 1983. "Broken Windows: Police and Neighborhood Safety." *Atlantic Monthly* 249 (March): 29-38.

Wilson, William Julius. 1987. *The Truly Disadvantaged: The Inner City, the Underclass, and Public Policy.* Chicago: The University of Chicago Press.

Index

For Product Safety Concerns and Information please contact our EU
representative GPSR@taylorandfrancis.com
Taylor & Francis Verlag GmbH, Kaufingerstraße 24, 80331 München, Germany

www.ingramcontent.com/pod-product-compliance
Lightning Source LLC
Chambersburg PA
CBHW070358270326
41926CB00014B/2611